PREMIUM

C1 level | Coursebook

GW00401826

Tell it like it is

04

Be your own boss

12

Get smarter

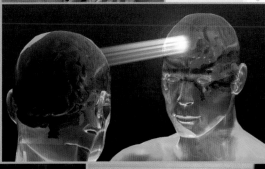

07

10

Eye witness

Recycle, restyle

08

09

Elaine **Boyd**
Araminta **Crace**

Wonders of the world

PREMIUM

Welcome to the **Premium C1 level Coursebook**. This book is part of a course that has been developed to meet the needs of advanced students who might be considering sitting an international English exam at C1 level.

Premium has been developed both for students who want to take an exam and for those who would like to improve their English but may not wish to take an exam. It provides thorough preparation for exam success as well as comprehensive language development for students who simply want to improve their ability to understand and communicate in English.

Language development

Premium C1 Coursebook offers skills-based development and practice for advanced level students through engaging topics. These topics have been carefully chosen to generate discussion and provide students with opportunities for expressing their own thoughts.

Each unit contains core skills development in Reading, Writing, Listening and Speaking and practice in the specific functional language needed for Writing and Speaking. There is extensive coverage of Grammar and Vocabulary throughout the book, plus a full reference section at the back. There is also a Writing reference section containing models and tips for a range of different writing genres. Additionally, there are learner tips in each unit to help students maximise their own learning.

The **Exam Reviser** booklet provides a personalised and comprehensive store of vocabulary and functional language. Students can record not only essential words and phrases but also words and phrases that they like and want to use.

The **Premium C1 Workbook** offers plenty of further self-study practice. There is also a **Multi-ROM** with interactive language activities as well as the audio CD for the listening practice.

Exam preparation

For students wishing to maximise their chances of exam success, **Premium C1** develops the key language and exam skills required to achieve success in C1 level skills-based exams. This Coursebook focuses on practice in the Certificate in Advanced English but the exam skills are transferable to other exams at this level. There is also an interactive CAE test on the **iTest CD-ROM** at the back of the Coursebook, giving feedback on students' progress and test performance.

The **Exam Reviser** booklet provides students with a record of useful language they will need for a C1 level exam. It includes topic-based vocabulary, multi-word verbs and other useful language chunks. It also contains useful functional language for use in speaking and writing tests at C1 level. Additionally, there are ideas on how to prepare for an exam and specific tips for each paper of the Certificate of Advanced English exam.

Further exam practice can be found in the **Workbook** as well as useful tips and hints on how to tackle exam-style questions.

For students who really want to maximise their chances of exam success, there is the **www.iTests.com** website where you can do more interactive test practice, get feedback on your performance and chart your progress towards exam success.

Whatever your reason for learning English is, we hope you enjoy using this book and wish you every success with your studies.

Elaine Boyd
Araminta Crace

Unit	Unit title	Page	Vocabulary	Grammar	Reading	Listening
1	Friend or foe?	p7	Multi-word verbs – relationships; Describing people	-ing forms and infinitives; Articles	Hit-and-run kindness; multiple choice	Clash of the siblings; sentence completion; *taking notes
2	Sensational eating	p17	Multi-word verbs with up; Senses in eating	Modifying comparison; Ability, possibility and obligation	The Nano diet; gapped text; *understanding cohesion in a text	Eating experiences; multiple matching
3	Game on	p27	Compete, win and lose; Achievement	Present perfect 1; Present perfect 2	Wimbledon's unsung heroes; multiple matching; *predicting content	Chaos training; multiple choice
4	Tell it like it is	p37	Memories; Powerful adjectives	Narrative tenses; Emphasis with what, all and it	Classic stories today; themed texts; *identifying reason for writing and intended reader	Myths and legends; unrelated extracts; Dickens World; multiple choice
5	Man's best friend	p47	Metaphorical language; Multi-word verbs with out	Cohesion in text; Relative clauses	Red Riding Hood; gapped text	How animals help us; multiple matching; *thinking of topic words
	Progress Check 1		pages 57–58			
6	Making movies	p59	Films; Word formation – prefixes	Linking words; Future forms	'Clip culture'; multiple choice	The film industry; unrelated extracts; *identifying positive and negative opinion
7	Get smarter	p69	Multi-word verbs with two particles; Fixed phrases with brain and think	If-structures; Linking phrases	The mind; themed texts	Total recall; multiple choice; *predicting from world knowledge
8	Wonders of the world	p79	Tourist sights; Effects of the weather	Degrees of certainty; Confusable structures	Seven wonders of the world; multiple matching; *guessing unknown words	Blue skies; sentence completion
9	Eye witness	p89	Multi-word verbs – crime; Breaking the law	Passives; Introductory it	Crime and punishment gone mad?; themed texts	Surveillance society; multiple choice; *identifying what to focus on
10	Recycle, restyle	p99	Environmental issues; Dependent prepositions with verbs and nouns	Participle clauses; Reported speech	The carbon coach; gapped text; *understanding the flow of a text	Celebrity Earth; unrelated extracts
	Progress Check 2		pages 109–110			
11	What's in a name?	p111	Word formation – suffixes; Words with multiple meanings	Verb patterns; Using noun groups	'Are you Dave Gorman?'; multiple matching	Bonfire of the brands; sentence completion; *paraphrasing and keeping track
12	Be your own boss	p121	Work; Using precise vocabulary	Countable and uncountable nouns; Question forms	What not to wear at work; multiple choice; *inferring underlying meaning	Making a living; multiple matching; *building up answers from clues
13	New science, old beliefs	p131	Verb and noun collocations; Multi-word verbs – science and research	Quantifiers – phrases; Emphasis with inversion	The science of luck; themed texts; *understanding an abstract idea from an example	Superheroes; multiple matching
14	A different perspective	p141	Word pairs; Fixed phrases with change	Using complex sentences (Writing); Causative have and get	Tribes; gapped text	Coming home; sentence completion; *ensuring your answers are accurate
15	Learning zone	p151	Further education; Dependent prepositions with adjectives	Hypothetical meaning; Punctuation (Writing)	Taking an exam?; multiple matching; *finding a paraphrase of the whole question; *timing a reading task	How to improve your listening; sentence completion
	Progress Check 3		pages 161–162			

Exam information 6 | Selected audioscripts pages 163–164 | Communication Activities pages 165–168

Speaking	Writing	CAE close-up	Learning tip	Pronunciation
Friendship and happiness – discussion *showing an interest in what other people are saying	Reference *formal phrases	Use of English key word transformations (Paper 3, part 5)	Learning from other people	Word stress: multi-word verbs
Dining experiences – discussion *describing how good or bad something is	Review *using range	Use of English open cloze (Paper 3, part 2)	Keeping a vocabulary notebook	
Competitive sports – talking about photographs *giving opinions Keeping fit – personal questions and talking about photographs	Article *opening paragraphs	Speaking interview and individual long turn (Paper 5, parts 1 & 2)	Routine and 'chaos' in learning	
Stories – telling stories and exaggerating *making a story sound dramatic	Article *planning paragraphs	Listening multiple choice (Paper 4, part 3)	Reading is good for you	Stress and intonation: dramatic effect
Working animals – talking about photographs *describing feelings and attitudes	Contribution *getting ideas Letter of application	Writing letter of application (Paper 2, part 2)	Remembering words	
Films and acting – discussion *ways of justifying your opinion	Essay *giving opinions	Reading multiple choice (Paper 1, part 3)	Expanding your vocabulary	Sentence stress: reinforcing your opinion
The Queen remembers – discussion *taking turns How to improve your brain power – decision-making	Report *using formal language	Speaking decision-making (Paper 5, part 3)	Remembering multi-word verbs	Intonation: turn-taking
Vote for the Alhambra – presentation *ways of being persuasive	Proposal *being persuasive	Listening sentence completion (Paper 4, part 2) Use of English multiple-choice cloze (Paper 3, part 1)	Using a dictionary	
Surveillance society – discussion *thinking aloud *staying on topic	Information sheet *thinking about format and layout	Reading themed texts (Paper 1, part 1)	Watching and listening	Shifting word stress: multi-word verbs/ nouns
Celebrities and the environment – discussion *talking about effects and influences	Essay *outlining problems and suggesting solutions Report	Listening unrelated extracts (Paper 4, part 1) Writing report (Paper 2, part 1)	Recycling your vocabulary	
'Pointless' projects – collaborative task *negotiating and decision-making	Report *getting a balance of points *differences between a report and a proposal	Reading multiple matching (Paper 1, part 4)	Expanding your vocabulary	Vowels and diphthongs
Aspects of work – discussion *giving extended responses	Letter *expanding and developing notes Essay	Use of English word formation (Paper 3, part 3) Writing essay (Paper 2, part 2)	Improving your English for work	
Inventions and discoveries – talking about photographs *ways of contrasting pictures and ideas	Proposal *topic sentences Contribution	Listening multiple matching (Paper 4, part 4) Writing contribution (Paper 2, part 2)	Improving your pronunciation	Weak forms
Difference in cultures – discussion *expressing uncertainty	Set text *avoiding repetition *checking your work	Reading gapped text (Paper 1, part 2) Use of English gapped sentences (Paper 3, part 4)	Understanding varieties in pronunciation	Varieties in pronunciation
Further education – collaborative task *summarising your views Studying and skills – discussion	Competition entry *awareness of marking criteria Proposal	Writing proposal (Paper 2, part 1) Speaking collaborative discussion (Paper 5, part 4)	Preparing for the exam and planning your revision	

Grammar reference 169–189 | Writing reference pages 190–207

Exam information

The Cambridge Certificate in Advanced English consists of five papers. Each paper tests a different area of your ability in English and is worth 20% of your total result. After you take the exam you will receive a grade: A, B and C are pass grades; D and E are fail grades.

Paper 1 Reading

This paper contains four parts. Each part has at least one text with a task. There are thirty-four questions. A variety of types of texts may be used, including newspaper and magazine articles, reports, fiction, and informational material. You will have 1 hour and 15 minutes to answer all the questions.

Part 1: Multiple-choice

You choose between four alternatives to answer questions or complete statements about three texts. There are six questions.

Part 2: Gapped text sentences

Six paragraphs have been removed from a text. You decide where in the text these paragraphs should be placed. There is one extra paragraph that does not fit any of the gaps.

Part 3: Multiple choice

You choose between four alternatives to answer questions about a text. There are seven questions.

Part 4: Multiple matching

You read a text divided into sections and then match various prompts to each part of the text. There are fifteen questions. Sometimes more than one part of the text will match to one prompt.

Paper 2 Writing

In this paper you have two tasks. You will have 1 hour and 30 minutes to complete the two tasks. You will be required to write 180–220 words for part 1 and 220–260 words for part 2.

Part 1: this is compulsory and requires you to write an article, a report, a proposal or a letter based on information and prompts.

Part 2: in this you have a choice from five tasks. Two of these tasks relate to the set texts. The tasks will be a selection from an article, a competition entry, a contribution to a longer piece, an essay, an information sheet, a letter, a proposal, a reference, a report or a review.

Paper 3 Use of English

This part contains five parts with a total of fifty questions. You will have 1 hour to answer all the questions.

Part 1: this consists of a multiple-choice lexical cloze. This is a text with twelve gaps, followed by twelve four-option multiple-choice questions.

Part 2: this consists of an open cloze. This is a text with fifteen gaps which you must fill with an appropriate word.

Part 3: this consists of a word formation exercise. You will read a text in which there are ten gaps. You are given the stem of the word which you must use to complete each gap.

Part 4: this consists of gapped sentences. Each question has three sentences with one gap in each. You must find one word that completes all three sentences. There are five questions.

Part 5: this consists of eight 'key word' transformations. You are required to complete a sentence using a given word, so that it means the same as a previous sentence.

Paper 4 Listening

This paper contains four parts with a total of thirty questions. In each part you will hear the text(s) twice. The texts will be a variety of types, for example, announcements, radio broadcasts, speeches, talks, lectures, anecdotes, etc. There will be a mixture of native and non-native speaker accents. This will last approximately 40 minutes.

Part 1: you will hear three short unrelated extracts of about thirty seconds each. The extracts are from monologues or conversations between two people. You have to answer two multiple-choice questions about each one. For example, you may be asked to decide on the general subject of the text, the relationship of the speakers or the purpose of the conversation.

Part 2: you will hear a monologue lasting about 3 minutes. There are eight questions in which you will have to complete the sentences with missing information.

Part 3: you will hear a monologue or conversation lasting about three minutes. You will have to answer six multiple-choice questions.

Part 4: you will hear five short related extracts of about thirty seconds each. The extracts could be from monologues or conversations. While you listen you complete a multiple matching task in which you match the speakers to given prompts. There are five extracts to listen to and eight prompts. One prompt does not fit any of the extracts.

Paper 5 Speaking

This paper contains four parts. The standard format involves an interview between two candidates and two examiners. One of the examiners is an interlocutor who speaks to the candidates; the other examiner only assesses the candidates and does not speak. In parts 1 and 2 of this paper, candidates speak mainly to the interlocutor. In parts 3 and 4, the candidates speak mainly to each other. This will last approximately 15 minutes.

Part 1: the interlocutor asks each candidate to say a little about themselves, for example where they come from, what they like doing in their free time, etc. This will last approximately 3 minutes.

Part 2: candidates compare three photographs they are given by the interlocutor. The candidates will talk to each other about them in relation to themselves and their own experience. This will last approximately 4 minutes.

Part 3: candidates are given visual prompts and are asked to carry out a task together which may involve planning, problem solving, decision-making, prioritising or speculating. This will last approximately 4 minutes.

Part 4: the interlocutor develops the topic covered in part 3 and asks the candidates to discuss and give opinions on more general questions related to the same theme. This will last approximately 4 minutes.

Friend or foe?

kindness

rivalry

siblings

Introduction

Unit 01

1 Look at the pictures. What do you think the relationship is between the people shown?

2 Which three of the pictures are closest to your experience? Discuss with other students, explaining how and why. Use the phrases in the box and those in the Exam Reviser to help you.

> best friends   close friends   casual acquaintances   extended family
> nuclear family   step family   adoptive family

exam reviser   p3 | 1.1

3 Work in pairs. Check that you understand the meaning of the multi-word verbs in *italics*. Use a dictionary if necessary.
  1 Do you *take after* anyone in your family (in looks or personality)?
  2 When you were younger, was there anyone in your family who used to *wind* you *up*? If so, what did he or she do?
  3 Do you (or do you think you will) *keep in touch with* many of your school friends? Why/Why not?
  4 If you need *cheering up*, who do you usually *turn to*? Why? How does he or she help you?

4 Discuss the questions in Exercise 3 with another student.

premium plus   01

Reading

Hit-and-run kindness

PAUL CHAMBERS TALKS TO DANNY WALLACE ABOUT HIS 'KARMA ARMY' AND SPREADING HIS OWN BRAND OF KINDNESS.

1 Think about the different kinds of people in the box and discuss these questions.

In what situations, if ever, would you:

1 hug them?
2 kiss them on the cheek?
3 give them a present?
4 buy them a drink?
5 buy them a meal?
6 pay for their bus/train fare?

> one of your parents   one of your siblings
> your best friend   a friend of a friend
> a colleague   your next-door neighbour
> a stranger in the street

2 Read the text quickly and answer these questions.
1 Who is Danny Wallace and what did he do?
2 What does he intend to do next?

In London, just as in many other large urban, multi-cultural centres, it is easy to just keep your head down and not engage with anyone. The majority of us avoid making any kind of contact and walk that little bit quicker if anyone so much as looks at us. One person who decided to do something to change at least some of this was journalist and author, Danny Wallace. And when I met him, I realised he was just the man for the job; a friendly, open person, I took to him immediately. 'There is a social barrier in places like London,' says Danny. 'Sometimes you might see someone who needs help, or perhaps you just fancy starting a conversation with someone, but the social norms step in. Part of your brain wants to make contact, but another part says "No, they'll think I'm mad or they'll mug me." So you walk away.'

Feeling bored one day, Danny, twenty-six, posted an advertisement on the Internet which read simply: 'Join Me. Send a passport photo to this address …'. At first, even Danny wasn't really sure what he wanted to achieve or where it would all lead. He admits that he started the whole thing as a bit of a joke, just to see what would happen. A year and a half later, however, his east London flat is the headquarters for a global Internet-based group – his so-called 'Karma Army' – which carries out thousands of good deeds for strangers each week all over the world. His motives have evolved over time and the objective has now become to try to break down some of the social barriers that exist in many big cities. It's about giving people an excuse to cheer someone up … to do something nice – even something very small.

So who can join and what exactly do they do? The answer to the first question is simple – basically, anyone can join. You just send an email with a passport photo to Danny. You then sign a so-called 'Good Friday Agreement', agreeing to carry out some random act of kindness towards complete strangers every Friday. That's as far as the commitment goes, however, and the rest is really up to you. Over 4,000 people across the world, in countries as diverse as the UK, France, Norway and Puerto Rico have now signed up to take part in these 'Good Fridays'. Each one can make up their own rules as to how many or what kinds of acts they do, or indeed where.

The acts of kindness themselves are many and various. One simple one that Danny describes is the 'unsolicited drink'. 'You're sitting in a pub and see an old guy in the corner,' he says. 'So you walk up to him with a drink, say "I've got you a drink" and walk away. The look of pleasure mixed with bewilderment on his face is a pleasure to see.' There was one lady who told him about getting on a bus. She got on and put a £10 note down and said: 'That's for me and the next nine people.' So at every stop, everyone who got on was told that their fare had been paid for. Danny says he is not only struck by the acts of kindness themselves and the obvious happiness of the people receiving them, but also by the enormous pleasure of the people doing the deed. Being nice clearly makes you feel nice.

'You have to walk up with confidence and humour'

It hasn't always gone smoothly, however. When Danny and his Karma Army first started doing their Good Fridays, they were sometimes met with a certain amount of suspicion. He feels that has changed now mostly because in the early days, he and his fellow good-deeders didn't really know how to do it properly. Feeling a bit like naughty schoolchildren, a lot of people felt that they were doing something they shouldn't. 'I would walk up quite nervously like I was doing something wrong and I didn't know when to leave,' he confesses. 'It's hit-and-run kindness,' he says. 'You have to walk up with confidence and humour and don't get in their faces. You say, "This is for you." Then you go.'

His Karma Army idea has gone further than Danny ever hoped or expected when he wrote that first advert. It started as a bit of fun which also had a serious and important point to it. Danny felt that because of our social barriers, many people – both givers and receivers – were missing out. So what next for Danny and his Karma Army? Well, he intends to launch the American Karma Army and firmly believes that the simplicity of his message will have an impact in the US. 'Don't mug me. Hug me!' is one of his slogans that Danny believes will be particularly effective in combating street crime there. That sounds rather ambitious to me, but if anyone has a chance of doing it, believe me, it's Danny.

3 Read the text again. For questions 1–6, decide which answer A, B, C or D fits best according to the text.

1 According to the article, people often don't make contact with strangers because
   A they are afraid it might be seen as the wrong thing to do.
   B they are reluctant to mix with people of different cultures.
   C they are unwilling to put the effort in and feel they haven't got time.
   D they are concerned that people might be over-friendly towards them.

2 What is the best way to describe how Danny's plan changed?
   A A joke became a profit-making business.
   B A vague idea became a concrete aim.
   C A part-time hobby became a full-time job.
   D An individual effort became a London-wide plan.

3 Danny's 'Good Friday Agreement' states that people should
   A do something kind at least every week.
   B do a certain number of acts of kindness.
   C perform their acts of kindness in a certain area.
   D develop at least one new rule for acting kindly.

4 How do many of the members feel about doing the acts of kindness?
   A bewildered that people are so happy
   B embarrassed about approaching people
   C pleased with themselves
   D surprised that it is so easy

5 Danny has learned that when you do your act of kindness you should
   A try to look nervous.
   B leave as soon as you've done it.
   C talk to the person about what you're doing.
   D pretend that you're doing something wrong.

6 How does the writer feel about Danny's plans for the US?
   A He thinks his approach is too simple.
   B He thinks they will have a huge impact there.
   C He thinks his plans are overambitious and unlikely to happen.
   D He thinks it will be hard but Danny is the right man for the job.

4 Discuss these questions with other students.

1 Look again at the list in Exercise 1. How would you feel if a stranger did any of these things to you? Why?

2 Do you think that the way of 'spreading kindness' described in the text is a good thing or not? Why?

3 How do you think people in your country would feel if people did similar kinds of things to Danny's 'Karma Army'? Why?

Vocabulary | multi-word verbs – relationships

1 Work in pairs. What does each of the multi-word verbs in *italics* in these sentences mean? Check your answers in the Exam Reviser.

1 He was a friendly, open person and I *took to* him immediately.
2 It's good to be able to *cheer* someone *up* by doing something nice.
3 I've always *got on* really well *with* my sister.
4 I feel very comfortable with everyone I work with in my new job. I *fitted in* immediately.
5 I know I can always *turn to* my parents for support if I need to.
6 I find it difficult not to get annoyed when my brother *winds* me *up*.
7 She *went out with* her boyfriend for six months before they got engaged.
8 He's really upset because he *broke up with* his girlfriend yesterday.
9 I *fell out with* my flatmate after we argued about the washing-up.
10 I argued with my best friend last week but I *made up with* her today.

> exam reviser   p3 | 1.2 ▶

2 Look at the groupings of the multi-word verbs in the table. Why have they been grouped in this way? Look at the Exam Reviser to help you if necessary.

A	B	C	D
fit in	take to someone	cheer someone up	get on with someone
	turn to someone	wind someone up	go out with someone
			break up with someone
			fall out with someone
			make up with someone

> exam reviser   p30 | ▶

3 There are mistakes in these questions. Find the mistakes and correct them.

1 What do you usually do to cheer up yourself if you're feeling down?
2 How well do you get your parents on with?
3 For what reasons do flatmates often fall off with each other?
4 Do you think most people turn for family or friends when they need help?
5 When you were a child, what did you do to wind your parents on?
6 How important do you think it is to fit up at work?
7 For what reasons do couples often break each other up?
8 Can you remember someone who you took for the first time you met?
9 At what age do people in your country start going with someone out?
10 When was the last time you made for with someone after having an argument?

4 R.02 ▶ Listen to the sentences in Exercise 3 and <u>underline</u> the stress on each multi-word verb. Listen again and repeat the sentences.

5 Choose five of the questions in Exercise 3 to ask and answer with other students.

> premium plus   02 ▶

Speaking

1 R.03 ▶ Listen to two people discussing one of these questions. Which question are they discussing? Do they mostly agree or disagree with each other?

1 Are people around us more unfriendly now than in the past?
2 What different things do people look for in friends? Does this change as you get older?
3 Do you think that your family is more important than your friends?
4 Are old friends better than new ones?

2 R.03 ▶ Listen again and say how each person showed an interest in what the other one was saying.

3 Write the headings 1–4 in the correct place in the skills box. Look at the Exam Reviser and add one more phrase to each category.

1 Reacting with agreement/ understanding
2 Reacting with disagreement
3 Reacting with agreement but adding an alternative viewpoint
4 Reacting with agreement and adding another similar point

> exam reviser   p20 | 1 ▶

SPEAKING SKILLS
Showing an interest in what other people are saying

A _____

I see what you mean.
Yes, I hadn't thought of that.

B _____

Yes, plus you've got to remember that …
That's true, and don't forget that …

C _____

True, but don't you think that …?
Well, you may be right about … but what about …?

D _____

I'm not so sure about that.
I don't think I can agree with you about that because …

4 Work in pairs. Discuss one of the questions in Exercise 1. Show an interest in what your partner is saying by using some of the phrases in Exercise 3. Change partners and discuss another question.

premium plus   03 ▶

Grammar | *-ing* forms and infinitives

1 Choose the correct alternative in these sentences. Use the Grammar Reference to help you if necessary.

1 The majority of us avoid *making/to make* contact with each other.
2 He wasn't really sure what he wanted *achieve/to achieve*.
3 The aim is to try *break/to break* down social barriers.
4 I tried *sending/to send* her flowers but the shop was already shut.
5 He encouraged me *joining/to join* them every Friday.
6 *Being/Be* nice clearly makes you *feel/to feel* nice.
7 One lady told him about *to get/getting* on a bus.
8 He took her out to dinner *cheer/to cheer* her up.
9 It's worth *to make/making* the effort to be nice to other people.
10 Anyone can *join/joining* in if they want to.

•• see grammar reference: **page 169** ••

2 Work in pairs. Look at the verbs in the box and answer the questions. Use the Grammar Reference to help you if necessary.

> manage   risk   start   regret   let   keep on
> persuade   help   remember   advise   agree   intend

Which two verbs in the box:

1 are followed by an *-ing* form?
2 are followed by an infinitive with *to*?
3 can be followed by an *-ing* form or an infinitive with *to*, with almost no change of meaning?
4 can be followed by an *-ing* form or an infinitive with *to*, with a change of meaning?
5 are followed by an object + infinitive with *to*?
6 are followed by an object + infinitive without *to*?

•• see grammar reference: **page 169** ••

premium plus   04 ▶

3 Read the text and answer these questions. Then complete the text by writing the verb in brackets in the correct form.

1 What reason does the writer give for the success of social networking sites (like *Facebook* and *MySpace*)?
2 What does the writer hope for the future of such sites?

Social networking and the world of virtual friends
The phenomenon of social networking among Internet users keeps on _____[1] (grow). In the next thirty days, 20% of Internet users are expected _____[2] (visit) a social network like *Facebook* or *MySpace*. _____[3] (visit) these sites is now a significant way for adults to make 'friends' globally. So, what is it about these sites that has made them _____[4] (become) so successful?
One theory which tries _____[5] (explain) their success is the idea of 'collecting'. For many people, collecting things taps into not only our basic psychology of 'having more', but also many people's insecurities about _____[6] (be) popular. In other words, people want to have a large number of friends _____[7] (prove) they are popular.
I can see that these reasons are valid in a sense. I feel sure, however, that actually it's completely pointless _____[8] (have) all these virtual friends. I'd like to encourage people _____[9] (spend) time with their real friends. They may otherwise regret _____[10] (waste) years of their lives in front of a screen before they realise they actually have no friends at all.

4 Discuss these questions.

1 How often do you use social networking sites?
2 Do you spend more time with your real friends or your virtual friends? How do you feel about that?
3 How far do you agree with the opinions in the last paragraph of the text?

CAE close-up | Use of English Key word transformations (Paper 3, part 5)

Exam information

This part of the exam consists of eight key word transformations (plus an example). Each question contains three parts: a lead-in sentence, a key word and a second sentence with a gap in the middle. You have to fill the gap in the second sentence so that the completed sentence is similar in meaning to the lead-in sentence. The answer must be between three and six words, one of which must be the key word. The key word must not be changed in any way.

The focus of this part is grammar and vocabulary. A wide range of structures is tested e.g. *-ing* forms and infinitives, modals, verb tenses, *if*-structures, comparison, passive voice and reported speech. Multi-word verbs are also often tested, as well as lexical phrases such as *It doesn't make any difference …, I was wondering if …*, etc.

Approach

1 Read both sentences carefully.

2 Look at the key word and try to identify what kind of word it is (e.g. verb, noun).

3 Look at the words before and after the gap and try to work out what kind of grammar or vocabulary the question is testing (e.g. modals, phrasal verbs, reported speech).

4 Write between three and six words in the gap including the key word. Don't change the key word. Remember that contractions count as two words (e.g. *don't = do not =* two words).

5 Read your sentence to check that it makes sense. Also check for spelling and verb form mistakes.

6 In the exam, remember not to write the complete sentence. You should write only the missing words in the space on your answer sheet. Remember, too, that you should always write something in each gap: you do not lose marks for a wrong answer.

Practice task

For questions **1–8**, complete the second sentence so that it has a similar meaning to the first sentence, using the word given. **Do not change the word given.** You must use between **three** and **six** words, including the word given. Here is an example (**0**).

Example:

0 If you need any more information, you can always phone me.

HESITATE

If you need any more information, _____ me.

The gap can be filled by the words '*don't hesitate to phone*', so you write:

Example: | 0 | D O N ' T | H E S I T A T E | T O | P H O N E |

Write the missing words in **CAPITAL LETTERS**.

1 I'm sorry not to have taken the chance to go travelling with my friends.
REGRET
I _____ with my friends when I had the chance.

2 What I'm saying is very important and you need to listen carefully.
ATTENTION
It's very important that everyone _____ what I'm saying.

3 I had an argument with Sally and she hasn't spoken to me for three weeks.
OUT
Sally and I haven't spoken to each other since _____ ago.

4 I'm glad my parents were supportive of my playing the piano when I was a child.
ENCOURAGED
I'm glad my parents _____ the piano when I was a child.

5 The party was much better because you were there.
ALL
The party was _____ there.

6 My friends said they would take me out to dinner to make me feel better.
CHEER
My friends wanted _____ me out to dinner.

7 She tried very hard to make me decide to go camping with her.
PERSUADE
She tried very hard _____ camping with her.

8 Maria is nicer than most of the people I work with.
ONE
Maria is _____ people I work with.

Go to www.iTests.com or your CD-ROM for interactive exam practice

Listening

1 Read this introduction to a radio programme and answer the questions.

SHOWBIZ SISTERS

'Ashlee and Jessica, Sienna and Savannah, Britney and Jamie Lynn – showbiz is full of sisters who work side by side. But, as our correspondent Penny Driver asks, is keeping it in the family a recipe for disaster or success?'

1 What do you think she means by 'keeping it in the family' and 'a recipe for disaster or success'?
2 What do you think about the question she asks?

2 **R.04** Listen to the radio programme. What does Penny Driver say is the main factor that determines whether a relationship is disastrous or successful?

3 **R.04** Listen again and take notes of any key points you hear.

LISTENING SKILLS

Taking notes

Being able to take notes of the important points while listening is a very useful skill. A good set of notes will help you remember and understand the most important things from what you have heard. Try to write down only the key words you hear. Don't put them into grammatical sentences at this stage.

4 **R.04** Read these sentences. Then listen again and complete them. Compare your sentences with another student, making sure that they make sense.

1 Many _____ sisters have been seen at various award ceremonies and film premieres recently.
2 There is likely to be a lot of _____ when a famous woman's sister also starts becoming famous.
3 Privately, Penelope Cruz is probably a little _____ about being used by her sister.
4 People have noticed that Britney's sister is just as _____ as her and may be ready to take her place.
5 Differences in personality and issues from _____ often cause clashes between people.
6 Research shows that a younger child may be more _____ than his or her older sibling.
7 People in the _____ are often driven by a need to be in the limelight.
8 If sisters have a good relationship to start with, they will probably be _____ of each other's successes and failures.

5 Discuss these questions.
1 If you were a celebrity, how do you think you would feel about a younger sibling using your fame or success to get what he or she wanted? Why?
2 Where are you in the 'birth order' in your family? Use some of the phrases in the Exam Reviser to help you.
3 How much do you think birth order has affected the personalities and lives of you and your siblings?

exam reviser p3 | 1.1

Learning from other people

You can increase your learning opportunities by thinking about how people around you can help.
1 Which of the following would you recommend?
  • Speak in English to other students during classroom activities.
  • Create opportunities for speaking to people in English outside class (e.g. start a 'conversation club', arrange social activities).
  • Ask people for tips and learning strategies that work for them.
  • Ask a friend to test you on new words, phrases, etc.
  • Arrange with a friend to write emails to each other in English.
2 What other things can you suggest for learning from other people?

learning tip

13

Grammar | articles

1 Complete these sentences with the zero article (Ø), *the, an* or *a.*

Penelope Cruz is _____[1] actress whose sister, _____[2] Monica has used her sister's success to her own advantage.

Being _____[3] celebrity certainly makes _____[4] sibling rivalry more difficult.

_____[5] entertainment industry is full of _____[6] people who want to be 'The One'.

Sibling rivalry may lead to _____[7] relationship breaking up. When this happens it's usually because _____[8] relationship was poor to start with.

Sisters with a good relationship often give each other _____[9] support and _____[10] advice.

_____[11] relationship with our siblings is one of _____[12] most important factors in shaping our personality.

2 Look at the rules for the use of articles in the Grammar Reference and answer these questions.

1 Which rule matches each example in Exercise 1?
2 Which rules are different from those about the use of articles in your language?

•• see grammar reference: **page 170** ••

Grammar note | articles – difficult cases

Look at these pairs of sentences. In each case, do we use *the* or not? Why?

1 A _____ life is not always easy.
  B _____ life of celebrities is not always easy.

2 A I first went to _____ school when I was five.
  B I went back to _____ school I attended as a child and it had completely changed.

3 A She started her _____ own very successful fashion business.
  B _____ fashion business she started was very successful.

---

3 Complete the text by writing the zero article (Ø), *the, an* or *a.*

A good argument

Conflict is part of _____[1] life, most commonly starting at home with your brothers and sisters. Indeed, most psychologists agree that one major benefit of having siblings is learning how to handle conflict. It does not stop there, however. As we get older, almost all of us continue to argue, especially within _____[2] family.

Another point that _____[3] psychologists generally agree on is that arguing is, in itself, _____[4] good thing. A good row allows both sides to express their feelings and to clear the air. A good row, however, often degenerates into a bad row, with insults and shouting and eventually at least one person storming off.

So, how do you make sure that your arguments remain in _____[5] 'good row' category? Dr John Gottman, _____[6] American psychologist, says there are a number of key points. First, catch an issue early before you have built it up in your _____[7] own mind as a major crisis. Secondly, keep your language as positive as you can – don't just list a string of complaints. Thirdly, one of _____[8] most important points is to try to respect _____[9] other person's opinion and learn to live with _____[10] difference.

Gottman says that it's really worth trying to put things into perspective in this way. If we can train ourselves to use compromise and affection instead of criticism and contempt, then we can argue constructively and _____[11] world will be _____[12] better place.

4 Work in small groups and discuss whether you agree or disagree with these statements. Give reasons to justify your opinions.

1 Arguing is an inevitable and useful part of life.
2 One benefit of having siblings is to learn how to handle conflict.
3 Arguments usually end up with people shouting and storming off.
4 Humour, compromise and affection are essential in good arguments.

Vocabulary | describing people

1 Work in pairs. Think about the meaning of the phrases in the box. Which ones:

• are you sure you know?
• do you think you might know?
• are you sure you don't know?

General personality	Attitude to others	Thinking and decision-making
be easy-going	be diplomatic	be decisive
be good company	be fiercely loyal	be spontaneous
be considerate	be brutally honest	be level-headed
have a selfish streak	be a natural leader	have a vivid imagination
be painfully shy	lose your temper easily	have a razor-sharp mind
have a strong sense of responsibility	(often) put others first	have a tendency to make snap decisions

2 Ask other students about the ones you don't know or you're not sure about. Use a dictionary if necessary.

3 Complete these sentences using phrases from the box in Exercise 1.

1 When I was a child I was _____ and would never open my mouth to speak to anyone.

2 I'm the kind of person who _____ but I usually calm down quite quickly afterwards.

3 I'm a very _____ person who doesn't like to plan things in advance too much.

4 I am a _____ person and would do anything to support my friends.

5 I think I'm quite a _____ person – I generally make considered decisions and keep calm in a crisis.

6 I'd say that I've got _____ and I always try to do the right thing morally.

4 Add one more phrase for describing people to each column in the Exam Reviser.

exam reviser p3 | 1.3

5 Discuss with other students whether the sentences in Exercise 3 are true about you. Explain your reasons with examples about your personality. Which student in the class do you think is most similar to you? In what ways?

premium plus 05

Writing | reference

1 Look at the writing task and answer these questions.

1 What is the task asking you to write?

2 What three things do you need to include in your answer?

Writing task

A friend of yours is applying for a job with a travel company as a tourist guide for English-speaking tourists visiting your country. The company has asked you to provide a character reference for your friend.

In your reference, you should:

- say how you know the person;
- describe the person's skills and qualities which make him/her suitable for the job;
- describe his/her relevant work experience.

2 Discuss these questions with a partner. Then check your ideas in the Writing Reference.

1 How do you think you should start the reference?

2 How do you think you should finish it?

3 Do you think the language should be formal or informal?

4 How do you think the paragraphs could be organised?

3 Look again at the model in the Writing Reference and find the formal equivalents of the following phrases and sentences.

1 to whoever wants to read this

2 Everyone can see that she works very hard.

3 She is definitely very responsible.

4 Everyone knows that she works well in a team.

5 She is very organised and sensitive about other people as well.

6 when you first meet her…

7 She is much more confident now.

8 She can deal with pressure very well.

9 because of all these reasons, …

10 I definitely think she's the best person for the job.

•• see writing reference: page 200 ••

4 You are going to write a character reference for either this task or the one in Exercise 1. Think about someone you know who you could write a character reference for and decide which task you're going to answer.

Writing task

You have been asked to provide a reference for a friend of yours who has applied for a job as a Social Programme Organiser in an English language college.

Your reference should provide information about your friend's personal qualities and skills, their previous relevant experience and reasons why they should be considered for this job.

5 Plan how many paragraphs your reference will have. Then make some brief notes for each one, including relevant phrases for describing people from the Vocabulary section on page 14.

6 Write your reference in 220–260 words using your paragraph plan and notes. Make sure the language you use is appropriately formal.

Vocabulary

1 Read the email and decide which word A, B, C or D best fits each gap.

```
●○○
⊟Send 🖫 🖨 📝 ✓ 📎 ✉ ❗ ⬇ 📋 Options... ❓ Help

To...      Ben Holt
Cc...
Bcc...
Subject:   Party!
```

Hi Ben

Thank you so much for the party last weekend. Even though I didn't know many people, I fitted _____1 immediately and felt very much at home! It was nice to meet your friend Florence. She was so friendly and I took _____2 her as soon as I met her. We've got a lot in common, I think – we certainly got _____3 really well at the party. It was good to see Danny again, too – although whenever I see him, he spends the whole time _____4 me up and trying to annoy me. I don't know why!

Going to that party really _____5 me up actually as I'd been feeling a bit down that week. I fell _____6 with a friend about some money he owed me, which wasn't very nice. We did _____7 up with each other and we're friends again now, but the whole thing made me feel rather upset. It's really good to know that I can always turn _____8 you when I need some help – and also some fun!

Anyway, I hope you're OK. Hope to speak to you soon.

James

1 A up	B on	C in	D out
2 A for	B off	C on	D to
3 A up	B on	C from	D to
4 A whisking	B winding	C wondering	D willing
5 A cheered	B chatted	C took	D went
6 A up	B on	C out	D for
7 A do	B talk	C take	D make
8 A to	B from	C at	D up

2 Complete the text with the words in the box. Five of the words cannot be used.

brutally   fiercely   heavy   level   livid   painfully
shape   sharp   snap   streak   stripe   strong   vivid

To whom it may concern

Daniel Fellows

I have worked with Daniel for nearly ten years and in that time, as well as being a colleague, he has also become a personal friend.

Daniel has a _____1 sense of responsibility, is always punctual and always tries to do the right thing. He is always considerate of other people. In fact, I would describe him as a _____2 loyal friend who always puts others first. He certainly hasn't got a selfish _____3 at all. He can be _____4 honest sometimes, but people respect him and therefore value his opinion.

He is not someone to make _____5 decisions but always thinks about things very carefully. He is always calm in a crisis and remains _____6-headed when faced with a difficult decision about something. Daniel is a very intelligent person with a razor-_____7 mind and a great sense of humour. He is also a very creative person and has a _____8 imagination – he can always come up with a good idea or a creative solution to a problem.

I have no hesitation in recommending Daniel for the position he has applied for in your company.

Grammar

3 There are mistakes in these sentences. Find the mistakes and correct them.

1 Daniela is one of best friends I've had in my life.
2 To have a good relationship with my sisters is important to me.
3 Their father has been in and out of a prison all his life.
4 It's hopeless to try to talk to him about it – he won't listen to anyone.
5 I love music you sometimes hear in pubs around Ireland.
6 I distinctly remember to give the money back to you last week.
7 You'll need a coat and some boots – and make sure a coat is waterproof.
8 I'd be grateful if you could help me carrying all these boxes upstairs.
9 My brother plays the guitar very well and he also loves the tennis.
10 He decided making the decision after he had had a chance to talk to his friends.

Language Review

Sensational eating

Premium | Unit 02

takeaway

b

c

nano-food

bland

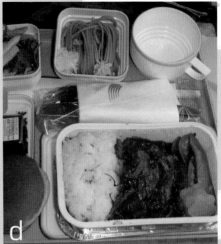
d

e

Unit 02

Introduction

1 Which eating experience in the pictures do you think you would enjoy most? Why?

2 Work in pairs. Talk about food you don't like, giving your reasons. Think about these aspects of food:
- smell
- texture
- appearance
- taste

3 What are the differences between the restaurants in each of the pairs A–C? Which ones would you prefer to eat in? Why?

A a family-run restaurant / a high-class restaurant

B an old, established restaurant / a new, trendy restaurant

C a self-service restaurant / a takeaway restaurant (e.g. Taco Bell, Domino's Pizza, McDonald's)

4 Discuss these questions with other students.
- Are you affected by where you eat and who you eat with? In what way?
- Do you think your feelings are typical of most people? Why/Why not?

Listening

1 Discuss these questions with other students. Look at the Exam Reviser for words and phrases to help you.
- What different types of atmosphere can you get in a restaurant? Think about decor, noise levels, expense, number of diners, etc.
- Which type of atmosphere do you prefer? Why?

exam reviser p4 | 2.1

2 R.05 You will hear five people talking about a restaurant they went to recently. Listen to the extracts and decide which type of restaurant, A–F, each speaker went to. Use the letters once only. There is one extra letter you do not need to use.

A a family-run restaurant
B a traditional, established restaurant
C a self-service restaurant
D a high-class restaurant
E a trendy restaurant
F a themed restaurant

3 R.05 Listen again and decide what opinion, A–F, each speaker has about the restaurant they went to. There is one extra letter you do not need to use.

A It is in a good location.
B It has excellent service.
C It served good quality food.
D It is worth the money you pay.
E It offers a good variety of dishes.
F It is too noisy.

4 With a partner, decide how important you think each of these aspects is. Put them in order from 1–6, with 1 as the most important. Give your reasons.
- the service
- the decor
- the ingredients in the food
- the presentation of the food
- the noise level
- the customers

Vocabulary | multi-word verbs with *up*

1 The meaning of *up* can help you understand the multi-word verb it is part of. In this sentence does *up* mean a) creating, b) completing or c) increasing?
He's built up a lot of custom.

2 Decide which meaning applies in each of these sentences. Be careful! Sometimes the same multi-word verb has two different meanings.
1 He's managed to *build* the business *up* from almost nothing in only three years.
2 She *thought up* a brilliant idea for the restaurant opening party.
3 Complaints to the council about this restaurant are beginning to *pile up*.
4 It's getting harder to *conjure up* new dishes these days.
5 *Eat up* before it gets cold!
6 You'll have to *speak up* – the music is very loud in here.
7 It's her own recipe – she *made it up* from scratch!
8 If you've *used up* all the milk, get some more.

3 Complete the sentences with the correct form of the most appropriate verb in the box.

> add   hang   dream   think   save   heat

1 When the waiter tried to _____ up the bill, he made several mistakes.
2 I don't know where he _____ the dish up from – it was really awful!
3 It's a good restaurant but expensive so you need to _____ up to go there!
4 The food industry is always _____ up new ways to get money off us!
5 You must make sure you _____ the soup up gently otherwise it'll taste burnt.
6 I called the restaurant three times but they kept _____ up!

4 Look at the Exam Reviser. Choose one verb from each column and add three more questions to ask your partner.
1 Do you *save up* for special things you want?
2 What's the best idea you have ever *dreamt up*?
3 _____
4 _____
5 _____

exam reviser p4 | 2.2

5 Work in pairs. Ask and answer the questions in Exercise 4.

premium plus 06

Speaking

1 Look at the picture and discuss whether you would like to try this extreme dining experience.

2 R.06 ▶ Listen to someone telling a friend about her experience of this restaurant. What is her opinion of:
1 the food?
2 the atmosphere?
3 the experience?

3 Discuss these questions.
1 Which of these occasions do you think Dinner in the Sky would be most suitable for and why?
  • a birthday dinner
  • a business lunch
  • a wedding celebration
  • a family get-together
  • a romantic dinner
  • a meal for a special festival
2 What kind of restaurant would you choose for each of the remaining occasions?

4 R.06 ▶ You can describe your feelings about something by turning adjectives into adverbs. Listen again and tick the phrases you hear.

Describing how good or bad something is
perfect – perfectly cooked food ☐
unusual – unusually slow service ☐
incredible – an incredibly thrilling edge ☐
delicious – deliciously juicy steak ☐
pleasant – I was pleasantly surprised by ... ☐
unexpected – it was unexpectedly delicious ☐
sad – it's sadly lacking in atmosphere ☐

5 Which of the adjectives in the box change their meaning when they are used as adverbs? How?

> wonderful unbelievable strange terrible
> incredible dreadful absolute positive pleasant

6 In pairs, take turns to describe a place or an object that was:
  • extremely good
  • strangely silent
  • absolutely perfect
  • positively dangerous
  • unbelievably beautiful

7 Choose an experience from your life and describe it to your partner. Use your own combinations of adverbs and adjectives and say whether or not you think he or she should try this experience and why.

exam reviser   p20 | 2
premium plus   07

Keeping a vocabulary notebook

1 How can you learn more vocabulary?
2 What can you do to help you remember vocabulary?

When you learn a new word, make a note of it in your own vocabulary book. Make sure you note down any other forms it can take, including negative forms and any typical collocations or fixed phrases, e.g.

perfect perfectly perfection perfectly cooked

This will increase your vocabulary and make words easier to remember. Writing down collocations will help you remember the typical context for the word.

Look back at Exercise 5. Choose three words and write down what you would include in your notebook.

learning tip

Grammar | modifying comparison

1 Match the sentence halves 1–7 and A–G to make complete sentences.

1 It is one of the cheaper	A than we expected for what we had.
2 It would be better for a bigger group	B the less you get.
3 It was far better value	C as other places.
4 The more you spend	D restaurants in the area.
5 The food was better	E for not being crowded.
6 It's twice as expensive	F than in many similar restaurants.
7 It was all the better	G rather than an intimate supper.

2 Complete these sentences using one word from each box.

> much   worse   better   later   more   times   most

> than   to   noisier   that   for   less   better

1 It would be _____ suited _____ a quiet supper than a celebration.
2 We spent _____ money _____ was wise.
3 It was _____ _____ than we anticipated it would be.
4 The chef is one of the _____ charming people _____ I've ever met.
5 I think the pie was _____ _____ being served cold.
6 The service was ten _____ _____ than when I had been there before.
7 The _____ you arrive the _____ choice there is.

3 Complete the second sentence so that it has a similar meaning to the first sentence, using the word given. Do not change the word given. You must use between three and six words.

1 Other tables do not have such a good view.
   far
   This table _____ other tables.
2 The meal cost double what we were expecting.
   twice
   The meal _____ we expected.
3 I find if you book early then you get a better table.
   earlier
   The _____ your table.
4 The salmon tasted much better when it was served warm.
   all
   The salmon tasted _____ served warm.
5 It's less busy at 7.00 p.m. than at most other times.
   quieter
   7.00 p.m. is one _____ times.

4 Write three sentences comparing two different restaurants you know. Use some of the expressions in Exercise 2. Discuss your comparisons with a partner, giving reasons for them.

> premium plus   08 ▶

5 Put these modifiers of degree into the correct columns in the table.

> rather   very   absolutely   fairly   terribly   really
> quite   extremely   completely   pretty

used with gradable adjectives (e.g. *cold*)	used with ungradable adjectives (e.g. *freezing*)

6 Look at this sentence. Which is the only modifier of degree you can use with the comparative?

The meal was *quite/rather/very* better than I expected.

> **Grammar note | *quite***
> Choose the correct alternatives in each sentence:
> 1 I thought the meal was *quite/fairly/totally* good.
> 2 It was *quite/very/completely* impossible to work out the bill.
> What is the difference in meaning in *quite*?

> •• see grammar reference: **page 171** ••

7 Complete the gaps with *quite*, *rather* or *absolutely*. Sometimes more than one option is correct.

HARD ROCK CAFÉ

The Hard Rock Café in London is the world's first Hard Rock, and if you are looking for a plump chargrilled burger with a healthy portion of _____¹ delicious fries, there is very little competition that comes close. Its appeal is in the memorabilia which is on show everywhere. You can even buy merchandise as a souvenir although it costs _____² more than you might want to pay! Yet the food is _____³ good. When I went, my burger was _____⁴ well cooked and juicy, although the normally fast service was _____⁵ slower than usual. I was expecting to hate it, but I was pleasantly surprised by my experience; the atmosphere was _____⁶ wonderful. But be warned – it's _____⁷ difficult to get a table. Hard Rock is busy and queuing is the norm.

8 Think about the last restaurant you visited. Write three sentences using *quite*, *rather* and *absolutely* to describe your experience there. Compare your sentences with a partner.

Writing | review

1 Look at the pictures of the Ninja restaurant in New York and discuss these questions.

- Would you like to go to this restaurant? Why/Why not?
- What aspects do you think would be enjoyable or not enjoyable?
- What problems do you think a restaurant like this would have?

2 Read a review of the restaurant in the Writing Reference. Discuss these questions with a partner.

- How enthusiastic do you think the review is?
- If you were interested in visiting this restaurant, do you think the review contains all the information you would need?
- Would this review persuade you to visit the restaurant?

•• see writing reference: **page 206** ••

3 Choose a restaurant to write a review for in this task.

Writing Task

You see this announcement on a website:

> Have you been to a restaurant that is special or different? If so, write a review for our website. Your review should describe the restaurant and its atmosphere, explain why the restaurant is different or special and say whether or not you would recommend it to other people.

4 Put the points A–G into the most appropriate paragraph in the plan. Use the model in the Writing Reference to help you.

A why other people would enjoy the restaurant
B the type of food served
C the name of the restaurant
D the efficiency of the service
E any problems you experienced
F the features that made it special or different
G the atmosphere

Para 1/Introduction:	
Para 2:	
Para 3:	
Para 4/Recommendation:	

•• see writing reference: **page 206** ••

5 Make your review interesting by using a variety of language. Write synonyms for these words and phrases, then compare your synonyms with those in the review on page 206.

1 memorable
2 not typical
3 nicer
4 very
5 surprisingly
6 very nice
7 thought it was good
8 fast

6 Discuss these aspects of your chosen restaurant with a partner. Try to use a range of language.

- the atmosphere
- the food
- the service
- the cost

WRITING SKILLS

Using range

Your writing will be more interesting if you use a range of language, especially when you are describing something.

1 Remember to use a variety of adjectives, e.g. *good = excellent, superb, wonderful, first-class, exceptional, top quality.*

2 If you are describing something, describe a variety of aspects, e.g. a meal – the appearance, the flavour, the ingredients.

7 Which of these opening sentences would make you want to read a review? Why?

1 I went to The Fat Duck with my husband last week. It was a really nice building set in the countryside.

2 Have you ever tried egg and bacon ice cream? Or chocolate jelly with risotto? Well, if you want to, The Fat Duck is the place to go.

3 Many people never try anything new. They know what they like and are reluctant to try anything different. But The Fat Duck offers a very different menu.

8 Write your review in 220–260 words using your paragraph plan and the writing model in the Writing Reference. Think carefully about how to get the reader's attention in your opening sentence.

Reading

1 Look at the pictures and read the title and sub-heading in the article. What do you think the article will be about?

2 Now read the article quickly. Don't worry about the gaps at this stage. Were your predictions correct?

The future of food

The scientific dream of creating food that is both small and gives you a choice is fast becoming reality.

Willy Wonka, the hero from the novel *Charlie and the Chocolate Factory*, is the father of nano-food. The great chocolate-factory owner invented a chewing gum that was a full three-course dinner. 'It will be the end of all kitchens and cooking,' he told the children on his tour – and produced a prototype sample of Wonka's Magic Chewing Gum. When chewed, one strip of this would[1] deliver tomato soup, roast beef with roast potatoes and blueberry pie and ice cream – in the right order.

1 F

Far-fetched? In fact, a group of research laboratories are busy working towards this kind of 'programmable food'. For example, one new idea they are working on is a colourless, tasteless drink that you, the consumer, will design after you've bought it.

Once you get home, you zap the product with a microwave transmitter. This will activate nano-capsules containing the necessary chemicals of your choice: green-hued, blackcurrant-flavoured with a touch of caffeine and omega-3 oil, say. They will dissolve, while all the other possible ingredients will pass unused through your body.

2

Nano-technology is the science of the tiny – the precision engineering of substances at molecular and atomic level. The industry exploits the fact that physics and chemistry change at nano-scale and common substances behave very differently – thus they can[2] take on startling new properties. 'It's like having a brand new tool box,' says one enthusiastic scientist.

3

What's to be afraid of, from a technology that offers so much – healthier food, fewer, better targeted chemicals, less waste, 'smart' (and thus less) packaging, and even the promise of a technological solution to the problem of the one billion people who don't get enough to eat?

4

Food manufacturers also plan to use nano-encapsulation to improve shelf life and engineer taste sensations in fat-based foods like chocolates, ice creams and spreads. There could[3] be huge reductions in fats and salts in processed foods. They believe they can[4] reduce the fat content of ice cream from 15% to 1%.

5

Atomic-level encapsulation techniques will get more sophisticated. Nano-encapsulation could[5] let chefs choose, exactly, how strong a taste or smell should[6] be and when it should[7] be delivered, and design a food's mouth-feel. The capsule can[8] be tailored to break down and release its contents to order. A chef might[9] decide that some flavours in his dish would only be released to the eater a certain number of seconds or minutes after chewing.

6

Further ahead, the industry is looking at food that is pre-engineered to cater for your tastes, your dislikes and your allergies. Or just built from scratch. 'Ultimately,' says Franz Kampers, a scientist at the Netherland's Wageningen University, 'The Holy Grail of the food industry is to create a roast turkey with all the trimmings from plant protein. That would be really something!' You may[10] not want it, but the scientists are already halfway there.

3 Six paragraphs have been removed from the article. You have to choose which paragraph A–F best fits in each gap 1–6. The first one has been done for you as an example. First look at the example and study the highlighted cohesive devices in the text and the missing extract. Decide what each one is an example of from the list in the skills box.

READING SKILLS

Understanding cohesion in a text

A text can be connected through a variety of cohesive devices. You need to recognise and understand these to be able to follow a text effectively. Examples of these cohesive devices are:

1 reference, e.g. *him*, *her*, *it*, *these*, etc.
2 ellipsis, e.g. '*So I told him* (what to do).'
3 referring nouns, e.g. *experiment*, *idea*, *information*
4 linking words/phrases, e.g. *However*, *In addition*, etc.

A
Aside from altering nutrients for health reasons like this, an American company has claimed to have created 'the Holy Grail of chewing-gum design' – chewing gum with real chocolate in it. Hazelnut-cappuccino flavour is next. Even better, when it comes to chewing gum, nano-particles will shortly be able to carry teeth-cleaning chemicals that you won't be able to taste.

B
Other benefits could[11] include less use of chemicals and heat treatments in food processing plus significant nutritional benefits. For example, lactose can[12] now be filtered from milk, and replaced with another sugar, making all milk suitable for the lactose-intolerant. As well as these more practical applications, in lab experiments, the colour has been removed from beetroot juice, leaving the flavour; and red wine has been turned into white.

C
Not everybody is so positive. 'Matter has different behaviour at nano-scales,' said Dr Kees Eijkel from the Dutch Twente University. 'That means different risks are associated with it. We don't know what the risks are.' With nano-tech, the food industry has once again got it back to front, he feels. 'Such innovation must[13] be consumer-led – the consumer must[14] be able to see what's in it for them.'

D
An off-shoot of this is the possibility that if you're going out to a restaurant, or even food shopping, you could[15] carry your own nano-nose, a personal tasting sensor programmed to test food for things you don't like, or chemicals and allergens which may make you ill.

E
The end of cooking? Probably not. Catch me having friends round for a programmable nano-cola? Not more than once. But our reaction to some of the dafter promises of the new science is not really relevant. You may[16] not want it, but the food industry does. Every major food corporation is investing in nano-tech because the food industry has spotted the chance for huge profits. But what exactly is it?

F (example)

4 Now decide which paragraph A–E best fits in each gap 2–6. Look carefully at the paragraph before *and* after the gap.

5 Discuss these questions with a partner.
1 Find two advantages and two disadvantages of nano-food mentioned in the text. Can you think of any more advantages or disadvantages?
2 How do you feel about the prospect of this kind of food? Why? Use the adjectives in the box to help you.

> concerned   amused   fascinated   terrified   bored

Grammar | ability, possibility and obligation

1 Match the modal verbs 1–16 in the text on page 22 to the uses A–E. Use the Grammar Reference to help you.

A general possibility
B ability
C obligation
D negative possibility
E looking at the future in the past

•• see grammar reference: **page 171** ••

2 Choose the correct alternatives. Think about which meaning you need from the list in Exercise 1.

CHOCOLATE CAN BE GOOD FOR YOU!

Should/Would[1] chocolate be an essential component of a balanced diet? Back in the 17th and 18th centuries people expected that chocolate *can/would*[2] become known for its medicinal virtues. In fact, the jury is still out on whether or not it *could/should*[3] be good for us.

Chocolate *can/must*[4] help prevent tooth decay! The husks, usually discarded in chocolate production, *should/can*[5] help fight plaque and in future they *could/would*[6] be added back in to chocolate to make it dental-friendly. However, we know that decay *can/could*[7] be caused by chocolate's high sugar content, so chocolate isn't going to replace toothpaste any time soon.

Researchers have carried out experiments that suggest that if you eat chocolate three times a month you *must/might*[8] live almost a year longer than those who forego such sweet temptation. But it *might/would*[9] not all be good news – the research also suggested that people who eat too much chocolate *should/could*[10] have a lower life expectancy because of the high fat content in chocolate.

It looks like the old adage of 'everything in moderation' holds. But if you *must/would*[11] eat chocolate, you *should/might*[12] stick to dark. It's higher in cocoa than milk chocolate and helps prevent fat clogging up arteries.

3 Rewrite these sentences using a modal verb to replace the highlighted words.

1 Did you know how to **cook** when you were a teenager?
2 It's possible we will all be eating nano-food within the next ten years.
3 There's a chance she won't like chocolate chewing gum!
4 In Italy I first tried a dish that I later came to love.
5 There's a possibility that you won't like this new food.
6 A nano-restaurant is an amazing idea but I don't think it'll happen.

4 Write three things that you think are possibilities for the future and three things you think are unlikely to happen. Compare your list with a partner using modal verbs from Exercise 3.

premium plus 09 ▶

Vocabulary | senses in eating

1 Put the words related to food into the correct columns in the table. Some words can go in more than one column. Check your answers in the Exam Reviser.

refined   stodgy   tender   bitter   acidic   spicy
bland   smooth   appetising   lumpy   creamy
sweet   off   pungent

Appearance	Flavour	Aroma	Texture

exam reviser   p4 | 2.3 ▶

2 Choose the correct alternative in these questions.

1 In the winter do you like eating *smooth/stodgy* food to fill you up?

2 Have you got a *sweet/refined* tooth?

3 Do you prefer soups that are *bland/smooth* or chunky?

4 What do you think is the most *appetising/tender* food to eat when you're hot?

5 Do you like hot and *spicy/acidic* food?

6 Why do you think so many people find chocolate so *refined/tempting*?

7 Why do you think adults have a more *refined/clean* palate than children?

3 Ask and answer the questions in Exercise 2 with a partner.

4 Work in pairs. Look at Exercise 2 again and add one more word to each column in the Exam Reviser.

exam reviser   p4 | 2.3

5 Describe your favourite dish to a partner. Say how it looks, tastes, smells and feels when you eat it.

CAE close-up | Use of English Open cloze (Paper 3, part 2)

Exam information

This part of the exam consists of a text in which there are fifteen gaps (plus one gap as an example). The answer will always be a single word (never a phrase) with the focus on grammar and grammatical vocabulary. Occasionally there may be more than one possible answer, but you must only write one word. It is important that your spelling is correct.

Approach

1 Read the text quickly before filling in any of the gaps in order to get a general sense of the meaning.

2 Read the whole sentence that contains a gap and decide what type of word is missing, e.g. a preposition, a linking word, a negative, etc.

3 Read the words before and after the gap carefully before you try to decide on the correct word.

4 Think about collocations (e.g. *take a break*), dependent prepositions (*depend on*) and grammatical patterns (e.g. *bigger than expected, can be seen*).

5 Only use one word to fill each gap. Do not fill any gaps with a contraction (e.g. *didn't, I'll*) and never use abbreviations (e.g. *TV*).

6 Remember that in the exam you should always write something in each gap: you do not lose marks for a wrong answer.

Practice task

For questions 1–15, read the text below and think of the word that best fits each gap. Use only one word in each gap. There is an example at the beginning (0).

Write your answers IN CAPITAL LETTERS.

Example: | 0 | B E |

Why does food taste worse when airborne?

The perceived blandness of airline food can **(0)** _____ attributed largely to the limited space available on aircraft, and the pressure **(1)** _____ airlines to keep costs low. Meals are generally frozen and **(2)** _____ to be re-heated before takeoff, rather **(3)** _____ prepared fresh. It has also been suggested that the taste buds are **(4)** _____ sensitive at higher altitudes, **(5)** _____ everything taste bland. The reduced supply of oxygen can cause a significant increase in your sensitivity to sweet tastes, a mild increase in your salt sensitivity and a decrease in your sensitivity to sour and bitter tastes. However, most airline meals are bland because they are designed to be **(6)** _____ way. They are designed **(7)** _____ this because of two factors: food safety and passenger comfort.

Food safety is paramount in **(8)** _____ airline catering industry. A case of mass food poisoning among the passengers on **(9)** _____ airliner could have disastrous consequences. **(10)** _____ to the safety considerations, there are also the issues of passenger comfort. **(11)** _____ designing a meal service for a passenger flight, caterers must keep in **(12)** _____ that the passengers have no other sources of food **(13)** _____ what the airline is offering – they **(14)** _____ buy a meal elsewhere when stuck in the air. Accordingly, the food must be palatable to almost everyone on board. Any particular strong spice is likely to be disliked by a percentage of the passengers. This is **(15)** _____ most western airline meals consist of a large serving of protein, a small green salad, some potatoes and a dessert.

Go to www.iTests.com or your CD-ROM for interactive exam practice

Grammar

1 Choose the correct alternatives.

The Chinese Takeaway

My grandfather is from China and he came to this country and did *quite/ rather*[1] better than his friends because he set up his own takeaway shop selling typical Chinese dishes. At first it was *quite/completely*[2] hard as Chinese food was not *terribly/fairly*[3] popular as it has *as stronger/much stronger*[4] flavours than a lot of British food. Slowly he began to sell *more and more/all the more*[5] as customers found it was *twice as cheap/one of the cheaper*[6] ways to eat and it saved them cooking. The menu has expanded over the years and now it's *incredibly/totally*[7] varied. I would love to turn it into a cosy restaurant. We get *twice as many/far more*[8] students as family customers because we're near the university. We have a lot of regulars, especially on a Saturday night. We find *all the more/the more*[9] they eat our food, the more they want – it's *very/really*[10] delicious!

2 There are mistakes in these sentences. Find the mistakes and correct them.

1 There was a possibility the table would to be booked.
2 You mustn't expect him pay for the meal.
3 Unfortunately, the research must not be completed in time for the conference.
4 Is it right that we shall expect the food industry to control our diet?
5 We know that too much salt must be very bad for your blood pressure.
6 The pudding was so stodgy that I shouldn't eat it.
7 It would be incredible we could control what flavours were released.
8 It can be that in the future we won't need fridges.

Vocabulary

3 Replace the highlighted word with a multi-word verb using *up*.

1 Have you finished all the milk?
2 Can you say that more loudly – I can't hear you?
3 She invented some amazing dishes from scratch.
4 When I complained, she put the phone down on me.
5 We've managed to increase our list of regular customers.
6 You have to make sure the pudding is warm.
7 Can you please finish your meal quickly? We're going out.
8 He's hopeless at calculating the bill.

4 Complete the text with the words in the box.

> stodgy off spicy bitter appetising acidic
> sweet smooth pungent bland

Is taste genetic?

Humans have evolved certain common taste preferences, such as sugar and fat and also taste aversions for food which smells _____[1]. However, scientists have found specific genes that control individual taste variations within this, and this affects how strong or _____[2] we find different flavours. A single gene has been found that controls our sensitivity to PTC, a chemical present in many _____[3] foods, such as black coffee. There is also some research to show that our preference for _____[4] foods made with chilli is partly governed by the same gene. Perhaps we will discover that there is a gene to control our sensitivity to other things, such as the _____[5] taste of fruit or the _____[6] flavours in puddings. We may even find genes that control our reaction to texture, leading us to prefer _____[7] soups or chunky stews, or giving us a fondness for heavy, _____[8] puddings. Smell also affects how we feel about food and perhaps this, too, is genetically controlled so that the _____[9] smell of some spices makes the dish _____[10] to some but off-putting to others!

Language Review

Game on

competitive

champion

achievement

Unit 03

Introduction

1 Discuss these questions with other students.

1 Which of these international sporting events can you see in the pictures?

> Winter Olympics   Formula One   Golf Ryder Cup
> Football World Cup   Wimbledon Tennis Championships

2 What are your 'top three' international sporting events? You can use the events in the box or think of your own. Compare your ideas with other students, giving reasons for your choices.

2 Which of these words/phrases in *italics* are only used to talk about sport and which can be used to talk about other things as well?

1 What do you think is your greatest *achievement*? Give details.
2 Are you the type of person who *rises to a challenge*? Why/Why not?
3 When was the last time you *set yourself a goal*? Give details.
4 Do you prefer *individual sports* or are you more of *a team player*? Why?
5 Are you more of *a spectator* or *an active participant*? Give reasons.

3 Discuss the questions in Exercise 2 with other students.

premium plus   10 ▶

Listening

1 How do you feel about keeping fit? Choose an opinion from the list A–D, or write your own sentence. Then compare and discuss with other students.

A I love keeping fit – I go to the gym at least three times a week.

B I like going to keep fit classes, partly to keep fit and partly because it's sociable.

C I keep fit by doing things like jogging, but I'm not that keen on it.

D I don't like doing any kind of keep fit exercise – I find it boring and I always give up.

2 R.07 ▶ You are going to listen to a radio programme about a new fitness craze called *chaos training*. First look at the pictures. How do you think these things might be used in this fitness craze? Listen and check your ideas.

3 Before you listen again, read the questions and options and <u>underline</u> key points to listen out for.

1 What is the interviewer's attitude to the fitness industry?

A She thinks they make keeping fit too expensive.

B She thinks they create new ways of exercising just for the money.

C The new fitness crazes they think up make her laugh.

D She is pleased that they encourage everyone to take part.

2 According to Rob, why is it good that 'you never know what's coming' in these classes?

A Because it makes people more competitive.

B Because it gives the classes a clearer purpose.

C Because you are exercising both mind and body.

D Because it encourages people to make more effort.

3 What does Rob think about the props (e.g. ladders and drinking straws) that are used in the classes?

A They all work very well in the classes.

B Some of them are more useful than others.

C They are just there for effect but aren't really used.

D They are too extraordinary for most people's taste.

4 What is the advantage of including difficult activities in these classes, according to Rob?

A It stops people getting bored.

B It encourages the more advanced participants.

C It means people come back to the gym more often.

D It makes people more confident of their own abilities.

5 Why does Rob think chaos training will be successful in Europe?

A Because people want to copy what has been done in New York.

B Because people want to exercise a few muscle groups in this way.

C Because people want to try fitness crazes whenever they can.

D Because people will be motivated by the different nature of this kind of exercise.

4 R.07 ▶ Listen again. For each question in Exercise 3, choose the best answers A, B, C or D.

5 Discuss these questions with a partner.

• How would you feel about having a go at chaos training? Why?

• Do you think the fitness industry 'is having a laugh at our expense'? Why/Why not?

premium plus   11 ▶

Routine and 'chaos' in learning

Look at these different ways of studying and organising your studies.

• Which ones do you already do?

• Which ones would you like to do more?

• Can you add any ideas that work well for you?

Routine	'Chaos'
1 Keep a vocabulary notebook of new words and phrases. 2 Learn five new words every day. 3 Organise a quiet place to study. 4 Decide when you study best.	1 Pick ten words at random from your notebook to test yourself on. 2 Have conversations with people you meet. 3 Sometimes allow yourself to speak without worrying about any of your mistakes.

learning tip

Vocabulary | compete, win and lose

1 Complete these sentences with an appropriate word in the box.

> win   beat   lose   competitive   competition

1 Most of us have a pretty strong _____ streak.
2 Many of us thrive on _____.
3 Most people want to succeed and _____ the others.
4 They need to use that inbuilt desire to _____.
5 Not many people actually like to _____!

2 Look at the words and phrases in *italics* in each sentence. Which one, two or three of the options in brackets collate correctly with them?

1 I've got a strong *competitive* _____. (streak/instinct/spirit)
2 He's *competing in a* _____ tomorrow. (race/match/tournament)
3 There are some _____ *competitors* in this race. (strong/intense/stiff)
4 I came up against _____ *competition* in yesterday's match. (strong/intense/stiff)
5 She's got an *inbuilt desire to* _____. (win/succeed/beat)
6 He _____ *me* every time we play tennis together. (wins/succeeds/beats)
7 They *won by a* _____ *margin*. (slim/huge/thick)
8 He _____ *a record* every time he races at the moment. (sets/holds/breaks)

3 Check your ideas in the Exam Reviser.

> eHam reviser   p5 | 3.1 ▶

4 Look at this picture of James Cracknell (Olympic gold medal rower) and Ben Fogle (TV presenter). Read the text quickly and answer the questions.

1 What did they do and why?
2 How easy or difficult was it?

TWO MEN IN A BOAT

For James Cracknell and Ben Fogle, their 4,726-km row across the Atlantic started at a party, when Ben asked James to join him for this epic race for charity.

They made an odd couple. Cracknell had trained all his life for three Olympic Games. He has a huge competitive _____[1] with only one aim – to _____[2]. Ben, on the other hand, is a TV presenter and very laid-back – not _____[3] at all. He likes challenges but has no _____[4] desire to win. They both knew it was going to be a huge challenge.

James's wife was worried about how he would cope with competing _____[5] a race in which he couldn't see the other _____[6] and had little control over his ability to _____[7]. And they were certainly up against some _____[8] competition. Some of the rowers they were_____[9] against had spent over two years preparing themselves physically and psychologically. James and Ben only had two months.

They rowed in horrendous conditions – often too miserable and exhausted to speak. Sometimes they were scared for their lives. But they made it, arriving in Antigua after seven weeks of near-torture. That was extraordinary enough. Even more incredible was that they _____[10] all the other competitors, winning _____[11] a considerable margin. They may not have _____[12] any existing records as such, but they certainly put in a personal best.

5 Complete the text using the correct option A or B for each gap.

1 A instinct   B inbuilt
2 A beat   B win
3 A competitive   B competition
4 A instinct   B inbuilt
5 A for   B in
6 A competitors   B competes
7 A beat   B succeed
8 A stiff   B slim
9 A succeeding   B competing
10 A won   B beat
11 A in   B by
12 A broken   B set

6 Discuss these questions with a partner.
- How would you feel about competing in a race like this?
- How would you describe your competitive instinct in sport and at work or school? Why?
- Do you think you could be a serious competitor in a particular sport if you trained hard? Why/Why not?
- When was the last time you won something? What happened? How did you feel?

> premium plus   12 ▶

Grammar | present perfect (1)

1 Complete these sentences with the correct verb in the box. Which words in the sentences helped you decide?

> have been   was   am

1 I _____ a member of my local gym now.
2 I _____ a member of my local gym for nearly six months now.
3 I _____ a member of my local gym until I broke my leg.

2 How do you choose between the present perfect and the past simple? Complete these rules with the correct tense (present perfect or past simple). Check your answers in the Grammar Reference.

A The _____[1] is often used to describe a situation or event which started in the past and continues up to the present time. The specific starting point or the length of the period is given.

The _____[2] describes an event which happened at a particular time in the past or a situation which no longer exists. It is also used to talk about repeated actions in the past.

B The _____[3] is often used to introduce an event, an action or an idea without specifying details about it. It is often used to talk about an experience when the specific time is unknown or unimportant.

We then use the _____[4] to talk about the details, including exactly when and where something happened and how people felt, etc.

•• see grammar reference: **page 172** ••

3 Complete this dialogue with the correct form (present perfect or past simple) of the verb in brackets.

A: Is 'chaos training' really popular then? I _____[1] (never hear) of it before.

B: Well, yes. It _____[2] (be) a huge success in New York and now it _____[3] (start) to become popular in Europe, too.

A: Can you do it at your local gym?

B: Yes, in the last few months, loads of gyms around here _____[4] (decide) to start classes and I _____[5] (have) two sessions so far.

A: Oh, really? What _____[6] (be) it like?

B: Well, I _____[7] (think) it was great fun, actually. Like they said on that radio programme, I _____[8] (find) doing so many different and unpredictable things really motivating. I _____[9] (not like) all the tasks, but it _____[10] (be) really good exercise, that's for sure!

4 R.08 ▶ Listen and check your answers.

5 Use the ideas in the box to ask your partner questions starting with *Have you ever ...?* or *How long have you ...?* Continue your conversation using other appropriate tenses.

> do a dangerous sport   break a leg   run a long distance
> think about taking up a new sport/type of exercise
> see/meet a famous sportsperson   join a gym

premium plus   13 ▶

Speaking

1 Work in pairs. Look at the pictures and say briefly what you can see in each one.

2 R.09 ▶ Listen to two students talking about the pictures. What do they say about these three questions?

1 What different aspects of competition do the pictures show?

2 How might the people be feeling?

3 Do you think that having a competitive element to sport is a good thing for young people or not?

3 R.09 ▶ Listen again and number these ways of giving opinions in the order you hear them. Some of them are not used. Then look at the Exam Reviser for more ways of giving opinions.

Giving opinions
- As I see it ... ☐
- If you ask me ... ☐
- In my view ... ☐
- What I think is ... ☐
- The way I see it is ... ☐
- I don't really feel that ... ☐
- I would say it depends on ... ☐

exam reviser   p20 | 3 ▶

4 Look at the pictures again and discuss the questions in Exercise 2 with a partner. Use some of the phrases in Exercise 3.

CAE close-up | Speaking Interview and individual long turn (Paper 5, parts 1 & 2)

Exam information

Usually, the Speaking part of the exam is done in pairs, with one other candidate. In part 1, the examiner asks a selection of different personal information questions to each candidate in turn. There is also a second examiner in the room who listens but doesn't say anything. This part lasts about 3 minutes. (The whole Speaking exam lasts about 15 minutes.)

The examiner starts by asking you one or two basic questions (e.g. *What do you do?*). He or she then asks you two or three more questions. The topics are all connected with personal information about you and your opinions, including some of the following: leisure time, learning, future plans, travel and holidays and daily life.

In part 2, the two candidates take turns to speak for 1 minute without interruption. You answer two or more questions based on three photos on the same topic. It is not necessary to describe the photos in detail. Each candidate will talk about a different set of photos and you should not interrupt the other candidate. You must pay attention while the other candidate is speaking, however, as you will be asked to comment briefly when they have finished.

Approach

In part 1:

1 Listen carefully to the questions the examiner asks you. If necessary, ask the examiner to repeat anything you don't understand, e.g. *Could you say that again, please?*

2 Make sure you answer the questions the examiner asks you. Don't start talking about something else.

In part 2:

3 Make sure you have revised how to describe contrasting pictures and ideas (see Exam Reviser page 25) and the language of describing feelings and attitudes (see Exam Reviser page 21).

4 Don't just describe what you see in the photos, but make sure you answer the questions which are written next to the photos. (The examiner asks you these same questions.)

5 You don't have to give very long answers, but try to show off the range of vocabulary and structures that you know, e.g. *The way I see it is that if there were more sports facilities, more young people would take part and ...*

6 While the other candidate is speaking, look at their photos and listen carefully to what they say. Be ready to answer the examiner's question to you when they have finished speaking.

7 Keep talking until the examiner tells you to stop. Don't worry if the examiner interrupts you while you are still talking – it does not mean you have done something wrong!

Practice task

R.10 ▶ Follow the instructions on page 165.

Go to www.iTests.com or your CD-ROM for interactive exam practice

Roger Federer

Reading

1 Look at the pictures and discuss these questions with a partner.

1 Do you like playing or watching tennis?
2 How many champion tennis players can you name?
3 What do you know about the Wimbledon Tennis Championships?
4 Look at the pictures 1–6 of people who work at Queen's Tennis Club in Wimbledon. What do you think each of their jobs involves?
5 Look at the title of the text. Why do you think they are called 'unsung heroes'?

READING SKILLS

Predicting content before reading

It is a good idea to think about the content of a text before you read it and try to predict what it will be about. This will help you understand what you read better. You can use different clues to help you think about the content, e.g. the title or any accompanying pictures.

2 Skim the text quickly and match each picture 1–6 to the correct paragraph A–F.

WIMBLEDON'S UNSUNG HEROES

Immaculate courts, orderly queues, strawberries and cream … they just wouldn't happen without Wimbledon's unseen army of workers. Here, we give these unsung heroes some well-deserved credit for their amazing achievements behind the scenes.

A

Twice a week, all year round, Wayne Davis and Finnegan, a magnificent falcon, go up onto the centre court roof. Finnegan's job is simply to do what comes naturally – fly up to about 500 ft and then dive-bomb any pigeons he sees.

'They can be distracting for the players and mess up the courts. There can also be issues with disease,' says Davis. 'We've been scaring off pigeons since 2002 and it's been a resounding success. Pigeon numbers have dropped dramatically and it's much more ecological than poison,' he says. During the championships, Davis is up on the roof from 6.00 a.m. every day. 'I've trained him not to kill the pigeons, so he just plays with them a bit, and they disappear!'

B

'You can't play tennis on your own lawn because the soils are wrong, the grasses are wrong and it's not maintained properly,' says Eddie Seaward, the man in charge of the upkeep of the playing surfaces on all of Wimbledon's forty-one courts. As Head Groundsman, he clearly has incredibly high standards.

'The soil beneath each court is made to a special formula and the playing surfaces have been tested for wear using specialised machines that mimic a tennis player's footfall. The grass is also specially cut, using a machine that leaves all the blades pointing skywards. We've got to reach our goals in order for players to have the best chance of reaching theirs.'

3 <u>Underline</u> the key words and phrases in these questions to help you know what to look for in the text.

For which person are the following true?

he/she uses particular technology to do his/her job 1 _____

his/her job is to keep the courts in perfect playing condition 2 _____ 3 _____

his/her work is directly affected by the weather 4 _____

he/she gets to know the competitors quite well 5 _____

his/her work happens mostly during the actual championships 6 _____ 7 _____

he/she is concerned with environmental issues 8 _____

he/she mentions an accident that he/she witnessed 9 _____

he/she sometimes has to deal with difficult members of the public 10 _____

he/she has worked at Wimbledon for over a quarter of a century. 11 _____ 12 _____

4 For each of the questions in Exercise 3, choose from the people A–F. The people may be chosen more than once.

5 Discuss these questions with other students.

- Which of the jobs in the text would you most like to do? Why?
- Are you someone who prefers to work behind the scenes or to be in the limelight? Why?
- Do you go to live sporting events? If so, talk about a particularly memorable one. If not, why not?

C

Around 150 teenagers will be responsible for ensuring tennis balls get to where they should be with the minimum of fuss, and in charge of them – as she has been for more than twenty-five years – is Anne Rundle. Training takes place on Wimbledon's covered courts for about three months before the championships.

The youngsters do a series of exercises to improve fitness and refine their skills. They are encouraged to achieve their own personal best. 'Temperament is also vital, however,' she says. 'The ones who get on the main courts may not be the most skilful, but they're the ones best able to cope with it. Like the boy who broke his arm banging into the net post – but carried on!'

D

In his twenty-eighth tournament, Andrew Gairdner heads a team of more than 200 stewards who are the public face of Wimbledon, informing people where to go and, in particular, managing the famous queues outside. 'We're quite strict in ensuring that people stay in the correct order. It's important that the people who get there first are treated fairly.'

'We get about 10,000 through the turnstiles in two-and-a-half hours every day,' he says. The stewards sometimes have to help in 'unexpected situations'. 'For example, a lady with a huge hat on that she refuses to remove. We would gently encourage her to do so.'

E

One and a half million strawberries, or about twenty-five tons, will be eaten at Wimbledon this year, and every one will have come from Marion Regan's farm in Kent. 'It's really good strawberry-growing land,' she says, 'with sunny, south-facing slopes.' Her farm has been the sole provider of strawberries to Wimbledon for fifteen years and has gained a reputation for providing exceptional fruit. The variety Regan supplies is Elsanta, which is at its best during Wimbledon fortnight.

'You never know what's going to happen – if the sun's going to shine, if a popular player is going to do well – and it all affects consumption. But our pickers start at 5.00 a.m. so we can adapt to fit the order,' says Marion.

F

Doug Dixon's job over the Wimbledon fortnight could best be summarised as the players' surrogate mother: he assigns lockers, gives them towels, does their laundry and tends to their every need. 'Demands vary,' says Dixon. 'They might have just got off a plane and have a bagful of washing, or they might just want a restaurant recommendation …'.

Working so close to the players for more than thirteen years, Dixon has seen a thing or two, including some rather quirky behaviour among some of the tennis idols. 'There was a player, a long time ago, who would stare at his locker for an hour after he lost. Suddenly, he would jump up and rip his shirt down the middle. Then he was fine.'

Vocabulary | achievement

1 Complete each sentence with an appropriate word in the box. Then check your ideas in the text on pages 32–33.

> goals   reputation   resounding   best   credit   idols   standards

1 We give these unsung heroes some well-deserved _____ for their amazing achievements

2 As Head Groundsman, he clearly has incredibly high _____.

3 We've been scaring off pigeons since 2002 and it's been a _____ success.

4 Her farm has gained a _____ for providing exceptional fruit.

5 Dixon has seen some rather quirky behaviour among some of the tennis _____.

6 We've got to reach our _____ in order for players to have the best chance of reaching theirs.

7 They are encouraged to achieve their own personal _____.

2 Look at the picture of Martin Strel and read the text about him quickly. What did he do and why?

Taking on the Amazon

A Slovenian man battled crocodiles and exhaustion to become the first person to swim the entire length of the Amazon River. Martin Strel, fifty-two, *achieved/gained*[1] his goal sixty-six days after setting out, swimming over 5,265 km.

At the end of his swim, Strel was suffering from dizziness, nausea and sunstroke. He has incredibly high *expectations/standards*[2] of himself, however, and was determined to finish. He not only finished, but did so in record time, averaging fifty-two miles a day. It was an outstanding *achievement/goal*[3]; he even completed the swim four days ahead of schedule.

Over the last ten years, Strel has continued to achieve new *recognition/personal*[4] bests and has gained a *reputation/status*[5] for setting long-swim records. These include the Danube (3,004 km), the Mississippi (3,797 km) and the Yangtze (4,003 km). During his Amazon challenge, he also gained minor celebrity *reputation/status*[6] with his blog, and he was well-received by local people along his route. He is particularly pleased to have become a role *model/idol*[7] for young people who are determined to aim as high as him.

When asked 'why', Strel simply says 'to prove that he could *break/reach*[8] the goals he set himself.' He also wants to gain *reputation/recognition*[9] as a record-holder and become part of an elite group in the *Guinness Book of World Records*. Like me, you might have little understanding of his reasons, but you have to admire him *of/for*[10] his enormous achievements.

3 Choose the correct alternatives in the text. Look at the words before and after the gap to help you. Then check your answers in the Exam Reviser.

exam reviser   p5 | 3.2

4 Prepare to talk about one of these questions by making some notes using the phrases in Exercise 3. Then in pairs take turns to speak for 1 minute about your question. While you are listening to your partner note down all the new phrses he or she uses.

1 Which famous sportsperson do you think is a good role model for young people? Why?

2 In which areas of your life do you think you have high standards? Why are high standards important to you in those particular areas?

Grammar | present perfect (2)

1 Work in pairs and answer these questions.

1 What is the difference in meaning between these two sentences? How do you know?

   A I've played tennis this morning.

   B I played tennis this morning.

2 Look at the words in *italics* in these sentences. How does the meaning change in each case?

   A I've *just* played tennis.

   B I've *already* played tennis.

   C I haven't played tennis *yet*.

   D I *still* haven't played tennis.

Grammar note | **position of *just*, *yet*, *already* and *still***

1 Which word(s) in the box can you add to each sentence below?

> just   yet   already   still

   A They've scored a goal.

   B They haven't scored a goal.

   C Have they scored a goal?

2 Where is the normal position of the word in each sentence?

2 Which sentence is more appropriate in each of these pairs? Why?

1 A Finnegan the falcon *has scared off* pigeons since 2002.
   B Finnegan the falcon *has been scaring off* pigeons since 2002.

2 A 10,000 spectators *have come* through the turnstiles this afternoon.
   B 10,000 spectators *have been coming* through the turnstiles this afternoon.

3 There are mistakes in some of these sentences. Find the mistakes and correct them. Look at the Grammar Reference if necessary.

1 Have you ever been thinking about getting tickets for Wimbledon?
2 She hasn't been able to play tennis since she's broken her arm.
3 Since he's been my coach, my game has improved considerably.
4 This is only the second time I'm going to a live sporting event.
5 I reckon I've done enough training for today.
6 He prepared as much as he can now for the match.
7 She knows she wanted to be a champion since she was a child.
8 I've been beating him the last three times we've met.
9 I'll continue my training as soon as my shoulder has recovered.
10 I didn't meet anyone who has higher standards than him yet.

•• see grammar reference: **page 173** ••

4 Look at these questions. Add three more questions using the present perfect (simple or continuous).

Find someone in the classroom who …

- … has taken up a new sport in the last year.
- … is interested in doing more exercise but hasn't done it yet.
- … has been a member of a gym for more than six months.
- … has been playing a particular sport for over five years.
- … is proud of something he or she has done in the last year.
- …
- …
- …

5 Ask and answer the questions in Exercise 4 with a partner. Then choose two of the questions you are most interested in. Continue your discussion, asking further questions to find out more details.

premium plus **14**

Writing | article

1 Work in pairs. Read the task and write an appropriate paragraph plan.

Writing task

Your sports club magazine is including a special section on role models in sport. You have been asked to contribute a short article profiling somebody involved in sport or a sportsperson you know about.

Write the article describing some of the achievements of this person and why you think he/she is a good role model for young people.

2 Look at this list of purposes of the opening paragraph of an article. Which do you think is the most important?

- to tell the readers what the topic of the article is
- to tell the readers how the article will be organised
- to grab the readers' attention and make them want to read on

3 Look at this list of ways of opening an article. Then read the two opening paragraphs A and B on page 166 and say which way(s) are used in each one.

WRITING SKILLS
Ways of opening an article
- A question
- A statement or definition of the topic
- A description or image
- A surprising fact or opinion
- A quotation or reference to a well-known phrase

4 Look again at the task in Exercise 1 and follow these instructions.

1 Decide who you are going to write about. You can choose either someone you're interested in or someone you've read about in this unit.
2 Write the introduction paragraph for your article (using about 50–60 words).
3 Read your paragraph and think about how you could improve it. Ask another student for his or her opinion.
4 Look at the writing model in the Writing Reference and say which of the tips (around the model) are most useful for you.

•• see writing reference: **page 204** ••

5 Write your article in 220–260 words. Use your paragraph plan from Exercise 1 and don't forget to think of an interesting title.

Grammar

1 Complete this email by writing the verb in brackets in the correct form. Use one of these tenses: present perfect simple, present perfect continuous, present simple or past simple.

Send 🖫 🖨 📝 ✓ 📎 ⇩ ❗ ⬇ | Options... | ❓ Help

To...	Ellie Robinson
Cc...	
Subject:	Fitness shoes!

Hi Ellie!

Sorry I _____[1] (not email) since I _____[2] (see) you at the party! Everything _____[3] (be) really busy here lately.
One thing I _____[4] (do) is finally trying to get fit. I think it's the first time that I _____[5] (take) it seriously – I mean, I _____[6] (join) the gym three times before, but this time I really am going to stick to it.
So, apart from joining the gym, two weeks ago I _____[7] (buy) myself a pair of these amazing shoes! They're called MBTs – that means Masai Barefoot Technology. I don't know if you _____[8] (hear) about them, but they're based on the fact that when you _____[9] (walk) barefoot, your body has to work harder, so you stay fitter.
I can tell you, I _____[10] (wear) them for two weeks and I _____[11] (notice) a big difference in my fitness already. The thing is, the sole of the shoe isn't flat – it's quite wobbly in fact, so that your muscles have to work hard to keep you balanced and upright. Anyway, sorry to go on about my shoes! I hope you're well and _____[12] (not work) too hard recently. Really hope to see you soon.
Best
Olivia

---

2 Choose the correct alternatives.

1 You're late – the training session has *still/already* started.
2 They have *just/yet* finished playing the match.
3 He *still/yet* hasn't won any gold medals.
4 I haven't done any exercise this week *yet/already*.
5 It's been a long time *since/when* I went to a match.
6 They haven't beaten their closest rivals *for/since* years.
7 I took up golf about three months *since/ago*.
8 *Since/When* she's been going jogging, she's lost weight.

Vocabulary

3 There are mistakes in these sentences. Find the mistakes and correct them. Sometimes there is more than one possible answer.

1 I've won him every time I've played him so far.
2 She's got a strong competitive stripe and has always hated losing.
3 Our team were clear champions and won by a strong margin.
4 Some racehorses seem to have an inbuilt desire to beat.
5 He's just broken a new world record with an incredibly fast time.
6 I'm expecting a hard match because he's a heavy competitor.
7 They came up against unexpectedly thick competition today.
8 I'm doing a lot of training because I'm competing on a sailing race next week.

4 Complete the sentences using an appropriate word in the box. Four of the words cannot be used.

> admire credit expectations gained goals idols models personal reached reputation recognition resounding status standards

1 Sports Day was a _____ success, despite the bad weather.
2 Somebody whom I really _____ for his achievements is Tiger Woods.
3 After taking part in the sponsored run, she gained minor celebrity _____ around the town.
4 He has gained a _____ as a bad-tempered player.
5 She didn't win the race, but she was very pleased to achieve a _____ best.
6 It's very important for young people to have good role _____ who they can look up to.
7 After sixty-six days of terrible conditions they _____ their goal and arrived at the top of Everest.
8 Her only fault is having almost impossibly high _____ for herself.
9 Successful people usually have clear _____ for themselves – things they want to achieve.
10 The team lost in the end, but you have to give them. _____ for never giving up.

Tell it like it is

Premium | Unit 04

myth

memories

author

Unit 04

Introduction

1 Look at the items in the box. Which is the odd one out and why?

> a fairy story   a fable   a fib   a legend

2 Discuss these questions with other students.

1 Which traditional fairy story can you see in picture a?
2 What other films do you know which are based on fairy stories?
3 Do you like this kind of film? Why/Why not?
4 Can you remember a story which you liked as a child? Why do you think it was appealing to you?

3 Who is the author in picture c? Have you read her books? Do you like them? Why/Why not?

4 Which of these are you most likely to read on a train journey? Why? Compare your answers with other students.

> a serious novel   a trashy novel   a non-fiction book
> a magazine   a comic   a puzzle book   an autobiography
> a professional journal   a newspaper

Reading

1 You're going to read three extracts from different texts, which are all connected in some way. Read them quickly and answer these questions.

1 What is the connection between them?

2 The reasons why the writers wrote these texts and their intended readers are all different. Match each text with one of the reasons/ intended readers A–D. One option cannot be used.

A to tell a story for adults to enjoy

B to give personal news to a friend

C to give information and comment to newspaper readers

D to describe and promote a product to potential customers

2 Read the extracts again and for the questions which follow each text, choose the answer A, B, C or D which you think fits best according to the text.

READING SKILLS
Identifying the reason for writing and the intended reader

It is a good idea to try to identify the author's reason for writing and the intended target reader. This will help you understand the overall message of what you read better. You can use clues like specific vocabulary and informal/formal language, as well as the use of questions, descriptions, etc.

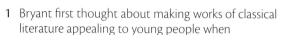

about us   news   edit this page   contact us

The Classical Comics Story

The idea for 'Classical Comics' came about in late 2006, after Clive Bryant, the founder, had been reading a book about reducing crime in cities. On reading the book, his mind immediately turned to the thought that people would not behave in an antisocial way if they appreciated fine literature. But the question remained in his mind: how do you get people who aren't interested in literature to get hooked?

Creating an appreciation of classical texts must surely start at school. But if you ask a hundred teenagers their opinion of Shakespeare, for example, the vast majority will probably say 'boring'. So, the major hurdle to overcome was how to turn 'boring' into 'cool'. Bryant felt sure that once enough people thought reading these classics was cool, the rest would just follow suit.

Earlier that same year, Clive had written a book about self-help and, in order to aid accessibility, he had used cartoon illustrations in the book. While he was researching the whole area of cartooning, he got interested in a particular comic-strip style. The comic, he soon realised, would provide the key; if Shakespeare's stories can look as exciting as Spider-Man stories, then that *would* be cool and young people *would* read them.

'Classical Comics' decided, too, that the language could be modernised in order to make following the story easier, so we publish a 'plain text' version as well as an 'original text' one. The response from the public has been extremely positive and sales have been increasing steadily. These engaging books are now introducing new generations of both teenagers and adults to the world of classic fiction.

1 Bryant first thought about making works of classical literature appealing to young people when

A he realised that most people thought they were boring.

B he remembered enjoying these books at school.

C he thought that crime could be reduced if people read them.

D he wanted the challenge of changing their opinion from 'boring' to 'cool'.

2 The way the stories in 'Classical Comics' are told is different from how Shakespeare originally intended because

A they have teenage versions as well as adult versions.

B they have versions with illustrations as well as versions without.

C they include new cartoon characters as well as the existing ones.

D they have simple English versions as well as Shakespeare's own language versions.

PUBLISHERS REJECT 'JANE AUSTEN'

She might have sold millions of books in the past 200 years, but a daring experiment has found Jane Austen would struggle to secure a book deal today.

DAVID LASSMAN, a frustrated author and director of the Jane Austen Festival in the English town of Bath, sent off manuscripts featuring several chapters of Austen's most famous works to eighteen publishers and agents, claiming it was all his work. He decided to send off the manuscripts in frustration at having his own original thriller rejected, which, although he accepts may not be a masterpiece, he certainly feels is publishable. He began to wonder, if Jane Austen were around today, whether she would have as much trouble being accepted by a publisher as he was having.

So Lassman decided to do an experiment, retyping parts of Austen's *Pride and Prejudice, Northanger Abbey* and *Persuasion*, to send to potential publishers. He made only slight alterations, such as names of people and places. To his amazement, all the publishers he contacted rejected the manuscripts. Perhaps, even more staggering was the fact that all but one failed to spot that he had ripped off opening chapters of these famous works.

The one publisher who did make the connection, wrote in his rejection letter to Mr Lassman: 'Thank you for sending us the first two chapters of *First Impressions*. I suggest you reach for your copy of *Pride and Prejudice*, which I'd guess lives in close proximity to your typewriter, and make sure your opening pages don't too closely mimic the book's opening.'

Great Expectations
Chapter one

My father's family name being Pirrip, and my Christian name Philip, my infant tongue could make of both names nothing longer than Pip. So I came to be called Pip. Having lost both my parents in my infancy, I was

5   brought up by my sister, Mrs Joe Gargery, who married the local blacksmith.

Ours was the marsh country, down by the river, within twenty miles of the sea. My earliest memory is of a cold, wet afternoon towards evening. At such a time

10   I found out for certain that this windy place under long grass was the churchyard; and that my father, mother and five little brothers were dead and buried there; and that the dark flat empty land beyond the churchyard was the marshes; and that the low line further down

15   was the river; and that the distant place from which the wind was rushing was the sea, and that the small boy growing afraid of it all and beginning to cry was Pip.

'Hold your noise,' cried a terrible voice, as a man jumped up from among the graves. 'Keep still, you little

20   devil, or I'll cut your throat.'

A fearful man, in rough grey clothes, with a great iron on his leg. A man with no hat, and with broken shoes, and with an old piece of cloth tied round his head. He moved with difficulty and was shaking with

25   cold as he seized me by the chin.

'I'm not alone,' he said, 'as you may think I am. There's a young man hidden with me, **in comparison with whom I am kind and friendly**. That young man hears the words I speak. No boy can hide himself from

30   that young man.'

3 Lassman felt that his own writing was
   A extremely good.
   B good enough to get published.
   C just as good as a classic Jane Austen novel.
   D a good modern version of a Jane Austen novel.

4 Lassman was very surprised because
   A only one of the publishers realised the manuscripts were fake.
   B one of the publishers wanted to publish the fake manuscripts.
   C only one of the publishers bothered to write him a rejection letter.
   D the fake manuscripts were turned down by all but one of the publishers.

5 The impression we get of Pip and his family is that
   A he takes after his father.
   B he was very close to his parents.
   C he has a bad relationship with his sister.
   D that he was orphaned when he was quite young.

6 When the older man describes the younger man by saying 'in comparison with whom I am kind and friendly' (lines 27–28), he means:
   A the younger man is a nicer person than him.
   B he knows he is horrible but the younger man is worse.
   C he is great friends with the younger man.
   D he thinks the younger man will like him better than Pip.

Grammar | narrative tenses

1 Look back at the first text (The Classical Comics Story) in the Reading section on page 38. Find at least one example of each of these tenses.

1 past simple
2 past continuous
3 past perfect simple
4 past perfect continuous

2 Discuss these questions with other students.

1 Which tense do we usually use to talk about events in stories?
2 In which part of a story do we often use the past continuous?
3 What is the main difference between simple and continuous tenses?
4 Which verbs do we generally not use in the continuous form?
5 What is the main use of the past perfect simple?
6 What is the main use of the past perfect continuous?
7 Which of these tenses do you use differently in your language?

3 Complete these sentences with the correct form of the verb in brackets.

1 The moment he walked into the room, a deathly silence _____ (fall).
2 We _____ (sit) in the exam room for about ten minutes, when the fire alarm went off.
3 As soon as the bus drove off, I realised that I _____ (leave) it at home.
4 While I _____ (get) dressed, I heard someone moving downstairs.
5 I _____ (not believe) a word he said until that day when everything changed.
6 She _____ (just step) into the house when there was a huge explosion.
7 I've never felt the same about that house since the day I _____ (go) down to the cellar.
8 I _____ (never be) so shocked in my whole life when he told me what had happened.

•• see grammar reference: **page 173** ••

4 R.11 ▶ Listen to three students playing 'Tell us a story' together. What do you think are the two basic rules of this game?

5 Work in groups of three and play 'Tell us a story'. Choose one of the sentences in Exercise 3 as the first sentence of your story. Take turns to say one sentence of the story each.

premium plus 15

CAE close-up | Listening Multiple choice (Paper 4, part 3)

Exam information

In this part of the exam you hear a conversation between two or more speakers, which lasts approximately 4 minutes. There are six multiple-choice questions, each with four options. You hear the extract twice.

Approach

1 Read the rubric to the task. It will tell you the general topic so you know what to expect when you're listening.
2 Read the questions before you listen for the first time and underline the key parts.
3 Listen and make brief notes for each question. Then try to answer the questions in your own words, before looking at the options.
4 Go through the options and choose the one which you think fits best.
5 Listen again and check each option again.
6 Remember that in the exam you should always choose an answer for each question: you do not lose marks for a wrong answer.

Practice task

R.12 ▶ You will hear part of a radio interview about 'Dickens World', a theme park based on the novels of the English writer, Charles Dickens. For questions **1–6**, choose the answer (**A**, **B**, **C** or **D**) which fits best according to what you hear.

1 What does the expert say is unusual about 'Dickens World'?
   A The buildings are recreated from original material.
   B The tours take you into the actual streets of London.
   C You can dress up in real Victorian costumes.
   D There are people who look like real Victorians.

2 What else can you do at 'Dickens World' apart from going on some small rides?
   A enter some Victorian buildings
   B go on some large, high-speed rides
   C taste some food from Victorian times
   D have a lesson in a Victorian school

3 What does the expert say about the 'Haunted House' ride?

  A It made him think that adults like having fun as well as children.

  B It made him want to go on another fairground ride.

  C It reminded him of outings he went on as a child.

  D It worried him that this generation doesn't get much adventure.

4 The expert says that people

  A would expect Disney film versions of Dickens's novels.

  B may be disappointed by the seriousness of the theme park.

  C might connect Dickens with the theme park and not the novels.

  D could be put off reading Dickens's novels because they didn't like the theme park.

5 The expert thinks criticism of the theme park is unjustified because

  A there is so much you can learn from going there.

  B evidence shows it is likely that people go home satisfied.

  C most visitors have already read a lot of Dickens's novels.

  D anything that motivates people to read Dickens is beneficial.

6 According to the expert, how would Dickens have felt about 'Dickens World'?

  A He would be happy that his writing was still reaching all sorts of different people.

  B He would be pleased about the money his novels were still generating.

  C He would disapprove of the overly modern feeling in the theme park.

  D He would be annoyed that the theme park didn't show all the social problems he wrote about.

Go to www.iTests.com or your CD-ROM for interactive exam practice

Vocabulary | memories

1 Complete the phrases in *italics* in these sentences with the words in the box.

> back   blank   brought   evokes   flooding
> go   memories   nostalgic   vaguely   vividly

1 Visiting the theme park *made me feel* _____ for my childhood.

2 I went on the haunted house ride and *the memories came* _____ *back*.

3 *One of my earliest* _____ is of my father reading to me.

4 *Looking* _____, I can see that he had a huge influence on my life.

5 *It* _____ *it all back* as soon as I set foot in the house.

6 This little book _____ *strong memories of* my childhood.

7 I know her very well – *we* _____ *back a long way*.

8 I _____ *remember* him reading to me – all the details are there.

9 I _____ *remember* meeting her once but I can't remember much about her.

10 *My mind's gone* _____ and I can't remember what the title was at all.

2 Check your ideas in the Exam Reviser.

exam reviser   p6 | 4.1

3 You are going to talk about a special memory you have. Follow these instructions.

1 Think of a special memory you have of visiting a theme park, fairground, museum, show or other activity.

2 Write brief notes about the main things you remember.

3 Look at the phrases in Exercise 2 and underline four that you could use.

4 Tell as many other students as possible about your special memory.

4 Discuss these questions with a partner.

• Which activity did most students talk about as their special memory: a theme park, a fairground, a museum, a show or another activity? Why?

• Which memory made the most impact on you? Why?

premium plus   16

Writing | article

1 Discuss these questions with a partner.

- Have you ever been a member of a book club, a conversation club or a film club?
- If so, what kind of things did you do? Did you enjoy it? Why/Why not?
- If not, what kind of things do you think you would do? Would you like to join one of them? Why/Why not?

2 Read the instructions to the writing task and answer these questions.

1 What different things must you include in your answer?
2 What different things must you read before you write your answer?

Writing task

You are a member of a book club at your company. The editor of the company's in-house magazine has asked you to write an article about the club in order to attract new members.

Read the extract from their last programme and the notes you have made in the notebook. Then, using the information appropriately, write the article, explaining what the book club does, describing a special event in more detail and saying why people should join the club.

Book Club – Kernow Advertising Ltd

Autumn programme:

	Book	Event	
Sep	*Romeo and Juliet* by Shakespeare	See play at Globe Theatre	*interesting guided tour*
Oct	*Murder on the Orient Express* by Agatha Christie	Murder mystery weekend	*fun game*
Nov	*Phantom of the Opera* by Gaston Leroux	See musical	*fantastic musical! fancy dress! meal after*

Don't forget!
- meet monthly
- wide range – books and events
- make friends
- practise your English

3 Read the writing task again, including the extract from the programme and the notes. Which of these paragraph plans A or B would be most appropriate and why?

Plan A

Paragraph 1: Introduction – grab readers' attention and say what book club does.

Paragraph 2: Describe one particularly successful event.

Paragraph 3: Describe another particularly successful event.

Paragraph 4: Conclusion – encourage other people to join and say how to join.

Plan B

Paragraph 1: Introduction – grab readers' attention and say what the book club does.

Paragraph 2: Say where and when it meets and describe one particularly successful event.

Paragraph 3: Encourage other people to join and say how to join.

Paragraph 4: Conclusion – Say again what makes this book club really enjoyable.

WRITING SKILLS

Planning your paragraphs

It is important to plan your paragraphs before you start writing your answer. Don't forget to include an introduction and a conclusion. You also need to make sure that you have covered all the points you need to include, and that you have put them in a logical order.

4 Look at the two extracts on page 168. Which one is not appropriate as an answer? Why?

5 Prepare to write your article by following these instructions.

1 Look at the Writing Reference and say which three tips for writing articles are most relevant to you.

2 Look again at paragraph plan B in Exercise 3 and make some more notes on it to prepare your article.

3 Look at the Writing Reference section on articles. Think about how to make your opening paragraph interesting.

•• see writing reference: page 204 ••

6 Now write your article in 180–220 words using your paragraph plan and your notes. Make sure you include all the information asked for and use your own words as far as possible.

Reading is good for you

Reading not only improves your reading skills, but also helps your writing skills and develops your range of vocabulary. It's also fun.

1 Explain to a partner which of these apply to you and why.
- I only read things I enjoy.
- I have to read a lot for my studies.
- I don't worry about unknown words when I read.
- I like reading 'graded readers'.
- I find English newspapers difficult to understand.

2 Finish this sentence. Then compare your sentence with other students.

My tip for increasing the amount of reading you do is ...

Listening

1 Look at the pictures and say what you can see in each one.

2 Match the types of stories in the box with the definitions A–C.

> legend   urban myth   conspiracy theory

A a story about an unusual event which happened recently that a lot of people believe although it is probably not true

B a story based on a belief that a powerful organisation has secretly done something harmful or illegal

C an old, well-known story, often about brave people, adventures or magical events

3 R.13 ▶ Listen to three extracts and match each one with the correct picture and the correct type of story.

4 R.13 ▶ Listen again and for questions 1–6, choose the answer A, B or C which fits best according to what you hear.

Extract 1
You hear two friends talking about New York.

1 The man says you should be careful in New York because
  A there are alligators in the streets.
  B sometimes alligators come up through the toilets.
  C people have put alligators into the drains.

2 What does the woman think about the man's story?
  A The whole thing is complete rubbish.
  B What started as a true story has been exaggerated.
  C The man has made the whole story up to scare her.

Extract 2
You hear part of an interview about conspiracy theories.

3 What does the expert say is the main reason why people are so interested in conspiracy theories?
  A People like spreading ideas and secrets on the Internet.
  B People are frightened when they haven't got anyone to blame.
  C People are reassured by being able to understand worrying things.

4 How does the expert feel about the conspiracy theorists' explanations about the Apollo moon landings?
  A They are mostly unbelievable.
  B They are fairly good proof that it was all faked.
  C Some are good reasons but many are rubbish.

Extract 3
You hear part of a radio programme called *Top Films*.

5 What do the man and woman agree about?
  A They generally both prefer the commercially less successful films.
  B Fans of these epic films are not concerned with the commercial success of the film.
  C Some of the commercially successful films are not such good films as the less successful ones.

6 What is the woman's opinion of the film *Troy*?
  A The acting, the visual images and the story are all good.
  B The acting and the story are good but the visual images are rather weak.
  C The visual images and the story are very strong but some of the acting is a bit weak.

5 Discuss these questions in small groups.
- Do you like films about old legends, e.g. the action film *Troy*, the cartoon film *Hercules*? Why/Why not?
- What do you think about the conspiracy theories they talked about in the extract?
- What is the most famous legend (or urban myth) from your country or area?

Vocabulary | powerful adjectives

1 Look at these sentences and say which one is more interesting and why.

1 It is surprising that some people don't know that fully-grown alligators are very big.

2 It is staggering that some people don't know that fully-grown alligators are immense.

2 Look at the adjectives in *italics* in these sentences. Think of other adjectives with a similar meaning that are more powerful and interesting.

1 Fully-grown alligators are *big* and certainly not suitable as pets.

2 I think the story about baby alligators is *silly*.

3 Some of the images in the film are *impressive*.

4 Many people found the death of President Kennedy *painful*.

3 Check your ideas in the Exam Reviser.

exam reviser | p6 | 4.2

4 Choose the correct alternatives A or B to complete the text.

Editor's recommendations of the month

I have rarely enjoyed a book as much as *Captain Corelli's Mandolin* by Louis de Bernières – it really is a _____¹ novel. Set on a Greek island in 1941, the book follows the troubling story of a young Italian officer during the _____² times of war. As well as upsetting the reader with some almost _____³ moments of sorrow, it also contains _____⁴ moments of joy and love, lifting one's spirits again.

Saving Private Ryan is an _____⁵ film; I really love it, and the book certainly does not disappoint either. Set during the war, Captain John Miller and his men go to look for Private James Ryan. At times I felt like crying; parts of it are _____⁶ and there are some fairly _____⁷ moments of sadness. In my opinion, it is _____⁸ how the writer can create such an action-packed book at the same time as writing in such a sensitive way.

The Beach is Alex Garland's _____⁹ first novel, which was highly praised by critics – and now it is also a _____¹⁰ film starring Leonardo DiCaprio. The main character, Richard, is travelling in Thailand and obtains a secret map to an idyllic beach. It's an area of _____¹¹ beauty, but after a series of _____¹² events, he realises that paradise is not what it seems.

1 A stunning	B colossal	7 A excruciating	B ludicrous
2 A distressing	B dazzling	8 A traumatic	B staggering
3 A fatuous	B unbearable	9 A astounding	B preposterous
4 A tremendous	B excruciating	10 A massive	B laughable
5 A astonishing	B agonising	11 A dazzling	B distressing
6 A laughable	B traumatic	12 A fatuous	B disturbing

5 You're going to try to persuade other students to read a book you know. Follow these instructions.

1 Choose a book to talk about.

2 Make some brief notes to prepare what you're going to say, e.g. about the characters, the plot, the main message, the style of writing.

3 <u>Underline</u> some powerful adjectives in the Exam Reviser to make the book sound interesting and attractive.

6 Tell as many other students as possible about the book you've chosen. Which books were you most persuaded to read?

exam reviser | p6 | 4.2

premium plus | 17

Grammar | emphasis with *what*, *all* and *it*

1 Which of these sentences is more emphatic? Why?

1 People want some kind of explanation.

2 What people want is some kind of explanation.

2 Complete these sentences using the phrases in the box to make them sound emphatic and dramatic.

> All I know is … It is when …
> What he told me was …
> All people want is … It's the way …
> What they'd do is …

1 _____ that it was once a fad among New Yorkers.

2 _____ go on holiday and bring back a baby alligator.

3 _____ you've been had and fallen for a load of nonsense!

4 _____ some kind of explanation.

5 _____ they start to come up with hundreds of detailed reasons that the whole theory loses credibility.

6 _____ he makes the characters seem like real humans that really works for me.

3 Complete these sentences with *what*, *all* or *it*.

1 Using _____ at the beginning of the sentence, emphasises an action or a series of actions.

2 Using _____ at the beginning of the sentence, suggests that this is the only thing that is important.

3 Using _____ at the beginning of the sentence, allows us to emphasise a noun (including an *-ing* form), the reason something is done or the time it is done.

4 Rewrite each sentence in two different ways starting with the words given.

1 The plot is important in a good book.
   a *What ...*   b *It's the ...*

2 I love literature more than anything else.
   a *What ...*   b *It's ...*

3 She's going to tell us about the main character.
   a *What she's ...*   b *All she's ...*

4 The only thing that matters is being honest.
   a *All ...*   b *It's ...*

5 When I saw him, I realised I'd met him before.
   a *What I realised ...*   b *It was ...*

6 We didn't notice the money was missing until the next day.
   a *It wasn't ...*   b *It was ...*

5 Work in small groups. Take turns to choose one of the topics in the box and to speak about it for 1 minute.

• When you're speaking, try to use emphatic sentences with *what*, *all* and *it*, using dramatic intonation.

• When you're listening, note down any emphatic sentences you hear with *what*, *all* and *it*.

> things that irritate me
> my perfect weekend
> a frustrating day
> my views on television
> the worst film/book I've ever seen/read

premium plus 18

Grammar note | more on emphatic *it* sentences

Emphatic *it* sentences can be used to emphasise a) the reason (with *because*) and b) the time (with *when* or *until*).

Complete these sentences with *because*, *when* or *until*.

1 It was _____ she spoke that I knew she was upset.

2 It wasn't _____ she spoke that I knew she was upset.

3 It was _____ she was upset that she couldn't speak.

•• see grammar reference: page 174 ••

Speaking

1 R.14 ▶ Listen to two people playing 'Something extraordinary'. In this game, you must tell a story that may be true or false, but it must *sound* exaggerated or completely made up. Answer these questions.

1 What does the woman say happened to her?

2 Does she sound bored, neutral or enthusiastic? What makes her sound like this?

3 Does the man believe her?

4 Is the story true or false?

2 R 14 ▶ Listen again and underline the stressed words in each phrase in the box.

> **Making a story sound dramatic**
> *Believe it or not, ...*   *Amazingly enough, ...*
> *Incredible though it is, ...*   *Difficult as it is to believe, ...*
> *To my astonishment, ...*

3 Complete the sentences in the Exam Reviser.

exam reviser   p21 | 4 ▶

4 You're going to play the game 'Something extraordinary'. First think of a story you can tell, using these suggestions or your own ideas. Remember it can be true or false.

• You had an accident.   • You got lost.
• You met someone famous.   • You won something.
• You found something important.

5 Prepare to tell your story, writing notes if it helps. Don't forget to include these things where appropriate:

• some of the phrases from Exercise 2
• some emphatic sentences with *what*, *all* and *it*
• some powerful adjectives

6 Tell your story to other students, starting with the words *Something extraordinary happened to me ...* . Make sure you use dramatic intonation.

7 Did the other students guess correctly if your story was true or false?

Grammar

1 Choose the correct alternatives.

Shakespeare on TV

The TV dramatisation of Shakespeare's *Macbeth* on BBC1 last week *is/has been*[1] quite simply one of the best bits of drama I have *ever seen/ever saw*[2]. While I *was studying/had been studying*[3] for my exams last year, I *read/was reading*[4] the play many times. At that time, I also *saw/have seen*[5] two productions of it at two different theatres. They *were/had been*[6] good, but not nearly as good as this version. What a clever idea to set the whole thing in a modern-day restaurant kitchen!

Since studying the play in depth, and before seeing this, I *had been wondering/have been wondering*[7] how it could be made relevant to a modern audience. To my mind, this TV drama provides the answer. I *have read/had read*[8] a short review of it before I saw it, but it *hasn't been/wasn't*[9] until I saw the whole thing that I *realised/had realised*[10] how good it was. *Macbeth is always/has always been*[11] one of my favourite Shakespeare plays and now I *feel/have felt*[12] even more positive about it.

2 For questions 1–5, rewrite the second sentence so that it has a similar meaning to the first sentence, using the word given. Do not change the word given. You must use between three and six words, including the word given.

1 I hate people gossiping more than anything else.
   most
   What _____ people gossiping.

2 What he wants most is to be a successful author.
   that
   It's _____ he wants most.

3 I didn't understand the story properly until I saw the film version.
   only
   It _____ I saw the film version that I understood the story properly.

4 The only thing I want to do when I'm on holiday is read all day.
   all
   When I'm on holiday, _____ to do.

5 I only realised she was lying when she finished the story.
   until
   It _____ of the story, I realised she was lying.

Vocabulary

3 Complete the text with the words in the box. Four of the words cannot be used.

> blank   black   back   vividly   lividly   memories
> nostalgia   nostalgic   brought   flooding   looking   going

_____Memories!_____

Memories are made of this! Of what exactly? Well, when I came across an old photo album the other day, I realised that memories are mostly made of people. And the memories came _____[1] back when I found pictures of my best friend Charlotte. There are many things that I remember well but my mind has gone _____[2] on some others.

We go _____[3] a long way, Charlotte and I, having first met at school, aged five. We are still friends now but there are some things I'd forgotten about. The photos _____[4] it all back – how we used to play together all day every day and _____[5] back, I can see that we had the happiest of times together. One of my earliest _____[6] of our friendship was always wanting to dress the same as each other. I _____[7] remember pleading with my mum to buy the same dress or shoes so that I could be the same as Charlotte. When my own children do the same, it is irritating, but it makes me feel quite _____[8], too!

4 Complete the sentences with an appropriate word starting with the letter given.

1 That is the most i_____ thing to say – don't be so stupid!

2 Losing her dog was a difficult and rather t_____ experience for her.

3 I left my last job due to the c_____ amount of travelling involved.

4 He's so annoying – always asking such f_____ questions.

5 After the car accident, I was left with the most e_____ pain in my leg.

6 She always gives the most t_____ parties with loads of fantastic food.

7 For such a young child, she's got a really d_____ voice.

8 He loved that house and moved out with i_____ difficulty.

Man's best friend

sentience

pony club

sniffer dog

Unit 05

Introduction

1 Look at the animals in the pictures. Which is your favourite and why?

2 How could the animals in the pictures help each of these people?
- a policeman or customs officer
- someone who cannot see or hear
- a teenager who gets into trouble
- someone who is trying to build something
- a small child
- a farmer

3 Which of these things do you think animals may be able to sense before humans? Why?
- changes in the weather
- the presence of an enemy
- another animal's unhappiness
- how near food is
- natural disasters

4 Discuss these questions with other students.
- What kinds of animals do you think humans can have a close relationship with? Why?
- Do you think it is important for children to have a relationship with animals? Why/Why not?
- In what ways do some people associate human feelings with animals?

Grammar: cohesion; relative clauses | Vocabulary: metaphorical language; multi-word verbs with *out* | Writing: contribution

Unit 05

Reading

1 Look at the picture and answer these questions.

1 Where do you think it was taken?
2 Why do you think the horses are in the city?

2 Read the title and sub-heading of the article. What other ideas do you have for the questions in Exercise 1?

3 Read the article and put paragraphs A–G in gaps 1–6. There is one extra paragraph you do not need. Underline the words and phrases that help you to decide where each paragraph fits.

RED RIDING HOOD

In a shabby street in Philadelphia, an unlikely pony club gives the city's youth an escape route from the ghetto.

Every morning, sixteen-year-old Jake rides his bicycle seven miles across Philadelphia from one ghetto to another. These neighbourhoods[1] crackle[2] with fights and bad feeling after sunset, but Jake barely notices the backdrop[3] of urban decay. Only when he arrives at Fletcher Street does he really wake up; the scene[4] is so jolting and original, it never fails to take his breath away.

> **1**

As Jake arrives, a white horse emerges from one home, walking out of the front door and down the steps to the street. 'There he[5] is!' beams Dan, who owns two of the horses here. Eternally optimistic, Dan works for the City of Philadelphia by day, but spends as much time as he can at the stables, where he is considered something of a father figure.

> **2**

At first Camarillo, a regular contributor to news magazines, had a battle[6] with the riders to persuade them to be photographed. Claiming they had been burnt[7] by the media in the past, they were suspicious of her. She managed to gain their trust and has now produced a book documenting this unique street culture.

> **3**

Take twenty-year-old Ben. His uncle first brought him here[8] when he was eight, but as he hit[9] his teens he drifted[10] into trouble. But now he is back with his horses, his life has some structure[11]. He says, 'I can count on the guys here. I can come here and talk to my horses. They never let me down.'

> **4**

Few know better than Dan how horses can rehabilitate a troubled youth – he spent his own teens in prison but now recognises his importance as a father figure to some of the boys. Fletcher Street is almost entirely male – three generations from grandfathers down.

PREMIUM | UNIT 05

A He doesn't mean strict employment. The stables are entirely supported in a loose co-operative fashion by horse owners such as Dan. Each horse costs $300 a month to look after. And the horses themselves are not cheap – some of the ex-racehorses cost up to $4,000. Most were bought at auction from farms nearby. Money is tight[14].

B There have been stables here since the Second World War, when it was a wealthy area and Philadelphia's horse tradition was quite strong. But as the ghettos have grown, the stables have fallen away, which to Dan only enhances their importance. 'Most of these kids come from broken homes so we are like a second family,' he says.

C Every teenager has a similar story. Karl, eighteen, gets into far less trouble now that he spends his time at Fletcher Street. And, Fernando, who has been coming here for four months, never misses a day. Some of the kids even come there to eat if they're being ignored at home.

D As recently as the 1980s there were as many as 500 cowboys in the city, but over the past decade six of the ten stables have been shut down. In their stead, a series of townhouses were built as part of the city's improvement programme and 146 horses were sold.

E The sight of former racehorses, packhorses and ponies in a Philadelphia ghetto is surprising enough, but it was the kids who first caught the eye of news photographer, Martha Camarillo. 'I was driving through here in January and there they were, riding in a posse. And I had never seen that combination before: black American youth and horses. It[15] breaks[16] the John Wayne myth.'

F Despite their good relationship, it isn't always easy to control these kids, but Dan claims it is the horses that make them come back again and again, not the adults. But, Dan says, 'They shouldn't be here in school hours. We're just trying to keep the kids here so they ain't out getting into trouble.'

G About eighty horses live here. Some wait in muddy pens on a patch of wasteland, others are being groomed in the street, waiting to be ridden out to the park, where the men race each other. Most of the horses live in regular houses that, behind their rundown suburban facades, have been converted into ramshackle stables.

'These kids need a man to tell 'em that if you don't work while you're here, you can't come back,' Dan says.

5

But the stables gets no grants or support from the City of Philadelphia and this problem[12] may mean the end. Although, the mayor used to ride horses right down Fletcher Street, the city has been aggressively closing down stables in recent years.

6

The stable's survival rests largely on Camarillo's shoulders; she plans to make a documentary about Fletcher Street. They[13] hope she's going to make people realise how important it is to keep it going. Some of the old-timers have lived their whole lives with horses and they're worried about what will happen to the kids if the stables closes down. There's a lot riding on these stables,' says Dan 'And we need to keep Fletcher Street alive.'

4 Answer these questions.
1 Why is the title 'Red Riding Hood'?
2 What is unusual about where the stables are?
3 How do the stables help teenage boys in Philadelphia?
4 Why are the stables having problems?

5 Discuss these questions with other students.
1 If you were mayor, would you support the stables financially? Why/Why not?
2 What other ways can you think of to get financial support for the stables?
3 What different ways can you think of for introducing animals into the lives of children who live in cities?

Vocabulary | metaphorical language

1 Discuss these questions with another student.

1 Which sentence uses metaphorical language?
   A The boys burst with pride as they ride the horses.
   B The boys are full of pride as they ride the horses.

2 Why do we use metaphors?
   A to suggest something has similar qualities to the metaphorical word or expression
   B to illustrate a contrast with what we are actually describing
   C to show two ideas or qualities that are the same

3 What is the effect of metaphorical language on the reader or listener?

2 Look at these words, which are numbered in the article on pages 48–49. Which meaning A or B is used?

1 crackle[2]   A be alive with energy
               B make repeated, short sounds

2 backdrop[3]   A the background scenery on a stage
               B the conditions in which something happens

3 battle[6]   A a very hard or difficult argument or competition to achieve something
               B a physical fight between two opposing groups, usually part of a war

4 be burnt[7]   A be destroyed by fire
               B be emotionally hurt by someone

5 hit[9]   A reach a certain level or number
               B touch someone hard with your hand

6 drift[10]   A do something without a plan
               B move slowly on water or in the air

7 structure[11] A something large that has been built
               B a situation where activities are organised or planned

8 tight[14]   A very limited
               B pulled or stretched

9 break[16]   A separate into two or more pieces
               B end or destroy

3 Look at the Exam Reviser and choose three verbs. Think of nouns they could be used to describe in a metaphorical way, e.g. **break – someone's heart**. Compare your ideas with a partner.

exam reviser   p7 | 5.1

4 Replace the words in *italics* with the correct form of the metaphorical expressions in the box. Look at the article on pages 48–49 to help you.

> rest on one's shoulders   father figure   riding on this
> keep something alive   took one's breath away   catch one's eye

1 The sight of the boys on the horses *was fantastically beautiful*.
2 The strange appearance of the boy and the dog *made me notice them*.
3 He's *an older man who the boys can trust and respect*.
4 We need to be successful as there is a lot *we could lose*.
5 The welfare of the horses *is your responsibility*.
6 It is important that the stables *continue to exist*.

5 Look back at a piece of writing you have done recently. Can you improve it and the range of language you have used by replacing some literal words and expressions with metaphorical ones?

premium plus   19

Grammar | cohesion in text

1 Look at these sentences. Match them with the correct rule A or B.

1 We don't know how to get money and we must address this challenge.
2 The kids turn up at the stables when they want.

> We can 'tie' a text together by:
>
> **A** referring back to a word or phrase
>
> or
>
> **B** leaving words out to avoid repetition.

2 Look at the article on pages 48–49. What do these numbered pronouns refer to?

1 *he*[5]   2 *here*[8]   3 *they*[13]   4 *it*[15]

3 Look at the article again. What do these numbered nouns refer to?

1 *neighbourhoods*[1]   2 *scene*[4]

3 *problem*[12]

4 Decide what is missing from these sentences, e.g. a noun, a verb, a phrase, etc. Write in the missing words.

1 Some (_____) wait in muddy pens …
2 Every teenager has a similar story (_____).
3 She managed to gain their trust and (_____) has now produced a book …

5 Look at the Grammar Reference. Then change the highlighted words and phrases in this text to improve the style.

> ### Get a cat!
>
> If you're worried about your blood pressure, a pet cat or dog may control your pressure[1] during stressful times. That, at least, is the implication of research done on some American stockbrokers. The research[2] found that when the brokers were put under pressure, pets were much better at reducing the stress-induced rise in blood pressure than a drug.
>
> Oddly, dogs and cats were equally effective at controlling blood pressure, and even more oddly, owners got the benefits from them[3], even if they were not paying attention to the animals. Why do pets work in controlling blood pressure[4]? Other observations during the study indicate that the pets[5] offer a non-judgmental presence that influences how owners see difficult events. For you[6] to have something in your life that's totally on your side changes your perception of what's going on from a threat to a challenge. In fact, it's even possible that a photo or a toy animal may provide restraint at work for soaring blood pressure. Despite the information from this research[7], pets will not work as a restraint[8] for everyone. If you treat a pet as a piece of furniture, you will derive roughly as much benefit as you would from your sofa. However, when the stockbrokers heard about this, many went out and – you guessed it – invested in some pets of their own.

•• see grammar reference: page 174 ••

6 Do you think doctors should recommend pets rather than drugs to treat some illnesses? Why/Why not?

7 Look at some writing you have done. Improve it by using the techniques in Exercises 2–5.

> premium plus   20 ▶

Speaking

1 Look at the pictures and say briefly what you can see in each one.

2 R.15 ▶ Listen to two students talking about the pictures. What do they say about these questions?

1 What different situations of working animals do they show?
2 How do you think the owners feel about the animals?
3 Would you like to work with animals?

3 R.15 ▶ Listen again and tick the expressions you hear.

Describing feelings and attitudes	
Positive feelings:	
He must feel very close to them.	☐
I think they expect them to work hard.	☐
She feels affectionate towards them.	☐
He was delighted (to be with the dog).	☐
Negative feelings:	
It would make me wound up.	☐
They were downhearted (when the dolphins wouldn't jump).	☐
They get irritated by them.	☐
I felt absolutely devastated when she told me.	☐
Metaphorical expressions:	
He must be on a high (when he gets them to perform).	☐
I expect he is touched by (the animal's devotion).	☐

4 Work with a partner. Student A look at the pictures on page 166. Student B look at the pictures on page 168. You have 1 minute to makes notes for your questions.

5 Discuss the questions for your pictures with a partner. Use some of the phrases in Exercise 3.

6 Look at the Exam Reviser for more ways of describing how people feel. Work in pairs and choose expressions to describe how you would feel in these situations:

- being found out when you have done something wrong
- falling out with a friend
- being given a dog as a present
- trying to learn how to do something

> exam reviser   p21 | 4 ▶

Writing | contribution

1 Read the writing task. Which three points do you need to include in your contribution?

> **Writing task**
>
> A friend of yours is writing a book on attitudes to animals in different countries and has asked you to write a contribution. In your contribution you should say what kinds of domestic animals are popular, explain the attitude people in your country have to animals generally and suggest whether you think attitudes to animals should change or not and why.

2 Work in pairs. Discuss the best way to organise your ideas for your contribution.

- make a list
- draw a diagram
- another method

WRITING SKILLS

Getting ideas

You can get ideas in various ways.

1 If you think analytically, you may find it easier to make a list. Use different headings to help you.

2 If you think visually, you might find a diagram works best.

3 Add another method, if you have one.

Try each method and see which works best for you.

3 In groups of three, discuss ideas for the writing task. Look at the model in the Writing Reference and decide what information to include in each paragraph. Put your ideas into the diagram.

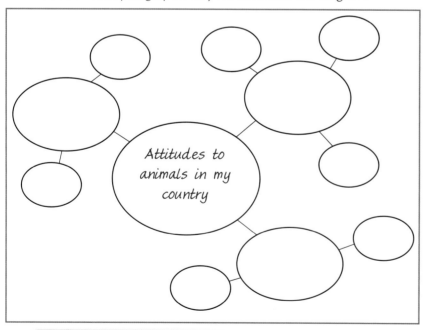

Attitudes to animals in my country

•• see writing reference: page 196 ••

4 Which of these sentences would you expect to read in the contribution? Explain why the sentences you have not selected are inappropriate.

1 I love animals because I think they're really cute.
2 Most people like animals but think they should be used for work.
3 They should treat animals better and not be horrible to them.
4 Other countries are not as kind as we are to our animals.
5 Attitudes are changing as society realises it needs animals.
6 I think we should all protect endangered species.
7 They should treat animals better by giving them proper care when they work.
8 Finally I like the way we treat animals and think we should all behave like this.

5 Write your contribution to the book in 220–260 words using your plan.

6 Read through your contribution. Try to improve your style by using the cohesive devices on page 50.

Listening

1 Work in pairs and follow these instructions.

1 Put these animals in order of how reliable you think they are in helping humans.

> dog   cat   bird   dolphin

2 Now put them in order of how sentient (able to experience things through the senses) they are.

2 Look at these animals with special abilities. What words would you expect to hear if someone was talking about them?

1 snakes which sense movement
2 fish which improve health
3 birds that respond to changes in air pressure

LISTENING SKILLS

Thinking of topic words

Try to think of words that relate to the topic area or context you are listening to, e.g. health: *medicine, disease, feeling ill, feeling well*, etc. You will find it easier to understand the difference between things you are listening to if you think about the relevant vocabulary before you listen.

3 ▶R.16▶ You are going to hear five short extracts of people talking about how certain animals help humans. Listen to the extracts and do the two tasks below. You must do both tasks while you are listening.

Task 1

Choose which animal each speaker is talking about from the list A–H.

A snakes which sense movement
B dogs which detect certain smells
C birds that respond to certain gases
D fish which improve health
E dogs which help people who can't hear
F birds that respond to changes in air pressure
G dogs which help children educationally
H insects which eat bad bacteria

Speaker

1 ____ 2 ____ 3 ____ 4 ____ 5 ____

Task 2

Choose the view each speaker expresses from the list A–H.

A It is unfair to use the animal to help humans.
B It is rewarding to teach these animals.
C It is surprising how effective the animals are.
D It is interesting to see how humans respond to the animal.
E It is unreasonable to expect too much from the animal.
F It is better to use other means of treatment in addition to the animal.
G It is worrying to see animals used in this way.
H It is reassuring that the animal can help.

Speaker

1 ____ 2 ____ 3 ____ 4 ____ 5 ____

4 ▶R.16▶ Listen again and check your answers.

5 Discuss these questions with other students.

- Which animal do you think is the most helpful? Why?
- Would you ever trust an animal to help you? Why/Why not?

Vocabulary | multi-word verbs with *out*

1 Match the multi-word verbs in *italics* 1–5 with their meanings A–E.

1 It's worth *checking out*.
2 It gives you time to *get out* of the trouble zone.
3 It would have been *ruled out* as an option.
4 Online shopping *cuts out* the need to queue.
5 We can *get* more *out of* dogs than we realise.

A leave
B find out if something is true or correct
C gain or achieve something
D decide it is not possible
E make something unnecessary

2 Complete this quiz with the multi-word verbs from Exercise 1.

How much do you like animals?

1 You go out for a high-class meal at a posh restaurant. Do you
A _____ how many kinds of meat are on the menu?
B try out an organic vegetable dish?
C eat fish because they're not animals, are they?

2 You go and see a circus. Do you think
A 'That was boring. I thought the animals would do more tricks'?
B 'I hated seeing those animals performing. They should phase it out'?
C 'Interesting – I really _____ something _____ of that'?

3 You find a spider in the bath. Do you
A grab it and chuck it out of the window?
B carefully try to catch the spider and find it a new home?
C scream and _____ of the bathroom quickly?

4 Someone asks you if you would wear a fur coat. You say
A 'Yes – they really suit me. I must dig out my granny's'?
B 'Actually I'm campaigning to get fur shops closed down'?
C 'I wouldn't _____ it _____ but I don't think so'?

5 You learn that dolphins can be caught in tuna fish nets. Do you
A eat tuna but give some money to a charity for dolphins?
B _____ tuna fish _____ of your diet immediately?
C work out where you can buy 'dolphin-friendly' tuna?

3 Do the quiz then look at page 166 and compare your answers with a partner.

4 Find five more multi-word verbs with *out* in the quiz. Add them to the Exam Reviser.

▶ **exam reviser** p7 | 5.2 ▶

5 Choose four multi-word verbs with *out*. Write sentences about events in your own life.

▶ **premium plus** 21 ▶

Remembering words

How do you remember new words that you learn?

1 write them down
2 try to remember them by heart
3 look at them every day
4 use another method, e.g. ...

Try this:

Write down 5–10 new words you need to remember on small cards or pieces of paper. Write an example sentence or a definition on the back of each one. Put the cards in you pocket as you go out. While you are travelling, take one card out at a time, look at the word and see if you can remember it. Check your answer on the back. If you are correct, put it in a different pocket. Keep doing this until all the cards are in a different pocket.

Grammar | relative clauses

1 Discuss these questions with other students. Look at the Grammar Reference if necessary.

1 Which extract contains essential information that identifies the subject and which contains extra information? How do we know?
   A *... tiny little fish, which have no teeth, ...*
   B *They evolved in hot springs where there was very little food ...*

2 Which sentence is more formal? Why?
   A *They become very responsible towards the people with whom they work.*
   B *They become very responsible towards the people they work with.*

3 Which sentence has a relative pronoun missing and which has had the pronoun replaced? Rewrite the sentences using relative pronouns.
   A *There've been tales of people seeing grass snakes disappearing.*
   B *Think of the time people worked in appalling conditions.*

4 What words can replace the highlighted words?
   Sometimes the air turned poisonous, in which case the bird would die.

•• see grammar reference: page 175 ••

Grammar note | *what*

What can be used as a noun + relative pronoun together to mean 'the thing which'. In this case, you do not use a noun. Which sentence is correct?

A *A study on literacy in the States looked at what happened when children read to their dogs.*

B *A study on literacy in the States looked at the thing what happened when children read to their dogs.*

2 There are mistakes with the relative clauses in some of these sentences. Find the mistakes and correct them.

Things you Didn't Know About Bees

1 Australian researchers discovered that honeybees can distinguish human faces. Most of the insects gave correct answers when shown pictures, which case they were given a treat.

2 In the Stealthy Insect Sensor Project, the thing what Los Alamos scientists have trained bees to do is to recognise explosives.

3 During World War I, honey was used to treat the wounds of soldiers because it attracts and absorbs moisture, makes it a valuable healing agent.

4 Bumblebees can estimate time intervals. Researchers have found that the insects extend their tongues in tandem with the rhythm of a sweet reward. This aids in the hunt for nectar, which availability varies.

5 The buzz that you hear when a bee approaches is the sound of its four wings moving at 11,400 strokes per minute. This means the speed which bees can fly is faster than many other insects.

6 A newly hatched queen is dangerous as it is a time which she immediately tries to kill all other hatched and unhatched queens in the hive.

7 In 1943, Austrian zoologist Karl von Frisch published his study on the dances bees perform to alert fellow workers. They do a round dance, that indicates that food is close by, or a waggle dance when it is distant.

3 Which fact about bees did you find most surprising? Why?

4 Rewrite each pair of sentences to make one sentence using a relative clause. Remember to punctuate your sentences correctly.

1 A man sold me this rabbit. He told me only to feed it lettuce!
2 By 6.00 p.m. the birds had all flown inland. At 6.00 p.m. the hurricane started.
3 The riding lessons were very good. I had already had ten.
4 Those are the stables. I learnt to ride there.
5 My uncle is a beekeeper. He is very good at his job.
6 This is the dog. His owner abandoned him.
7 The boys asked if they could help with the horses. I said that they should be in school.
8 I told them to pay attention. I was telling them about feeding the animals.

premium plus 22

CAE close-up | Writing **Letter of application (Paper 2, part 2)**

Exam information

In part 2 of the Writing exam, you may have the choice of writing a letter of application.

Approach

1 Read the question and make sure you understand:
- who you are writing to;
- what the job is;
- what you need to mention in the application.

2 Plan your answer. Remember to say why you are writing, why you are suitable for the job and why you are interested in the job.

3 It is very important that your application gives reasons why the company should employ you. Don't give a long list of jobs you have had, but mention what skills you have acquired, e.g. *When I was working in the coffee bar, I had the opportunity to improve my English with foreign tourists.*

4 If you mention a skill or personal quality you have, you should give some evidence for it, e.g. *I enjoy working with animals and have always had pets, such as a rabbit and a cat. I was responsible for my neighbour's dog when he was away and I have worked with horses at the local stables.*

5 Remember to be persuasive, e.g. *One of the main reasons I am applying is to …. / I have a lot of experience of … / I have always been interested in … / I can be contacted at …*

6 Make sure you use appropriate openings and closings, e.g. *Dear Sir or Madam, Yours faithfully.*

Practice task

You see this announcement in an international animal welfare magazine.

Wanted – Animal Lovers!

We run a small zoo for children, which attracts visitors from all over the world. We are looking for people to work over the summer in our zoo. Applicants must have experience of looking after animals, speak good English and be willing to talk to visitors about the animals. Are you this person? If so, write us a letter saying why you are the ideal person for this job and why you would like to work for us.

Write your **letter of application**. Write about **220–260** words.

Go to www.iTests.com or your CD-ROM for interactive exam practice

Grammar

1 Improve this letter by replacing the highlighted parts with cohesive devices (words that refer back or missing words out).

Dear Mr Graham

I am writing to apply for the position of zoo assistant, the position that[1] was advertised in *The Herald* on 6th September.

I have a lot of experience working with animals and I am also doing a biology course so I would be very interested in the position you advertised[2]. For several years, I was responsible for my neighbour's dog when she was away and I have also had a weekend job working at my local stables. While I have been working in this way[3], I have learnt how to care for animals and I have also become very interested in the animals[4]. To do the work[5] at the zoo would be a wonderful opportunity for me to work with rarer species and for me[6] to learn about wild animals. This work with the animals[7] will be critical for my future career as I would like to become a zoologist. In addition to the things I have mentioned[8], I am hard-working, patient and willing to learn.

I would very much like to work in the zoo as I have often visited the zoo[9] and am very impressed by the range of animals at the zoo[10] and the organisation of the zoo. I am available for interview for the job[11] any time next week and I[12] hope you will consider me for the post.

Yours sincerely

2 Which of these sentences are correct? Why are the others wrong?

1 A That's the dog which bit me!
   B That's the dog, which bit me!
2 A She's going to study zoology, about which I know nothing.
   B She's going to study zoology, which I know nothing about.
3 A We will do what we can to get him a guide dog.
   B We will do everything what we can to get him a guide dog.
4 A He came to the stables on Monday, which point I sent him to school.
   B He came to the stables on Monday, at which point I sent him to school.
5 A The plan which he had for the zoo was interesting.
   B The plan was interesting, which he had for the zoo.

Vocabulary

3 Complete the article with the metaphorical use of the words in the box.

shot   fly   display   handiwork
launch   rake   leap   fish

Clever stuff

In the wild chimpanzees use small branches to try to _____[1] termites out of their nests. In captivity, chimps _____[2] even greater ingenuity, wielding sticks to _____[3] in food from outside their enclosure and stacking boxes in order to reach bananas. But can a chimp use one tool to make another – the breakthrough that was to _____[4] early man's technological _____[5] forward?

First, the chimp was shown how to produce stone chips by striking one cobble against another; then how a chip could be used as a tool to cut the string securing the lid of a food box. After that, the chimp was left alone. His efforts weren't particularly impressive, and, after four months, he decided to have a _____[6] at a new technique – hurling the stone at the concrete floor and smashing it to fragments. Finally, he was turned out into an earth enclosure, and this time he placed a rock on the ground, took aim with the hammer-stone and let _____[7]. His _____[8] may not have been up to the standards achieved by early man, but he certainly learnt how to break rocks.

4 Complete the sentences with the correct form of the verbs in the box. You need to use one verb twice.

check   rule   get   cut   try
phase   chuck   dig   work

1 I can't _____ out how to get my dog to get my shoes for me!
2 Will you go and _____ out that article on snakes for me?
3 I'm not going to _____ out visiting a zoo, but I need to think about it.
4 Did you _____ out that old blanket I used for the cat?
5 Apparently, they're going to start _____ out the use of dogs by the police force because it is too expensive.
6 I'm going to try _____ out meat as I'd like to become vegetarian.
7 I'd like to _____ out this idea that cats can help lower your blood pressure.
8 In Australia, if you see a snake in your house you should _____ out immediately!
9 Many underprivileged kids _____ a lot out of dealing with horses.
10 They're going to _____ out a new way of training the chimps.

Progress Check 1 Units 1–5

1 Choose the correct alternatives, A or B.

1 She _____ part in a national swimming competition last year and got a silver medal.
   A took   B has taken

2 I _____ a fascinating article about how animals help us.
   A just read   B have just read

3 It's been a long time _____ I last went to a Chinese restaurant.
   A since   B when

4 He _____ on the phone for absolutely ages!
   A has chatted   B has been chatting

5 We _____ for over half an hour when the waiter came and told us the table was ready.
   A were waiting   B had been waiting

6 I'm sorry – I _____ haven't finished that book you lent me.
   A still   B already

7 I've been afraid of dogs ever since one _____ me when I was a child.
   A bit   B was biting

8 While I _____ to work, someone just came up and gave me a hug.
   A was walking   B have been walking

2 Complete the multi-word verbs in these sentences with the correct verb or particle.

1 Have you checked _____ that new café on the corner yet?

2 He did his best to _____ me up even though I felt miserable all day.

3 They are already _____ out the manufacture of video players.

4 I didn't _____ to him immediately because he seemed to have rather a selfish streak.

5 I'm surprised you're unhappy about your job. You seemed to _____ in so well there.

6 Someone has used _____ all the milk and left the empty bottle in the fridge.

7 I've tidied my living room and chucked _____ three bags of rubbish.

8 I _____ out with him over his patronising attitude and I haven't spoken to him for nearly a year now.

3 Complete the sentences with the correct article a/an, the or ø (no article).

1 She's got a cat and a dog, but it's _____ dog which she loves most.

2 After his skiing accident, he had to stay in _____ hospital for nearly two months.

3 One of her many interests is _____ music, but she is also quite sporty.

4 Winning a prize at school was one of _____ proudest moments of my life.

5 You need to work hard and to have _____ determination if you are to succeed as an athlete.

6 I can't believe that _____ friend of mine has just bought two horses.

7 I love playing _____ football with my friends but I wouldn't want to play professionally.

8 Hearing people play _____ piano makes me feel very nostalgic for my childhood.

4 Read the text and decide which answer A, B, C or D best fits each gap.

My grandfather

One of my earliest memories is of my grandfather. He was a very important person in my life – an integral part of the _____[1] to my childhood. Looking back, in some ways he was more influential than my parents; a kind of father _____[2] really. He made me realise what I could do with my life – certainly in terms of my creativity. I _____[3] remember him reading to me – his own stories mostly. I remember being completely enthralled; it was like magic to me that he could invent such _____[4] stories.

I wrote my first story when I was about eight. I can't remember what I called it; my mind's gone _____[5] on that. But it was about the adventures of a young girl, based on me, I suppose. I haven't got it any more; it was probably rubbish really, but I was really pleased with it at the time. I thought it was _____[6]!

My grandfather died last year, but I keep his memory _____[7] as much as I can by continuing to write stories myself. I found a photograph the other day of him and me together. He was reading one of his stories to me and the memories came _____[8] back. He was a very special person and always really good _____[9]. I feel very privileged to have had him as such a _____[10] influence in my early life.

1 A background   B backbone   C backdrop
   D backcloth

2 A person   B figure   C character   D model

3 A brightly   B powerfully C strikingly   D vividly

4 A excruciating B dazzling   C fatuous   D vast

5 A blank   B plain   C black   D bare

6 A preposterous B ludicrous   C tremendous
   D outrageous

7 A live   B alive   C living   D lively

8 A fleeing   B flailing   C flooding   D flapping

9 A company   B mate   C companion   D friend

10 A collusive   B colossal   C conclusive   D conniving

5 Complete the text with one word in each gap.

British man cycles round the world

Mark Beaumont from Scotland has set a new record for cycling round the world, arriving back in Paris 195 days and six hours after he set off. Completing this amazing achievement means that he has _____ 1 the previous record by a really _____ 2 margin – eighty-one days in fact.

His 18,000-mile trip, passing through twenty countries, was certainly not all plain sailing. He had a gruelling schedule; he lost a stone in weight, suffered food poisoning in Pakistan and was knocked off his bike three times. The twenty-five-year-old has a strong competitive _____ 3 and very high expectations _____ 4 himself, however, saying 'I love the idea of being the first and the fastest.' Mark has been dreaming of reaching this _____ 5 for a long time, and amongst his friends and family, he has always had a reputation _____ 6 pushing himself to the limit.

Mark's ambition for his world trip was not only to achieve a _____ 7 best, but also to set a new Guinness World Record. In addition, he was raising money for five charities, so he said there was never any question of giving up. Mark says that he has an inbuilt desire to _____ 8 and that he wouldn't rule _____ 9 doing something similar again. But when asked what he intended to do next, he said _____ 10 he really wanted to do was sleep for two weeks.

6 For each group of sentences 1–5, think of one word which can be used appropriately in all three sentences. The first one has been done for you.

1 She has a tendency to make _snap_ decisions and doesn't really think things through properly.
I tried to _snap_ the chocolate in half but it wouldn't break.
Please keep your dog under control – it just tried to _snap_ at me.

2 I really don't _____ if you want to come in and wait for a while.
He would be a great person on the team as he has a razor-sharp _____ and is incredibly hard-working.
I wish that just for once she'd _____ her own business and stop prying all the time.

3 She has a strong _____ of responsibility and I'm sure she would've called us if anything was wrong.
Many animals, like dogs, are able to _____ danger long before human beings can.
You're not making _____ at all. Can you explain it again, please?

4 I think you ought to throw this food away – it really smells _____.
He's painfully shy, but don't let that put you _____ as he's a really nice person when you get to know him.
I'm _____ really early tomorrow morning so I probably won't see you.

5 You really need to cut down on _____ foods if you want to get healthier.
I'm trying to keep dad _____ so that he'll lend me the car later.
How _____ of you to remember my birthday – you really shouldn't have gone to all this trouble.

7 Complete the second sentence so that it has a similar meaning to the first sentence, using the word given. Do not change the word given. You must use between three and six words, including the word given.

1 Why don't you get a personal trainer for yourself? I'm sure you'd like it.
encouraged
She _____ a personal trainer for myself.

2 Just tell me one thing: are you coming to the restaurant with us or not?
all
_____ whether you're coming to the restaurant with us or not.

3 You will increase your chances of succeeding if you train more.
harder
The _____ you have of succeeding.

4 I have great admiration for Charles Dickens's books and he has always been a huge inspiration to me.
admire
Charles Dickens, _____, has always been a huge inspiration to me.

5 Winning the championship is a brilliant thought, but I don't think it'll happen.
be
It _____ if we won the championship.

6 She looked at me in a strange way and it made me think she was upset about something.
it
_____ she looked at me that made me think she was upset about something.

7 You will certainly benefit if you join a gym and exercise regularly.
worth
It _____ a gym and exercising regularly.

8 I especially liked the film because the music was so wonderful.
better
The film was all _____ such wonderful music.

making movies

blockbuster

clip culture

red carpet

Unit 06

Introduction

(1 Look at the pictures. Which picture goes with each of these phrases? Why?

> a blockbuster   a clip   an Oscar nomination   an amateur video
> the red carpet   to download a video   video-sharing   a premiere

(2 Divide the words and phrases in Exercise 1 into two groups. Explain your groups to a partner.

(3 What kind of videos would you most like to watch on a video-sharing website such as YouTube? Why?

- amateur cinema
- video diaries
- family celebrations
- football compilations
- pet and baby videos
- comedy videos

(4 Discuss these questions with other students.

1 Which of these would make you want to see a film? Why?
- the trailer
- a review
- what your friends say
- your favourite film star is in it
- you've read the book
- the poster

2 Who is your favourite film star and why?

3 Why do you think people are interested in the Oscars and other award ceremonies?

CAE close-up | Reading Multiple choice (Paper 1, part 3)

Exam information

In this part of the exam, you read a text and then answer seven multiple-choice (A, B, C or D) questions. These questions may test your understanding of

- specific parts of the text;
- words or phrases in the text;
- the text as a whole, e.g. the attitude of the writer, the purpose of the text, text organisation features.

Approach

1 Read the opening instructions to the task. These will tell you where the text comes from and what type of text it is, e.g. a newspaper article.

2 Read the whole text quite quickly to get a general idea of what it is about.

3 Look at each question but *not* the options (A, B, C, D). Underline the important words, e.g. *why, believes, concludes,* etc. Then, mark the part of the text that each question refers to.

4 Now read the text carefully. When you come to a part you have marked, read through the relevant question and options (A, B, C, D). Choose the option that best matches what the text says. Make sure you read all the options carefully before you make a decision. Don't select by reading *only* the options – make sure you read each option with the question. Look for any words and phrases with similar meanings in the options and the text.

5 The last question may test your understanding of the text as a whole, so it may be appropriate to read the complete text from beginning to end one more time.

Practice task

You are going to read a newspaper article. For questions **1–7**, choose the answer (**A, B, C** or **D**) which you think fits best according to the text.

'Clip culture'

Could the short films on video-sharing sites such as YouTube ever rival films at the cinema?

In parallel with its own exponential growth, my fascination with YouTube has galloped into a raging obsession. Whole evenings, theoretically dedicated to writing, have been hijacked by a terrible need to click onto the Internet browser, and from there the lure of YouTube is inevitable. What's not to be fascinated by? However slick or however rickety, the best of these mini-films have an unmediated quality, a realness that is completely lacking in anything available in the cinema or on TV.

For a growing number of people, time spent surfing the web exceeds the time spent watching TV, so who knows if this way of making and watching films might not become a huge and serious rival to the mainstream. Many contemporary films-makers have become fascinated by the video aesthetic, and by camera work with a deadpan surveillance feel, which has risen in parallel to this Internet revolution.

The cinema, though, does have something in common with the confessional, video blog aspect of YouTube. The popularity of the horror film *The Blair Witch Project* was inflamed by a vast, grassroots Internet campaign which mischievously suggested that the film's horrors were real. Plus there's a cousin to this blurring of fact and fiction in YouTube – confessional blogs which turn out to be faked by ingenious actors. In the past, some documentaries that you could see on TV or at the cinema had YouTube qualities, in that the footage was shot by the participants themselves, although they needed a professional cinema practitioner to bring it to light. If the unhappy heroes of these films were making their videos now, they would probably bypass these directors and take them straight to YouTube.

Where straight cinema and YouTube come more closely into parallel is the use of the continuous shot: the persistent, unjudging, almost uncomprehending gaze; an unedited, deep-focus scene in which our attention as audience is not coerced or directed. The true YouTube gems are not the digitally carpentered mini-features. The most gripping material is raw, unedited footage in one continuous take. Outstanding examples range from domestic events in the home to windows on international events. Watching these, and going through the events in real time, is riveting yet disturbing at the same time.

Many film directors have tried exploiting the eerie, disquieting quality of video-surveillance footage. But they should look further as they might all be fascinated by, and even learn something from, what I think of as YouTube's comedy genre: bizarre things captured more by accident than design, which often have a sublime quality. One such clip of a woman falling down a hole was captured by CCTV; the camera is apparently fixed above a bar in a busy pub. Someone opens up a trap door directly behind a woman serving drinks, with results that Buster Keaton himself would have admired. The scene is shot and framed with unshowy formal perfection; a professional director and crew could work for months on a slapstick scene and not get it as right as this. It's something in the way the woman disappears so utterly from view.

Unlike the cinema, where we have to wait for reviews, you can get your material reviewed on YouTube instantly since there is a ratings and comments section for each video. Just as the videos are more real than films, this type of reviewing is also more honest. Cinema reviews may comment on the predictable elements, such as plot, setting, actors, etc., but YouTube reviews are boiled down to the essence of entertainment appeal. Are you interested enough to watch it to the end? Would you recommend it to your friends? Do you go back in and watch it again?

The cinema of YouTube has, at its best, an appealing amateurism, unrestricted by the conventions of narrative interest or good taste. It is a quality to be savoured, and quite different from documentary or the attempts at realism in feature films. What makes it so involving is that the viewers extend this amateur process in choosing, playing and sharing the files. Consequently, they supplement production with a new type of distribution. It's this that makes YouTube so addictive and unless the cinema learns from it, it may be outclassed.

1 What does the writer say about his interest in YouTube?

  A He enjoys watching YouTube while he is writing.

  B He prefers the short films on YouTube to the cinema.

  C He finds it hard to resist watching YouTube films.

  D He likes the fact that the films on YouTube are short.

2 The writer suggests YouTube will become more popular because

  A the films on it capture people when they are unaware.

  B people have changed how they use their leisure time.

  C people no longer have time to watch full-length films.

  D the films on it mimic real life with real people.

3 In the third paragraph, the writer says the similarity between YouTube videos and commercial films is that

  A they both produce realistic horror films.

  B they both have directors who are also actors.

  C they both depend on the Internet for publicity.

  D they are both effective at faking reality.

4 What does the writer say is the appeal of the continuous shot?

  A that nobody is managing the events on screen

  B that it can be used effectively in any setting

  C that we can see things we wouldn't otherwise see

  D that the camera acts as our eyes on the event

5 In the fifth paragraph, the writer uses the example of the woman falling to show that

  A YouTube uses a range of sources for its films.

  B It is difficult to replicate real-life comedy.

  C YouTube has funnier films than those at the cinema.

  D it is better when participants are unaware they are being filmed.

6 Why does the writer use questions at the end of the sixth paragraph?

  A to suggest what questions cinema reviews should address

  B to illustrate how YouTube reviews have a single focus

  C to guide the reader about what a review should contain

  D to show the broad range of views on YouTube

7 The writer concludes that YouTube is addictive because

  A it has so many potential viewers.

  B it offers films which have unique qualities.

  C it shows better films than those available commercially.

  D it has become part of the process of making films.

Go to www.iTests.com or your CD-ROM for interactive exam practice

Vocabulary | films

1 Work in two groups, A and B. Look at the words in the relevant box and check you know the meanings and the pronunciation. Use a dictionary if necessary.

A	
1	an extra, a lead role
2	the setting, the script
3	a scene, the set
4	direct, produce

B	
5	sound effects, a soundtrack
6	slapstick, comedy
7	mainstream, experimental
8	a shot, a take

2 Work in pairs (one from group A and one from B) and explain the difference between each pair of words.

3 Add the words and expressions from Exercise 1 to the Exam Reviser. Some words can go in more than one column.

exam reviser p8 | 6.1

4 Complete this article using the correct form of words in Exercise 1.

HOME | EQUIPMENT | SKILLS | RECENT ENTRIES | ARCHIVE

MAKING A VIDEO

Anyone can make a film nowadays and stick it on the web for their friends to share. But don't just film silly stuff with your camera phone – create a masterpiece!

- Get a decent camera and then take the filming process seriously. Actually _____[1] your film so it is how you want it to look.

- Make sure that, however short, you have a _____[2] for your film so you can get it to flow right.

- Don't have too much going on – give one of your friends the _____[3]; the rest of them can be _____[4].

- Think about the _____[5] and check you have enough light and no interruptions.

- YouTube videos are less than ten minutes so, to keep your viewers interested, make sure each _____[6] is only two–five seconds long. Also vary the _____[7] you take by using different camera angles.

- Remember, it doesn't matter how many _____[8] you do – just keep doing it till you get what you want.

- To make it even more professional, you could add a _____[9] by uploading some music when it's finished.

5 Discuss these questions with other students.
- Would you like to make your own video for a video-sharing website? Why/Why not?
- How difficult do you think it would be? Why?

6 R.17 Listen to a man talking about a film he has seen. Can you guess which film?

7 You are going to talk about a film you have seen, giving your opinion. Follow these instructions to prepare what you are going to say.
1 Think about the acting, the plot, the music, costumes, setting, special effects, etc.
2 Decide on your overall impression of the film and look again at the language for describing how good or bad something is

exam reviser p20 | 2

8 Tell another student about the film but do not say the title. Ask your partner to guess which film you are talking about.

9 Add any new words you used in Exercise 8 to the Exam Reviser.

exam reviser p8 | 6.1

premium plus 23

Grammar | linking words

1 Match the highlighted examples of linking words in the article on pages 60–61 with these meanings and functions.
1 meaning *and*: _____
2 meaning *if not*: _____
3 meaning *but*: _____
4 meaning *because*: _____
5 meaning *therefore*: _____
6 comparing: _____

2 Which two of the alternatives are possible in each sentence? Use the Grammar Reference to help you.
1 He got the part, *although/nevertheless/ yet* I didn't think he was very good.
2 *If/Unless/While* the leading man remained well, we would not need to use the understudy.
3 He took singing lessons *so/whereas/as* he could improve his chances.
4 He broke his leg. *Thus/Hence/Instead*, he was out of the competition.
5 The girl was very good, *unlike/as/ compared with* the boy, who was rubbish.
6 He ran several auditions, *yet/though/ while* he couldn't find anybody for the lead role.

•• see grammar reference: **page 175** ••

Grammar note | *position of linking words*

Remember that using linking words at the end of sentences can sometimes change their meaning. Using linking words at the end of sentences is much more common in spoken language.

1 What is the grammatical difference between the highlighted conjunctions?

   A *She went for the audition, though she was very nervous.*

   B *She went for the audition. She was very nervous, though.*

2 What is the difference in meaning?

3 Which one can be replaced by *although*?

4 How could A be written more formally?

3 Which of the words or expressions in the box can we usually use:

  1 at the beginning of a sentence?

  2 at the end of a sentence?

  3 in the middle of a sentence?

> although however since so (that) whereas
> consequently unless unlike for instead

4 Compare your answers with a partner and discuss the reasons for your choices.

5 Look at sentences 1–6 from informal, spoken English. Rewrite them in formal, written language using linking words in the box. You may need to make two sentences or change the order of the clauses.

> since provided hence
> nonetheless whereas additionally

  1 There are too many reality TV shows so they are declining in popularity.

  2 If people continue to buy celebrity magazines, the market for celebrity photos will remain.

  3 We increasingly watch videos on YouTube, but it's not good to get so involved in other people's lives.

  4 We are becoming a nation of couch potatoes because we watch too much TV.

  5 Stage shows are exciting because they are live and they are very involving for the audience.

  6 He is fascinated by famous people, but I find them boring!

6 Which other words could you use in sentences 1, 3 and 5 in Exercise 5?

Grammar note | *using two linking words*

Sometimes we can use two linking words in the same sentence. Which of these sentences are correct?

1 *He can dance well and he's also a good singer.*

2 *I can't come since, because I've got piano lessons.*

3 *Although he's good, I do, however, think he should practise more.*

4 *While she can certainly sing, she is, nevertheless, hopeless at dancing.*

5 *I called them for auditions three days ago, but so that they had some warning.*

•• see grammar reference: **page 175** ••

7 Look at a piece of writing you have done recently. Check through it and add some linking words from Exercise 1 in order to:

• make it easier for the reader to follow;

• connect sentences or ideas.

premium plus **24** ▶

Speaking

1 R.18 ▶ Listen to two people discussing a video they have seen. Did they both like the video?

2 Look at audioscript 18 on page 163. Find examples of these things that the speakers do in order to justify their opinions. Add them to the Exam Reviser.

  1 Explain why using facts.

  2 Explain why using an example.

  3 Explain their personal feelings.

  4 Make a comparison.

exam reviser p22 | 7 ▶

3 Look at this question and decide what your opinion is. Make notes of what you could say to justify your opinion using each strategy in the Exam Reviser.

> Do you think the best films on video-sharing sites are the ones where someone just happened to be in the right place at the right time or the ones which have been deliberately filmed for such a site?

4 Discuss the question in Exercise 5 with a partner, using your notes to help you.

premium plus 25 ▶

SPEAKING SKILLS
Ways of justifying your opinion

Explain why using facts, e.g.
He forgot his lines!

Explain why using an example, e.g.
The singing was good and the dancing was really energetic.

Give your personal response, e.g.
It made me cry with laughter.

Make a comparison, e.g.
It was much better than the last concert I saw.

Use stress to reinforce the strength of your opinion, e.g.
I didn't think it was very funny.

Listening

1 If you worked in the film industry, which of these jobs would you rather do and why?
- actor
- support work, e.g. stunt performer, make-up artist, set designer, director, cameraman
- ancillary work, e.g. film critic, film censor

2 You are going to listen to three extracts of people in the film industry talking about their work. First decide if these expressions they use are likely to introduce a positive or negative opinion.
1 *I'm looking forward to it.*
2 *... it'll be fine ...*
3 *... it doesn't help that ...*
4 *I can foresee big problems ...*
5 *... it's great ...*
6 *...*

3 What other ways can you tell if somebody's opinion is positive or negative?

LISTENING SKILLS
Identifying positive and negative opinion.

Opinions can be introduced by a range of expressions, not just *I think* or *I don't think*. When you are listening, be aware of language and intonation clues that tell you if somebody's opinion is positive or negative.

4 R.19 ▶ Listen to the extracts. For questions 1–6, choose the answer A, B or C which fits best according to what you hear. There are two questions for each extract and you will hear each extract twice.

Extract 1
You hear part of an interview with a cameraman, Mark, about his next job working on a James Bond film.

1 How does Mark feel about doing the filming on the Bond film?
   A confident in his abilities as a cameraman
   B comfortable with his colleagues on the film
   C secure about the planning of the project

2 What does Mark think about working on the Bond film?
   A He anticipates it will be the highlight of his career.
   B He is concerned about whether he will be successful.
   C He recognises it may be his last job as a cameraman.

Extract 2
You hear two people on the radio having a discussion about censorship in films.

3 What is the woman angry about?
   A the amount of violence allowed in films today
   B the lack of decision-making on the censorship committee
   C the length of time it takes to censor a film

4 What does the man disapprove of?
   A the type of people who sit on the censorship committee
   B the form of government controls on the censorship committee
   C the way the censorship committee is financed

Extract 3

You hear an interview with an actor at the Oscar film awards.

5 Why does the actor think the Oscars are important?
   A because actors are voted for by other actors
   B because they recognise the work of non-actors
   C because it is an opportunity for the industry to get together

6 The actor's mother did not come to the awards because
   A she was unhappy about appearing in public.
   B she was frightened by the number of photographers.
   C she was worried she didn't have the right thing to wear.

5 Discuss these questions with other students.
- What do you think would be the best aspect of being a cameraman? Why?
- Do you think it is more important to censor bad language or violence? Why?
- Which recent film you have seen do you think should win an Oscar? Why?

Vocabulary | word formation – prefixes

1 Look at the highlighted affixes in these words. What is the difference between a prefix and a suffix?

impossible   enjoyment

2 Look at these sentences and follow the instructions.
1 Underline the prefixes in these sentences.
   A I don't ever think you outgrow the job.
   B ... they're irresponsible ...
   C I think it's disgraceful ...
   D I can foresee big problems.
2 Write the prefixes at the top of the correct column in the table.
3 Put the words with prefixes into the correct column.

Negative prefixes e.g. un-	Time prefixes e.g. -	Quantity/level prefixes e.g. -

3 Read the text. Would you like to go to this film school? Why/Why not?

JOIN OUR FILM SCHOOL!

We are one of the most innovative and dynamic film and acting schools in the world. New York Film Academy offers an _____[1] (resistible) combination of Filmmaking, Screenwriting, Digital Video, Computer Animation and Acting For Film programs. Our philosophy of 'learning by doing' _____[2] (lies) every aspect of the curriculum.

Some of Hollywood's greatest have chosen to send their children to the New York Film Academy. Yet, the most _____[3] (standing) projects to come out of the Academy often come from students with no connections to the industry. Plus students develop an _____[4] (valuable) network of classmates that often provides opportunities for future work.

No film school can match the Academy's _____[5] (coastal) campuses in New York City and at Universal Studios in Hollywood. The Academy maintains the largest inventory of cameras, lights, etc. of any film school in the world, resulting in _____[6] (paralleled) access to film equipment for our students.

Click on our website for a _____[7] (taste) of our programs! We are normally _____[8] (subscribed), so apply early!

4 Complete the text by using the word given in brackets to form another word that fits the gap.

5 Look at the text again and choose three words you would like to add to the Exam Reviser.

exam reviser   p8 | 6.2
premium plus   26

Expanding your vocabulary
When you learn a new word, it's a good idea to write down all the words you can make from it, e.g.
dishonest, honest, honestly, honesty
How many words can you make from these 'roots'?
ambition   elegant   perfect

learning tip

Grammar | future forms

1 Look at this list of ways we can talk about the future. Find examples in audioscript 19 on page 163.

Extract 1

A present simple for timetables and schedules

B *will* for spontaneous decisions

Extract 2

C *going to* for predictions based on current evidence

D future perfect for something that will finish before a certain time

Extract 3

E infinitive future for commands

F future in the past for looking back at past intentions

2 Match each sentence 1–6 with their uses A–F. Check your answers in the Grammar Reference.

1 They will have been showing that film for over three weeks on Friday.

2 Are you working at the cinema on Saturday?

3 She thinks the film will bomb at the box office.

4 Do you know anybody who'll be working with you on that job?

5 I heard they were going to close the cinema down.

6 I'll help you write the review if you like.

A present continuous for arrangements

B *going to* for plans and intentions

C *will* for offers

D *will* for probability

E future continuous for an action in progress in the future

F future perfect continuous

•• see grammar reference: page 176 ••

3 Explain the difference in meaning between each pair of sentences. Two pairs have no difference in meaning.

1 A Don't worry about your dress – I'll pick it up for you.

   B Don't worry about your dress – I'm picking it up for you.

2 A I was going to apply for *Pop Idol*, but I was too late.

   B I'm going to apply for *Pop Idol* if it's not too late.

3 A She's about to leave for LA.

   B She's on the point of leaving for LA.

4 A In the summer I'll be taking a drama course.

   B In the summer I'll take a drama course.

Grammar note | *choosing your future*

Often a sentence can make sense with two or three different future forms. Sometimes the context is clear (e.g. in Exercise 3, question 2) but if several future forms are possible, then the difference may depend on the speaker's intention. Compare these sentences:

1 *I'm going to see him at the weekend.*

2 *I'll see him at the weekend.*

3 *I'm seeing him at the weekend.*

In which sentence is it most likely that:

A the speaker is expecting this to happen but has not arranged to meet?

B the arrangement is fixed and the time decided?

C the speaker is planning to do this but perhaps not yet fixed a time?

4 Choose the correct alternatives. Explain your choices to a partner.

Pop Idol – the movie!

Reality TV producer Simon Cowell *is going/will be going*[1] to produce a movie set behind the scenes of a TV singing competition similar to 'Pop Idol'. The idea is that the project, tentatively called 'Star Struck', *will follow/follows*[2] ten contestants trying to make it to the top. The leads *will be being/are being*[3] cast next month through US auditions similar to those used on the reality shows. Cowell told 'Hollywood Reporter': 'I'm determined that the story *is going to be told/will have been told*[4] through the eyes of those ten contestants. We want it to be the musical version of 'Rocky' – an underdog story, a feel-good film.' Cowell said casting unknowns for the lead roles was crucial for the film's authenticity. 'To enjoy the film, you *are going to/will*[5] have to believe that they are contestants on a reality show,' he said. He added that the film *is opening/will open*[6] with clips from the auditions and Cowell *will/will be going to*[7] attend the cast auditions. Apparently, the most important thing for the film was the timing. 'Pop Idol' *will be/will have been*[8] going for ten years this summer. They *will be filming/are filming*[9] for six months, and will get the movie out early next year. 'We knew that a TV show like "Idol" *will be/was going to be*[10] successful. I have the same feeling about doing the movie.'

5 Do you think the film of *Pop Idol* will be popular? Why/Why not?

6 Write a diary for your plans next week. Make sure you include fixed appointments and possible activities.

7 Tell your partner about your activities using an appropriate form of the future.

On Tuesday between 3.00 p.m. and 4.00 p.m. I will be preparing for my interview.

8 Work in pairs. Write three sentences predicting what you think your partner will do in the future.

Next month …

By this time next year, …

In five years' time …

9 Show your sentences to your partner and see if you guessed correctly!

> premium plus   27 ▶

Writing | essay

1 Discuss these questions with other students.

1 Do you prefer watching films at the cinema or at home on DVD? Why?

2 What can cinemas offer in order to attract people to them? Think about:

- the types of films
- the surroundings
- technological advantages
- extra services or facilities

2 Read this task and decide with a partner if you agree with the statement or not.

> **Writing task**
>
> You have been asked to write an essay giving your views on the following statement.
>
> *More and more cinemas are going to close down because people today just sit at home and watch DVDs on their TV and computer.*

3 Are these statements true or false?

1 An essay should be written in formal language.

2 You must give examples from your own life.

3 You can disagree with the essay title.

4 In the conclusion you should refer back to the title.

5 You should only give your own opinion.

6 If you prefer, you can present only one point of view.

7 The introduction should explain why the issue is under debate/controversial.

4 Look at the paragraph plans in the Writing Reference and answer these questions.

1 Which plan would you choose for this essay? Why?

2 Which paragraph plan would you choose and why if an essay contained the following words in the title.

A *How far do you agree?*

B *Discuss this statement.*

C *To what extent do you think … ?*

D *Give your opinion on …*

3 Which plan does the model in the Writing Reference follow and why?

> •• see writing reference: **page 194** ••

5 Look at these ways of giving opinions. Put them in the correct column in the table. Check your answers in the Exam Reviser.

> Giving opinions
>
> | | |
> |---|---|
> | *In my opinion …* | *As far as (X) is concerned …* |
> | *I disagree with …* | *I broadly agree that …* |
> | *In my view …* | *From (X) point of view …* |
> | *I agree with …* | *There is some truth in …* |
> | *It seems to me that …* | *People are mistaken when …* |
> | *I differ from …* | *I take the view that …* |

agreeing	disagreeing	introducing an opinion

> exam reviser   p21 | 6 ▶

6 Look at the model in the Writing Reference and decide what you need to include in the introduction and the conclusion.

> •• see writing reference: **page 194** ••

7 Write your essay in 220–260 words using your paragraph plan. Remember to:

- use linking words;
- summarise the argument and give your own opinion in the conclusion.

Grammar

1 Choose the best alternatives in these sentences.

1 I *will have seen/will be seeing* this film six times when this showing is over!

2 Did you know they *are going to make/will make* a film of *Pop Idol*?

3 Don't worry about the tickets – *I'm getting/I'll get* them for you.

4 I think he *will be/is being* very successful as an actor.

5 He *will have invited/was going to invite* her but he changed his mind.

6 This time next week I *will be touring/will tour* Universal Studios.

7 Quick! Move! The camera *is going to fall/will fall* on you!

8 I *meet/am meeting* her outside the cinema so join us if you want.

9 You *are not to start/are not starting* singing until I tell you.

10 Production *will be beginning/begins* next week on a new stage show based on *The Lord of the Rings*.

2 Put commas where necessary in these sentences.

1 I like watching reality shows and also I like voting on them.

2 Unless you're over sixteen you can't go to the audition.

3 The critics gave the show bad reviews. When we went however the singing was superb.

4 Since we haven't got any money we can't go to the concert.

5 I was late getting ready and therefore we couldn't go.

6 I booked the tickets so that we didn't have to queue.

7 He dances well just as his father used to.

8 Stuntmen train hard. Nevertheless their job is dangerous.

Vocabulary

3 Use the word in brackets to form a word that fits each gap.

What price fame?

Imagine what life is like for the _____[1] (win) of a TV talent contest. Suddenly they go from being a normal person, _____[2] (know) outside their circle of friends, to being someone who _____[3] (virtual) everybody in the country has heard of. Suddenly, it becomes _____[4] (possible) for them to go out without being mobbed. But this has its downside. Being in the public eye, they are not allowed to _____[5] (behave) in any way as this will damage their image. Nor can they be _____[6] (social) towards their fans as these are the people who buy their songs! Having been so _____[7] (patient) about finding fame, a lot of them then quickly become very _____[8] (illusion) with it as the restrictions are so great. The _____[9] (convenient) it creates in their lives starts to _____[10] (weigh) the benefits it brings. So don't envy these stars – feel sorry for them!

4 Complete the text with a word or expression beginning with the letters given.

Being an extra

Often when you start out as an actor, you get work as an extra on films. It's important they use u_____[1] for this job so we are not recognised. Usually you don't have to have an a_____[2] because you don't have to speak and you are given clear stage directions! There's an awful lot that goes on behind the s_____[3], though, as extras often have to have quite complicated make-up and costumes, like in the *Star Wars* films. Then if you're lucky, you progress to getting a walk-on p_____[4], where you just say one or two l_____[5].

If this opportunity comes and you get a chance to say something to one of the l_____[6] actors, then you will probably get yourself noticed and be offered bigger roles. As extras, we are not usually allowed to walk down the r_____ c_____[7] when the film has a p_____[8]. The thing I find frustrating is that the a_____[9] never know who we are but we are on the s_____[10] all day every day while the film is being made!

Get smarter

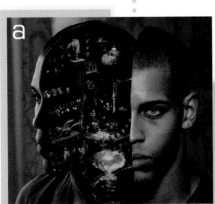

telepathy

mind control

use your brain

BUILD YOUR BABY'S BRAIN 2
through the power of
Mozart

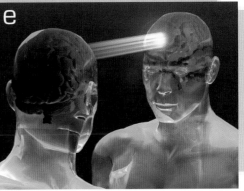

Unit 07

Introduction

1 Discuss these questions with other students.
1. What aspect of the brain do you think each photograph represents?
2. Do you think male and female brains differ in the way they approach certain tasks? Why/Why not? Can you think of any examples?

2 Do the words in the box refer to something positive, negative or neutral? Use a dictionary if necessary.

> a brainbox   the brainchild   the brain drain
> a brain teaser   to brainwash   a brainwave

3 Which of these statements do you agree with most? Why?
1. People are born creative; you cannot be taught how to be creative.
2. There is no such thing as knowledge, only what we believe to be true.
3. Some so-called 'intelligent' people can be very stupid.
4. Native intelligence is much more useful than academic intelligence.

Listening

1 Discuss these questions with another student.

- What kind of things do you find hard to remember? Why?
- What tricks can you use to help yourself remember things?

2 Study these faces and names for 1 minute. Then turn to page 166.

Anna
George
Maria
Steven
Helen
Peter

3 Compare your answers with a partner and discuss how you tried to remember the names.

4 You are going to listen to an interview with a professor about a new device that will store memories electronically. Choose what you expect the interviewer to ask the professor from this list:

A the professor's personal history
B what the device does
C the impact of the device
D the history of other devices
E any problems with the device
F what the professor does in his free time
G the advantages of the device
H how to construct the device

LISTENING SKILLS

Predicting from world knowledge

You can often predict what you will hear from your knowledge of the world and situations. For example, you may be able to predict:

- the types of questions an interviewer will ask;
- the feelings someone may have about a subject;
- the 'progress' of a discussion.

5 R.20 ▶ Listen to the interview and choose the best answer A, B, C or D.

1 According to the professor, what kind of information will the new device find it difficult to store?
A details of past events from our lives
B facts and figures that we need to remember
C the emotions and feelings we have had
D ways of solving problems and understanding things

2 The professor believes the new device may not be popular because
A it will select information for us.
B it will take too long to find information.
C it will remember things that are unimportant.
D it will remind us of things we wish to forget.

3 The professor thinks the new device will change our daily lives
A by recognising people we don't know.
B by storing details of people we meet.
C by recording details that could affect our health.
D by giving us access to information on the Internet.

4 What problem does the professor anticipate with storing memories electronically?
A developing a reliable method to protect the information stored
B training researchers in how to use the data banks properly
C controlling the input of data protection companies
D deciding who is responsible for storing the data

5 What is the professor's attitude to Keith Barrack?
A irritation
B gratitude
C concern
D astonishment

6 The professor says he supports the project because
A it is the only way to record the life we are living now.
B it is a way to automate a complex process.
C it is a unique way to record and transfer memories.
D it is a new way of creating photographs.

6 R.20 ▶ Listen again and check your answers. What topics from Exercise 4 were discussed?

7 Discuss these questions with other students.

1 Do you think it would be a good idea to store personal memories electronically? Why/Why not?
2 If you could store your memories digitally, what aspect of memory would you choose as a priority and why?
- information that you need, such as for studies
- feelings, sounds, tastes and smells
- details of events, such as parties
- details of other people

Grammar | *if*-structures

1 What is the difference between these four sentences? Use the Grammar Reference to help you if necessary. Think about time and probability.

1 If we had some way of recovering all this information, we could be happier.
2 If it weren't for this ability, our memory would be crowded with things which are unpleasant or unnecessary to remember.
3 Imagine we could store things like emotions, wouldn't it be wonderful to be able to revisit those?
4 If he hadn't been involved, it would have taken us much longer.

•• see grammar reference: **page 176** ••

2 Complete the sentences with the correct forms of the verb in brackets.

1 If you use rhymes, you _____ (find) it easier to remember facts.
2 If you _____ (write) a list, you would have remembered to do everything.
3 You might find it easier to remember things if you _____ (use) a diary.
4 If you should have to remember a lot, then _____ (try) memorising it in small chunks.
5 If it _____ (not be) for the alarm on my phone, I'd forget everything.
6 If you _____ (have) problems remembering people's names, try repeating their name when you meet them.

3 Some expressions with *if* are short forms and so some words after *if* are left out. Read sentences 1–5 and follow these instructions.

1 Check the Grammar Reference, then complete the gaps with one of the fixed expressions in the box.
2 Decide which words have been left out in each sentence.

> if necessary   if any   if in doubt
> **if not**   if ever   if about

You may want to go to the talk. **If not** you can work in the library. **If you don't want to go to the talk ...**

1 I'll help her practise her presentation, _____
2 There is little, _____ , evidence that her memory has improved.
3 He rarely _____ remembers the names of people he's met.
4 _____ , then don't say anything!
5 _____ to do a test, try to remember information in small chunks.

•• see grammar reference: **page 176** ••

4 Some words have a similar meaning to *if*. Choose the correct alternative in each sentence.

1 Would you like to store memories, *as long as/suppose* they were only happy ones? Why/Why not?
2 Would you like another person to be able to access your memories, *imagine/on condition that* you could control which ones?
3 Would you like to access memories from a previous generation, *provided/imagine* you could choose which ones? Which would you choose?
4 *Imagine/Providing* you could see into someone else's memory, whose memory would you choose to visit?

5 Ask and answer the questions in Exercise 4 with a partner.

6 Make questions to ask other students using these words and phrases..

Imagine ...   *Providing ...*   *If you weren't ...*
If necessary, ...   *If you had ...*

7 Ask each question to a different student. Make notes on each answer. Read out your questions and the answers. Can the class guess who gave each answer?

premium plus   28

Vocabulary | multi-word verbs with two particles

1 Match the multi-word verbs in *italics* from the interview on page 70 with their meanings A or B.

1 Will we really want to *go back over* stuff like this?
2 It could *get* you *out of* those tricky situations where you forget people's names!

A to escape from a state or condition
B to think about again and often

2 Check you know the meanings of these multi-word verbs with *get*. Use the Exam Reviser to help you. Choose the correct alternatives.

1 I have to do some work every day otherwise I'll *get down to/get behind with* my studies.
2 I'm going to work all weekend because I need to *get ahead with/get back into* this project before I go on holiday.
3 I wonder when he's going to *get behind with/get round to* sorting out his files. I don't know how he can find anything!
4 He'd like to *get back into/get out of* football as he used to play a lot, but he hasn't got the time.
5 I've told her a million times, but I can't seem to *get through to/get ahead with* her.
6 She doesn't want to go to the conference, but she doesn't have a good excuse for *getting round to/getting out of* it.

exam reviser   p9 | 7.1

3 Match these multi-word verbs with *go* to their meanings A–E.

1 Do you usually persuade others of your point of view or do you *go along with* the majority opinion?
2 Do you find it hard to *go through with* threats you make?
3 Do you think it's a positive or negative thing to *go on about* how good you are at something?
4 Do you think people who *go off with* other people's things are just forgetful or is it deliberate?
5 Do you *go in for* crosswords and other puzzles very much?

A to talk too much
B to do something you promised or planned even though you no longer want to do it
C to do or use something often because you enjoy it
D to agree with or support someone or something
E to take something away from someone without permission

4 Ask and answer the questions in Exercise 3 with a partner. Give reasons for your answers.

5 Make notes for a short story using four verbs from Exercises 2 and 3. In groups of four, tell your stories to each other using the verbs you chose. Decide who told the best story.

> premium plus   29

Speaking

1 R.21 ▶ Listen to two conversations in which people are talking about this photograph. Has each person finished speaking when the other person starts to speak? Listen carefully to the structure of what they say and their intonation.

Conversation 1

Speaker A:	*No* (doesn't finish clause; uses rising intonation)
Speaker B:	_____
Speaker A:	_____
Speaker B:	_____

Conversation 2

Speaker C:	_____
Speaker D:	_____
Speaker C:	_____
Speaker D:	_____

2 R.22 ▶ Listen to two more conversations and answer these questions.

1 In which one do we know that the second speaker wants to speak? How do we know this?
2 What kind of language does the second speaker use? Why do you think this is?

3 R.23 ▶ Listen to the second conversation again and complete the box with the 'fillers' the speakers use. Add these fillers to the Exam Reviser.

SPEAKING SKILLS
Taking turns

1 You will know when someone has finished their turn by:
 • the structure of what they say;
 • their intonation.

2 If you are not sure what you want to say, you can use 'fillers' to show you are about to respond:
 Right, …
 You know, …
 OK, …

> exam reviser   p22 | 8

4 Discuss these questions with another student. Remember to take turns.

1 Do you think the people in the photograph are really amused or are they just pretending? How can you tell?
2 How would you feel about having almost every moment of your life recorded by other people in the way that famous people do?

Remembering multi-word verbs

Use different methods to help you remember multi-word verbs. You can organise them by:

A particle – *up* (increase): *go up, build up*
B topic/meaning – relationships: *get on with, break up with*
C opposites – *bring forward/put back*
D three-word verbs – *come up against, do away with*

Remember always to include an example sentence when you make a note of new multi-word verbs.

learning tip

Writing | report

1 Choose from the list A–D two reasons why you would write a report.

A to tell someone about something you have done and you think they might be interested in

B to tell someone what you think they ought to do about something

C to give some feedback on something that other people may wish to do

D to offer suggestions for improvements to something you have done

2 Which sentence in each pair A and B uses formal language? In what way is the language formal?

1 A I think the content of the course was very good.

B In general, the content of the course was very good.

2 A We could not hear the lecture because we were at the back.

B We were unable to hear the lecture as we were at the back.

3 A The library had an impressive collection of books, giving us plenty to choose from.

B The library had an impressive collection of books. This was good as we had plenty to choose from.

4 A The meals weren't very good.

B The meals could have been better.

WRITING SKILLS

Using formal language

When you write a report or a proposal, you should use formal language. This means using:

- objective structures, e,g, the passive;
- full forms rather than contractions;
- complex sentences;
- more formal/less frequent vocabulary;
- dispassionate vocabulary (i.e. not too strong or emotional).

3 Read this writing task. Underline the three main points you need to include in your report.

Writing task

While studying in the UK, you recently attended a short course on improving your memory. The Course Director has written to you asking for a report.

Read the extract from the Director's letter below, the course programme and your diary. Then using the information appropriately, write a report for the Director saying what you enjoyed about the course, explaining what you were disappointed with and suggesting how aspects of the course could be improved.

> *We are asking some participants for a short report. Did you enjoy the course? Did your memory improve? Also please let me know if you have any recommendations.*
>
> *Many thanks*
>
> *Course Director*

COURSE PROGRAMME

Day 1: Lecture: 'Brain power'
         Seminar: discussions

Day 2: 'The skills you need'
         Practice sessions: increase your memory

Day 3: Film: 'What you can achieve'
         Memory test

Lunch is provided. Special library facilities.

Monday	All too technical. No choice for lunch!
Tuesday	Sessions brilliant. Library closed afterwards!
Wednesday	Test interesting …

4 Work in pairs. Decide:

- what information to include in your report;
- how many sections you need;
- what heading to give each section.

5 Make a plan of the points to be included in each section of your report. Discuss with a partner how to expand the points given in the task.

6 Write your report in 180–220 words. Use the skills box and the Writing Reference on to help you.

• • see writing reference: page 190• •

Reading

1 Try this test.

1 Look at this series of numbers for 5 seconds, then close your books and write them down in the same order.

3 7 2 6 9 5 1 8

2 Now try this again with this set of numbers.

4 6 2   5 3 7   9 8 1

Which set of numbers did you remember more accurately? Look at page 168 to check why.

2 You are going to read three extracts which are all concerned in some way with the mind. Read each one quickly and answer these questions.

1 Which text tells you how to do something?
2 Which text explains how something works?
3 Which text offers you something?

1 The advertisement states that the training programme

AWAKEN YOUR MIND'S POTENTIAL

The IMI Mind Power Plus Training offers practical formulas for stretching your mind and solving problems. The techniques taught in this programme have been gleaned from the best tried, tested and proven techniques studied and researched worldwide. Scientists and psychologists have estimated that we only use about 5–10% of our brains. The rest is there, waiting to be tapped, trained and used.

You will be impressed by the speed and effectiveness with which we can deliver tangible results using these techniques. In just three days you can unlock the power of your mind and awaken some of the genius potential you probably didn't even know you had.

You have many choices of dates to suit you and you can choose between mid-week and weekend training dates. Courses are held Friday to Sunday and also from Monday to Wednesday. Times are from 9.00 a.m. to 9.00 p.m. Deep relaxation sessions are also offered every day to ensure you'll be bright and fresh throughout the training, right to the end. Money back guarantee! We are sure you will be delighted, but in the event that you are not completely satisfied, we'll give you a full refund.

A has been newly developed.
B relies on other people's work.
C has been scientifically tested.
D works faster than any other programme.

2 The programme offers extra help for participants who
A are unhappy with the training.
B are unable to attend every day.
C find the training day very long.
D find it hard to relax at work.

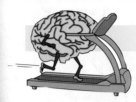

Book Review

Training Your Brain

Forget sudoku, crossword puzzles and computer games. If you really want to train your brain, then eat dark chocolate and follow the Scandinavian example of having cold meat for breakfast. You should also avoid watching soap operas, hanging out with serial complainers or pursuing fat-free diets, according to a new book on getting 'brain-fit'. The book should appeal to the growing numbers of people who are changing their lifestyle out of a desire to strengthen their mental ability. However, many of the suggestions in *Training Your Brain* are surprising, such as cuddling a baby, reading out loud and doing a university degree in business studies. Co-authors Terry Horne and Simon Wootton say their recommendations are based on the latest research by leading experts around the world. 'For decades we have thought that the cognitive capacity of our brains is genetically determined, whereas it's now clear that it's a lifestyle choice. This means that what we eat and drink, how we learn at school and what type of moods we have are all crucial,' said Horne. 'People can make lifestyle choices that will not only prevent what used to be seen as an inevitable decline in cognitive ability after the age of seventeen but will constantly increase our cognitive capacity throughout our adult lives.'

3 What are the writers advising readers to do when they say to 'forget' certain activities in the first line?
A to ignore the activities completely
B to put the activities to the back of your mind
C to consider the activities useless
D to resist doing the activities

4 One of the authors, Terry Horne, claims that brain function
A can be controlled so that it improves with age.
B will get worse as a result of getting older.
C has improved compared to previous generations.
D is a combination of genetics and the life we lead.

THE POWER OF PERSUASION

It's impossible to walk down the street without being bombarded with billboards and signs in shop windows and we are all influenced by the suggestions fed to us in advertising to some degree. Some suggestions we notice because we look at them directly, but lots of them we don't notice. You might not remember exactly what was on the last advertising billboard that you passed, even so on some level you have taken that information in and processed it. All the suggestions that surround us are meant to get us to buy into an idea, a person or a company's product.

The mind tends to work by association. So as to help you associate with the advertisement, the message might be something like 'If you buy this, you'll look as young and look as good as me'. These are positive suggestions, but negative suggestions are at work in advertising as well. There are also subliminal suggestions in advertising, sometimes given in such subtle ways that you might not even notice. Your unconscious mind picks up these messages and files them away and advertisers know this and use it.

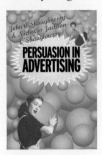

5 What does the writer say about advertisements on billboards?
   A They are most persuasive when they are more noticeable.
   B We absorb what they say even when we ignore them.
   C We have no control over the messages they send out.
   D They are effective at getting us to buy products.

6 What is the writer's purpose in this piece?
   A to show how advertisements are constructed
   B to criticise the advertising industry's methods
   C to suggest ways of avoiding advertising messages
   D to explain how we may all be susceptible to advertising

3 Read the texts more carefully. For questions 1–6 choose the answer A, B, C or D which fits best according to the texts.

4 Look at these statements. How true are they for you?

(1 = I don't agree; 5 = I strongly agree)

I find it easy to learn new things.	1	2	3	4	5
I would change my lifestyle to improve my 'brain-fitness'.	1	2	3	4	5
I am not influenced by advertising.	1	2	3	4	5

5 Explain your choices to a partner.

CAE close-up | Speaking Decision-making (Paper 5, part 3)

Exam information

In part 3 of the Speaking exam, you talk to the other candidate about some photos or pictures. You will be asked to complete two tasks. In the first task, you will be asked to talk about an aspect of each of the pictures in turn (e.g. what aspect of a problem they show). In the second task, you will be asked to reach a decision about something (e.g. which picture reflects the most important change).

The examiner will explain the two tasks, but these will also be written on the page with the pictures or photos.

Part 3 lasts about 4 minutes. (The whole Speaking exam lasts about 15 minutes.)

Approach

1 Make sure you have revised the language of:
- expressing and justifying opinions;
- agreeing and/or disagreeing;
- suggesting;
- speculating;
- negotiating and decision-making.

2 You will be marked on how you interact with the other candidate so don't try to dominate or interrupt the other candidate. Take turns, ask the other candidate for their views and make sure you give reasons for your own.

3 Make sure you talk about all of the pictures in the first task. Only move on to the decision-making task after you have discussed all the pictures.

4 Don't worry if you disagree with the other candidate; your 'decision' may be that you agree to differ. There is no right or wrong answer; the examiner just wants to hear how you each manage the discussion.

5 Don't sit in silence thinking as you only have a few minutes to do the tasks, but also don't worry if the examiner stops you before you have finished, as long as you have been discussing throughout the time available.

Practice task

R.24 ▶ Follow the instructions on page 167.

Go to www.iTests.com or your CD-ROM for interactive exam practice

Vocabulary | fixed phrases with *brain* and *think*

1 Look at these sentences and decide what the expressions with *brain* mean. Check the definitions in the Exam Reviser.

1 I've had that song *on the brain* all day.
2 She manages the finances, but he's *the brains behind* the project.
3 I've been *beating my brains out* trying to solve this maths problem.
4 I need to *get my brain in gear* before I can start working out what I want to do.
5 Could I *pick your brains* for a minute about this problem?
6 I've been *racking my brains* all morning but I can't remember his name.

> **exam reviser**   p9 | 7.2

2 Complete each sentence with the correct form of an expression from Exercise 1. Use extra words if necessary.

1 I _____ trying to remember her phone number.
2 Don't bother _____ about it – it's an insoluble problem!
3 Why don't you _____ – he knows a lot about the subject.
4 I woke up early but I couldn't _____ at all!
5 He's very crafty – I'm sure he's _____ the crime.
6 You've got computer games _____ – do something else for a change!

3 Match the expressions with *think* 1–6 with their meanings A–F. Use the examples in the Exam Reviser to help you.

1 think for yourself
2 can't hear myself think
3 have another think
4 don't think twice about it
5 think on your feet
6 think the world of someone

A think again about something, especially something you are trying to remember
B think of ideas and make decisions very quickly
C like or love someone very much
D come up with ideas without any help
E not worry about something
F be in a situation which is too noisy

> **exam reviser**   p9 | 7.2

4 Read the text and choose the correct alternatives.

Think ahead!

Giving a presentation involves a series of difficult skills, both on the day itself and while you're preparing for it. Firstly, don't ask other people to help you prepare. You need to *think on your feet/think for yourself*[1] so that when you give the presentation, you are talking about things you really know about. You can ask others to check it later. Make sure you go somewhere quiet to prepare where you can *hear yourself think/have another think*[2] and just allow your mind to wander to get new ideas. After you've planned your presentation, you will need to rehearse. *Have another think/Don't think twice*[3] about asking friends to watch you rehearsing your presentation. They won't mind being asked and may come up with some helpful suggestions. If they do criticise anything, then don't just hope it will be OK. *Have another think/Think on your feet*[4] about that section so you get it right before the day. On the day itself, try to stay calm and smile. If you do make a mistake, just apologise and move on. However, it is vitally important that you can *think on your feet/ think twice*[5] as you cannot predict what questions you may be asked. You may need to come up with an answer on the spot.

5 Would you be nervous about giving a presentation at work or in college? Why/Why not?

6 Discuss these questions with other students.

• Which song do you find most irritating because it's always on your brain? Why do you think you can't forget it?
• In what situations do you need to think on your feet? Why?
• Whose brains do you usually pick? Why?
• When you can't hear yourself think, which noise do you find most irritating? Why?
• Do you think it's better to be the front man or to be the brains behind something? Why?

Grammar | linking phrases

1 Match the phrases in *italics* from the texts on pages 74–75 with their meanings A–E. Check your answers in the Grammar Reference.

1 ... *in the event that* you are not completely satisfied ... (text 1)

2 ... people who are changing their lifestyle *out of* a desire to strengthen their mental ability. (text 2)

3 *This means that* what we eat and drink, how we learn at school and what type of moods we have are all crucial. (text 2)

4 ... *even so* on some level you have taken that information in and processed it. (text 3)

5 ... *So as to* help you associate with the advertisement ... (text 3)

A if

B in order to

C because (of)

D but

E therefore

•• see grammar reference: **page 178** ••

Do you believe in telepathy?

YES

Dr Martin Poole, Institute of Neuroscience

In view of/In the event of[1] recent studies, I believe that brain activity and conscious experience are tied together. At least three types of study indicate that there are genuine connections among people that are not controlled by ordinary senses. For example, *with the aim of/assuming that*[2] one person is actually trying to transmit an image to another, then there is a 32% success rate. *In addition/By contrast*[3] brain scans show increased activity in similar areas of their brains when two people are trying to communicate telepathically. A scientific test was also conducted of 'guessing who is on the phone', with a success rate of 42%. *In any case/For this reason*[4], I think something is definitely going on.

A lot of so-called telepathy is, in fact, just chance. The thing is, people have selective memories and, *in case/as a consequence*[5], they attach significance to weird coincidences and forget the times when they didn't work out. *In addition/As long as*[6] all these scientific experiments make no allowance for error, and I suspect this is what so-called telepathy will turn out to be. Studies of telepathy have been around for a long time; *whether or not/even so*[7], the methods of testing it keep changing. The key issue here seems to be that you must be able to replicate tests *in addition to/so as to*[8] ensure they are valid and reliable. If not, it could be that there is some fundamental flaw in the method.

NO

Professor David Needham, University of Westingdean

2 Read these texts and choose the correct alternatives. Use the Grammar Reference to help you.

3 Decide which viewpoint from Exercise 2 you agree with and why.

4 Draw a simple image on a piece of paper but don't show it to anyone. Take turns with a partner trying to 'communicate' your image telepathically while your partner tries to draw it. Check to see how close your images are.

5 Does this 'experiment' change your mind about your decision in Exercise 3? Why/Why not?

6 Rewrite these sentences to make one sentence, using a linking phrase from the Grammar Reference. Be careful – you may have to change the order of the information.

1 You can read someone's mind. You can also do this if they do not want you to.

2 Millions of people have been hypnotised. So we can say that it definitely works.

3 It is important to remember your dreams. Then you can understand what is going on in your mind.

4 It is ridiculous to say we have original thoughts. We can't because we are so easily influenced by other humans.

5 I believe that the mind can control pain. I continue to believe this even though the medical profession is sceptical.

•• see grammar reference: **page 178** ••

7 Discuss the completed statements in Exercise 6 with a partner. Say if you agree or disagree and why.

premium plus 30

Grammar

1 Complete the text with the linking phrases in the box.

> this means that   so as to   even so   as long as
> as a result   as a means of

How to give your brain a workout

- Use your daily commute _____[1] practising non-routine activities to stimulate your brain. Close your eyes and use other cues, such as the speed of the train or the bus to guess where you are.
- Try writing backwards or writing with your non-dominant hand. _____[2] you are creating a different neural pathway, and this is how you get new ideas. Da Vinci practised mirror-writing to keep his brain fresh.
- Chew gum. Normally dentists say this is bad for you. _____[3], chewing increases the activity in the hippocampus, the part of the brain important for short-term memory.
- Learn a second language. It forces your brain to switch tracks continuously and, _____[4], this is one of the most mentally demanding things you can do.
- Take up a new activity, such as the piano, _____[5] activate unused areas of your brain.
- Watch less television.
- _____[6] you eat plenty of berries, seeds, turkey and fish, you will be getting lots of Omega-3 fatty acids. These are said to be particularly good for the brain.

2 Complete the second sentence so that it has a similar meaning to the first sentence, using the word given. Do not change the word given. Use between three and six words.

1 Would you change your memories if you could?
   supposing
   _____ would you?

2 I only remember my keys because of my mum.
   weren't
   _____ I'd forget my keys.

3 I'll only help you if you agree to try harder.
   condition
   _____ you try harder.

4 Ask the teacher how to do it if you're not sure.
   doubt
   _____, ask the teacher how to do it.

5 I didn't try because I knew I would fail!
   had
   If I _____ failed.

6 I only needed another £20 to get that DVD.
   could
   If I had had another £20, _____ that DVD.

Vocabulary

3 Complete the crossword with the missing prepositions from these sentences.

CLUES

Across

1 I'm really getting _____ with my work because I'm so tired.

5 Why don't you go _____ over what you're going to say at the presentation?

8 I've told her five times but I can't seem to get _____ to her!

9 She went _____ with my keys so I'm locked out!

12 I keep meaning to phone her but I never seem to get _____ to it.

Down

2 I'd like to get _____ into art when I have some time.

3 I'm not sure she'll go through _____ leaving – it's a big step.

4 My brother's always going on _____ how hard he works.

6 I didn't agree but I went _____ with her to save an argument!

7 They're getting _____ with the project – it's nearly finished!

10 I didn't realise he went in _____ big dinners.

11 Have you any ideas how I can get _____ of going to the party on Saturday?

Wonders of the world

Premium | Unit 08

icon

storm chaser

blue sky

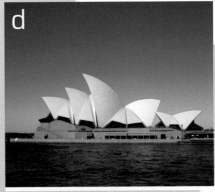

Unit 08

Introduction

1 Look at pictures a and d. Can you name the buildings and say why they are famous? Do you think either of them should be considered a 'wonder of the world'? Why/Why not?

2 Look at pictures b, c and e. Answer these questions.

1 What could be the connection between these pictures?
2 When was the last time you looked up at the sky properly? Do you like looking up at the sky? When and why?
3 What kind of extreme weather can you see in picture c? What kind of weather do you dislike? Why?

3 Discuss these questions with other students.

1 What's the most amazing ...
  • manmade sight you've ever seen?
  • natural sight you've ever seen?
  • weather you've ever experienced?
2 What do you think makes a 'wonder of the world'? Do you think it should be something manmade or something natural? Why?

Reading

1 The places in the extracts in Exercise 3 have all been suggested as wonders of the world. Look at the names of the places and the pictures. What do you think they might have in common?

2 When you are reading, you may need to guess the meaning of unfamiliar words. Look at this extract from a guidebook and decide on the meaning of the highlighted words. Think about what type of word each one is (e.g. noun, verb, etc.) and what the word refers to.

> In the heyday of the Etruscan era, Ferrara would have been a vibrant city which was the commercial hub of the society. Recently discovered carvings from the period show the sophistication of the Etruscans' daily lives, although today tourists are lured by the glorious Renaissance buildings.

READING SKILLS

Guessing unknown words

If you want to read quickly, you don't always need to use a dictionary. If there are words that you don't understand in a text, you may be able to guess their meaning. You can do this by thinking about the context and about the structure of the sentence in which they appear.

premium plus 31 ▶

3 Read these extracts from guidebooks about famous sights. For questions 1–15, choose from the descriptions A–G. You can choose each description more than once.

About which sight are the following mentioned?

the source of the wealth used to create it   1 _____ 2 _____

its relevance to modern life   3 _____

its role in becoming a recognisable symbol of its location   4 _____

the achievement of its designers   5 _____ 6 _____

the reason the wonder has survived   7 _____

the uncertainty about its purpose   8 _____

the fact that it was probably at the centre of a rich farming community   9 _____

the human effort required to create it   10 _____

its geographical situation being an attraction to visitors   11 _____ 12 _____ 13 _____

the religious nature of the site   14 _____

the fact that it is unrivalled   15 _____

A Petra, Jordan

Petra, nestled away in the mountains south of the Dead Sea, was once the glittering capital of a huge empire. It has been preserved because many of its buildings were carved out of solid rock walls, making it acclaimed for its engineering. Its ornamental carvings are also impressive examples of Middle Eastern culture. Once a fortress city, Petra is one of the earliest known settlements in the area, and control of key trade routes made it a commercial hub while also producing the funding for its monumental temples and tombs. The city may have housed 20,000–30,000 people in its heyday but by AD 700 its once-gracious buildings were in ruins. Tourists are lured by its spectacular setting on the edge of Wadi Araba and the beautiful rose colours of the rocks.

B Machu Picchu, Peru

The ancient city of Machu Picchu is an extraordinary settlement 2,350 metres above sea level, deep in the Amazon jungle. The settlement had been abandoned following the Spanish invasion and by 1532 had become a ghost town. It was brought to the world's attention in 1911 and several different theories were then developed as to what the settlement was. Some believed it could have been a luxurious mausoleum but a more popular belief was that it might have been built to control the economy of conquered regions and protect the Inca nobility. Certainly it had a large agricultural area bringing wealth and sophistication to this remote region. Today it is seen as a perfect example of a complete community and travellers to the site are enchanted by its elevated and isolated position.

C THE GREAT WALL, CHINA

The Great Wall of China was built to create a united defence system and keep invading tribes out of China. It is the largest construction ever built. Although not continuous, it stretches across deserts, grasslands and mountains, and the remarkable architectural grandeur and historical significance still attract thousands of tourists every year. However, rather than a feat of engineering, it is a symbol of perseverance, one which has been extended and repaired across several centuries. The wall was originally built of stone, wood and grass but later was made with bricks, laboriously transported up the mountains by men carrying them on their backs. It was once suggested that the wall was the only man-made object visible from space but this can't be true as nowadays even roads are visible.

D Chichén Itzá, Mexico

This famous temple city was the political and economic centre of Mayan civilisation. In 987 a Toltec king arrived with an army from central Mexico and, with local Mayan allies, made Chichén Itzá his capital. The city was built here as it is on the site of an underground well that provided water all year. Offerings were thrown into the well and occasionally, a human sacrifice, which can't have been very healthy! The central pyramid is supposed to be the greatest of all Mayan temples and had enormous religious significance for the community. It has staircases and terraces decorated with great sculptures of plumed serpents. Visitors can climb an older pyramid inside this and see the fantastic throne of the serpent god.

E Taj Mahal, India

The Taj Mahal is regarded as the most perfect jewel of Muslim art in India. This huge mausoleum was built by Shah Jahan in memory of his beloved wife and has become a great symbol of passion. It is a fairy-tale marvel of white marble and its gardens have been laid out formally around it. The material to build it was brought in from all over India with the help of elephants. The exterior decorations are as beautiful as the interior, and the colossal height of the tomb, along with its setting, make it look as if it is climbing into the skies. Visitors are struck by how romantic it must be to have such a tomb built in your honour, especially as no one has built anything since to equal this devotion.

F The Statue of Christ Redeemer, Brazil

This icon of the city of Rio de Janeiro, with its open arms, is a symbol of the warmth and openness of the people of Brazil. It is an important landmark on top of Corcovado mountain, overlooking the bay and the city. The statue was paid for by contributions from people all over Brazil, making it truly a people's monument. Its outer layers are made of soapstone as this is resistant to extreme weather. The railway was used to bring the large pieces of the statue to the top of the mountain. In the past it must have been quite hard work to climb the mountain and the 220 steps in order to appreciate the breathtaking views from the top, but today panoramic elevators whisk visitors up the statue.

G THE COLOSSEUM, ITALY

The design concept of this great amphitheatre in the centre of Rome has influenced almost every sports stadium since, including those still built today. Largely made of stone, its innovative design divided the seating into sections to allow maximum viewing. The first level was for the important senators and the emperor, the second for the aristocrats and the third for citizens, with the poorest at the top. Today the wooden arena floor no longer exists, but the walls and corridors which ran underneath are visible in the ruins. Despite its sophisticated design, it couldn't have been very pleasant to work in the conditions of darkness and fear that existed underground. The skeleton exists today as a symbol of the celebration and suffering that took place at the events the building hosted.

4 Discuss these questions with other students.
- Which of these sights would you most like to visit and why?
- If you had to select one of these sights as a wonder of the world, which one would you choose? Why?

Vocabulary | tourist sights

1 Complete these sentences with the words and phrases in the box.

> mausoleum   settlement   temple   amphitheatre
> commercial hub   setting   site   landmark   arena
> fortress   icon   symbol

1 A _____ is a place where people go to worship.
2 The _____ of a monument can make it appear more beautiful.
3 A _____ was usually built to defend a city or region.
4 The sports _____ was central to many Greek and Roman societies.
5 In Roman times, the public watched plays in an _____.
6 An _____ used to be a figure of religious worship but nowadays it can be someone who represents an idea or era.
7 Some buildings, such as the Sydney Opera House, are seen as the _____ of a city.
8 A _____ is a group of houses or buildings, usually where few people have lived before.
9 An archaeological _____ can provide many clues to how we used to live.
10 Although a _____ contains the body of a dead person, it can be a beautiful building.
11 Cities have grown up on places that were the _____ of a region.
12 Sailors in ancient times used the Pillar in Serapeum as a _____ to guide them.

2 Discuss these questions with other students.
- Can you name any examples of the places in the box in Exercise 1?
- Which type of places do you think would be the most interesting to visit and why?

3 Choose the best adjective in each sentence. Think carefully about the noun which follows the adjective.

1 The Colosseum reflects the *architectural/luxurious* achievements of the classical Roman empire.
2 Petra is very well-preserved and provides *monumental/impressive* evidence of a complex society.
3 The ruins of Machu Picchu are an *architectural/innovative* gem in an isolated region.
4 The Great Wall is a spectacular landmark, which is *panoramic/breathtaking* in its size.
5 Chichén Itzá is now in a tranquil setting very different from its *glittering/colossal* past.

4 Put the adjectives in Exercise 3 into the correct columns in the Exam Reviser.

> exam reviser   p10 | 8.1

5 Think of two places from the box in Exercise 1 in your country. Describe the places to a partner, using adjectives from Exercise 3. Ask your partner to say which of the places they would most like to visit and why.

6 Write a short description of a famous sight, but do not mention the name. In groups of four, read out your descriptions and see if anybody can guess which place you are describing.

Grammar | degrees of certainty

1 Look at sentences 1–8 and decide what degree of certainty A or B you think each one expresses. Use the extracts on pages 80–81 and the Grammar Reference to help you.

A certain or almost certain (based on evidence)
B likely, possible or fairly possible

1 The city may have housed 20,000–30,000 people.
2 It could have been a mausoleum.
3 It might have been built to control the economy.
4 It can't be true because even roads are visible.
5 It can't have been very healthy.
6 Visitors are struck by how romantic it must be.
7 It must have been quite hard work.
8 It couldn't have been very pleasant to work there.

> •• see grammar reference: **page 178** ••

Grammar note | *should(n't) have*
Which sentences express a logical conclusion and which express an obligation?

1 They should have arrived by now.
2 They should have booked the tickets earlier.
3 They shouldn't have taken a taxi as it's too expensive.
4 They shouldn't have had to wait long – there's hardly anyone here.

2 Choose the correct alternatives.

WHAT WAS STONEHENGE?

Stonehenge is a 2,000-year-old circle of huge standing stones set in the middle of green plains in the south of England. Astronomers believe Stonehenge *could have been/shouldn't have been*[1] used to predict the behaviour of comets. Archaeologists think the middle of the structure *may have been/couldn't have been*[2] the centrepiece for agricultural fertility rituals. Evidence from bodies buried near the site indicate it *might be/might have been*[3] a centre for miracle cures. However, the most commonly-held view is that it *can't have been/must have been*[4] a site of religious worship. Another mystery surrounds where the stones are from. Evidence suggests that they may have been transported from Wales but it *could have been/can't have been*[5] easy to do this, especially as the wheel had not yet been invented. To date, nobody has come up with a provable theory of how the stones got there or what they were for, so the mystery continues ...

3 Discuss these questions with other students.
1 Why and how do you think Stonehenge might have been built?
2 Would you like to visit Stonehenge? Why/Why not?

premium plus **32** ▸

Speaking

1 ▸**R.25** ▸ Listen to a woman giving a presentation about why the Alhambra in Spain should be considered a wonder of the world. What three reasons does she give?

2 ▸**R.25** ▸ Read the strategies you can use to be persuasive. Listen again and find examples of each strategy. You could also look at the audioscript on page 163.

SPEAKING SKILLS
Ways of being persuasive

1 using questions (engages the listener as they are forced to answer for themselves)
Do you realise the historical importance of the Pyramids in Egypt?
2 using adverbs and adjectives (makes what you are talking about special)
The Taj Mahal is a graceful and beautiful building.
3 giving details, especially describing the senses (helps the listener imagine their response to something)
The sun on the stone at Petra produces a captivating effect, making the colour even more intense.
4 using intensifiers (increases the emotional impact of what you are saying)
It was incredibly high and could be seen for miles around.
5 using personal pronouns (involves the listener in what you are talking about)
As you walk through the halls you can see yourself reflected in the vast mirrors.

---

3 Look at the Exam Reviser and add two more examples to each category.

exam reviser **p23 | 9** ▸

4 Imagine there is a competition to select a wonder of the world. It can be man-made, e.g. a building, or natural, e.g. a waterfall. Follow these instructions.
1 Choose somewhere you consider should be a wonder of the world.
2 Prepare a speech persuading others to accept your choice.
3 Remember you will need to:
   • describe your wonder;
   • talk about how you feel when you see it;
   • say why it is special.

5 Work in groups of four. Follow these instructions.
1 Try to persuade the others in your group to make your chosen place a wonder of the world.
2 Decide which place is the winner in your group.
3 The winners of each group give their speeches again to the whole class.
4 As a class, decide on an overall winner.

CAE close-up | Listening Sentence completion (Paper 4, part 2)

Exam information

In this part of the exam, you hear a monologue, which will last about 3 minutes. You complete sentences with information you hear on the recording. The missing information will be one to three words or numbers and will come from the recording. You listen to the recording twice. You have 5 minutes at the end to transfer your answers to an answer sheet.

Approach

1 Read the instructions for the task and the sentences that follow. Try to predict what kind of information is missing from each sentence.

2 As you listen the first time, complete as many of the gaps as you can. Remember that the sentences on the page will be worded differently from the recording but the words you need to write in the gap must be exactly the same as the words you hear. Use the exact words or number you hear, don't change them.

3 If you miss the words for one gap, don't worry, just move on to the next one.

4 When you listen for the second time, check the answers you put the first time and try to complete any gaps that remain.

5 Read through all the completed sentences. Check they make sense and are grammatical and that the gaps are completed with one to three words or numbers. Remember you cannot lose marks for an incorrect answer.

6 Pay attention to spelling. Remember that small spelling mistakes may be accepted by the examiners if the meaning is clear, but a small mistake may also alter the meaning of a word.

7 At the end of the Listening test, make sure you transfer your answers to your answer sheet very carefully. Check you have the right answer by the correct number and that your spelling is correct.

Practice task

R.26 ▶ You will hear part of a radio programme about where the bluest sky is. For questions 1–8, complete the sentences.

BLUE SKIES

An experiment to find the bluest skies in the world measured the light coming through the _____ **1**.

Variations in light levels can be caused either by bad weather, the _____ **2** of the sun or aerosols.

The blueness of the sky is dependent upon the _____ **3** of the light.

The experiment was conducted by a member of the _____ **4**.

Readings were taken at twenty-five holiday _____ **5**.

Readings were affected by the level of _____ **6**.

Our response to temperature can be dependent on our _____ **7**.

Although blue skies can be dangerous, they make us feel _____ **8**.

Go to www.iTests.com or your CD-ROM for interactive exam practice

Grammar | confusable structures

1 Look at these examples of similar structures. What is the difference between the sentences in each set? Use the Grammar Reference to help you.

1 A It looks like rain.
  B It looks as if it's going to rain.
  C It feels as if it's going to rain.

2 A Suppose it is cloudy later, what will we do?
  B It is supposed to be quite cloudy later.
  C I suppose it will be cloudy later.

3 A I used to be in the sun a lot as a child.
  B People who live in hot climates are used to being in the sun.

•• see grammar reference: page 179 ••

Grammar note | *was/were supposed to*

We normally use *was/were supposed to* to talk about a past obligation not *should* + infinitive. Which two sentences are correct?

1 *They should wear sunscreen when they went to the beach.*
2 *They should have worn sunscreen when they went to the beach.*
3 *They were supposed to wear sunscreen when they went to the beach.*

2 Complete these sentences with *like, as if, suppose, is/are supposed to be, used to, is/are used to.*

1 When _____ you _____ going to Africa? Is it still happening?
2 He _____ the cold so he never worries about rain on holiday!
3 It looks _____ he's going to be late.
4 The weather in Wales _____ be drier than it is now.
5 It seems _____ a nice hotel to me.
6 I _____ we ought to think about taking umbrellas!
7 It looks _____ a heat rash to me!
8 _____ we wear extra layers, do you think that will protect us?

3 Discuss with another student how true you think each statement is and why.

1 Sweating can make you feel as if you are cold.
2 Blue skies may look nice but they are supposed to be colder at night.
3 The weather seems as if it is getting hotter in many countries.
4 Hot winds like the Mistral are supposed to make people commit more crimes.
5 People used to think pale skin was more attractive than having a tan.
6 The Inuit who live near the North Pole are used to the cold so they don't get as cold as people in warmer countries.

4 Write two more sentences using the structures in Exercise 1. Ask a partner if they agree.

premium plus 33 ►

Vocabulary | effects of the weather

1 What kind of weather can have these effects on us? Put the words in the box into the correct column in the table.

> sweating shivering goosebumps sunburn exposure
> dehydration headaches depression lethargy

a heatwave	very humid	strong winds	freezing temperatures

2 Check your answers in the Exam Reviser. Can you add any more effects?

exam reviser p10 | 8.2 ►

3 Complete these questions with the correct form of the words from Exercise 1. Ask and answer the questions with a partner.

1 Which do you dislike most – _____ with the heat or _____ from cold?
2 Do you agree that strong winds make us feel unhappy and _____?
3 Does any kind of weather give you _____ which you can't seem to get rid of? What?
4 How much do we need to drink a day in order not to get _____?
5 Does hot weather make you lazy and _____ or lively and active?
6 Why do you think _____ can be so dangerous for people with pale skin?

premium plus 34 ►

4 Look at the examples of these fixed phrases in the Exam Reviser. Choose the correct alternative A or B.

1 If you are *as right as rain*, have you
   A taken a good decision?   B recovered well after feeling ill?
2 If you *weather a storm*, do you
   A fight somebody?   B come through a difficult period?
3 If you *feel under the weather*, do you feel
   A a bit ill?   B fed up?
4 If someone *has their head in the clouds*, are they
   A not very focused?   B very superior?
5 If you *blow hot and cold*, do you
   A have varying levels of energy?   B keep changing your mind?
6 If you *get your second wind*, do you
   A feel exhausted after trying hard?   B suddenly have more energy for something?
7 If you do *something in the heat of the moment*, do you
   A do it at the best time?   B do it without thinking?

exam reviser p10 | 8.3 ►

5 Work in pairs. Choose an expression from Exercise 4 and tell your partner about something that happened to you which illustrates your chosen expression. Your partner must guess which expression applies to your story.

CAE close-up | Use of English Multiple-choice cloze (Paper 3, part 1)

Exam information

This part of the exam mainly tests vocabulary. You read a text with twelve gaps. After the text there are four sets of words or phrases for each gap. You must choose the correct option to complete the gap. This part of the exam can test:

- words with a similar meaning, e.g. *bring, take, fetch, carry*
- common collocations, e.g. *take charge of*
- structures which follow certain words, e.g. *manage to do something, interested in something*
- multi-part verbs, e.g. *take up, take off, take on, take away*
- linking words, e.g. *however, although, nevertheless*

Approach

1 Read the title and then skim the text to get the general meaning. Don't worry about the gaps or the options at this stage.

2 Read the text again. Look at each gap and the words before and after it carefully. Think about what word could go in the gap. Remember the word must fit the grammar and meaning of the sentence.

3 Consider the options for each gap. Eliminate the ones you know are wrong. Think about the different reasons why a word might be wrong in the context. In the given example, only *caught* can be correct. *Captured* means taken prisoner by somebody, *gripped* is a way of holding something and *entrapped* means you have been tricked by someone. Make your choice. Make sure you read along the whole sentence to check if your choice fits.

4 Read the completed text all the way through to check your ideas. Don't leave any gaps. You do not lose marks for wrong answers.

Practice task

For questions **1–12**, read the text below and decide which answer (**A, B, C** or **D**) best fits each space. There is an example at the beginning (**0**).

Example:

0 A captured   **B** gripped   **C** caught   **D** entrapped

The storm chaser

I photograph extreme weather but getting the shots can be difficult. Once I got (**0**) __caught__ on the edge of a tornado and had to (**1**) _____ cover in an underground car park. The tornado was 75 m (**2**) _____ and completely destroyed the nearby buildings. As we (**3**) _____ in the car park, the tornado caught us and we were almost pulled (**4**) _____ the ground. Nowadays you can find out where a storm will be via a direct satellite link to your car. When the storm is a few miles away you might not be able to see it if the air is (**5**) _____ but you can track it on the radar. (**6**) _____, things don't always go to plan! A couple of my storm-chasing colleagues once saw an EF5 tornado coming their (**7**) _____ They realised they had to run so they jumped in their car but there was only the sound of (**8**) _____ metal as they tried to start it. They ran towards a storage barn and just (**9**) _____ it. They waited it out in the basement but when they came out the whole barn had disappeared! I've been (**10**) _____ no storm chasers have died in the last forty years though. Obviously, if you head right into the centre of a storm, you run a big risk. Your car will get (**11**) _____ in and you could die. Storm chasing is dangerous, but it's worth it because the excitement from being so close to a tornado is nothing (**12**) _____ of incredible.

1	**A** gain	**B** take	**C** accept	**D** enter
2	**A** long	**B** wide	**C** across	**D** round
3	**A** concealed	**B** shielded	**C** sheltered	**D** harboured
4	**A** off	**B** up	**C** away	**D** out
5	**A** blurry	**B** hazy	**C** obscure	**D** dull
6	**A** As such	**B** In case	**C** By contrast	**D** Of course
7	**A** route	**B** path	**C** way	**D** direction
8	**A** scraping	**B** squealing	**C** piercing	**D** roaring
9	**A** got	**B** made	**C** did	**D** passed
10	**A** said	**B** told	**C** reported	**D** mentioned
11	**A** gathered	**B** tugged	**C** towed	**D** sucked
12	**A** apart	**B** except	**C** short	**D** aside

Go to www.iTests.com or your CD-ROM for interactive exam practice

learning tip

Using a dictionary

As well as pronunciation and grammar, what do you use a dictionary for?

- to find out the meaning of a word
- to find out the frequency of a meaning
- to see what other words usually go with a word

Most dictionaries give you information on meaning, frequency and typical collocations. This can help you understand the difference between similar words. When you look up a word, make sure you pay attention to all three elements.

Look up three words that are unfamiliar in the Exam Close-Up exercise. For each word check the meaning, write down its two most frequent meanings and any words it usually goes with.

Writing | proposal

1 Discuss these questions with other students.

1 Do you think it is important to preserve historical buildings and ancient sites? Why/Why not?
2 What sort of problems do you think can destroy historical places?

2 Read the writing task and decide which place you would choose to write about. Explain to a partner why you have chosen this place.

Writing task

An international committee is giving money in the form of grants to preserve historical buildings and sites. You decide to write a proposal saying which historical place you think should be preserved, explaining what damage has been caused to the place, and why and giving reasons why it is important for your chosen place to be preserved.

3 Look at the model in the Writing Reference. Which of these is the purpose of a proposal?

1 to inform somebody about something
2 to persuade someone to agree with you
3 to suggest someone should do something

•• see writing reference: **page 192** ••

4 What is the difference between a proposal and a report? Do they have any similarities? If so, what are they? Think about:

- purpose
- layout
- style and tone
- language

5 Decide these things with a partner.

1 how many sections you need in your proposal
2 what to include in each section
3 how to balance the sections, e.g. do you need more in one section than another or are they all equal?

6 Decide why your chosen place should be preserved. Think about:

- what visitors to the area would like to see
- what it represents about the culture of the country
- what aesthetic value the place has

7 A proposal should be written in formal language. Find examples of formal language in the model in the Writing Reference.

•• see writing reference: **page 192** ••

8 Read the model proposal in the Writing Reference again. List the points that make it persuasive. Does writing use the same persuasive strategies as speaking?

WRITING SKILLS
Being persuasive

- Use facts to support your argument.
- Make your suggestion sound urgent.
- Be objective, but appeal to your reader's emotions.
- Where appropriate, use formal words and phrases that directly appeal to the reader, e.g.:

  I would urge you to …
  I would ask that you …
  Please consider …
  I appeal to …

9 Write your proposal in 220–260 words, using your plan and notes. Remember that you need to persuade the reader of your point of view.

Grammar

1 Match the situations 1–8 with sentences A–H.

1 I don't understand why they haven't arrived yet.
2 Why do you think Machu Picchu was abandoned?
3 Did they visit the Sydney Opera House when they were in Australia?
4 It's strange they haven't visited us while they are over here.
5 They emailed me to say they were in Moscow.
6 They said they climbed to the top of the statue.
7 Why didn't they call to say they would be late?
8 They said they saw the Sistine Chapel when they were in Rome.

A They might have done, but they didn't mention it.
B They can't be! They only left two days ago.
C They could have lost our number, I guess.
D They must have been held up at the airport.
E They can't have done because they don't like heights.
F I suppose all the inhabitants could have been wiped out by a disease.
G They couldn't have done because it's being restored.
H They must be staying in London longer than planned.

2 Choose the correct alternatives.

The North Pole

Did you use to/Are you used to[1] 'safe' holidays in well-known places? Well, *suppose/it is supposed*[2] you had the opportunity to visit the North Pole? This trip *was used to/used to be*[3] impossible for ordinary tourists, but now we can offer a journey like no other. Turn a dream into reality and join our exclusive North Pole Expedition. Encounter extraordinary scenery as you make your way across the ice to the Geographic North Pole. You will *feel as if/seems like*[4] you are on top of the world!

Your journey starts in the remote village of Longyearben in Arctic Norway, where the Northern Lights can be seen glowing in the sky. The best time to see them *is supposed/supposing*[5] to be between November and March. Then you will fly by helicopter to 89° North where you will strap on your skis and head True North to the Pole. For the next five days you will be a member of the expedition team as you face the challenges of circumnavigating thin ice, open water and drifting ice sheets. However, although it *seems as if/seems like*[6] hard work, an expedition to the top of the world is an incredible experience.

Celebrate your achievements on reaching the North Geographic Pole and spend a night sleeping on your ice bed … but don't be surprised to find you have moved overnight!

Vocabulary

3 Complete the text with the words and phrases in the box.

> breathtaking   stretch across   symbol   landmark
> be struck by   impressive   colossal   icon

New York, New York

Have you ever seen the Statue of Liberty? It's wonderful. It was a gift to the United States from the people of France and it's become a real _____[1] of the city of New York. It is supposed to be a _____[2] of the freedom and justice that the US offered to immigrants. From a distance it looks quite small, but when you get up close it is _____[3] because of its size. From the top there are _____[4] views which _____[5] the harbour and beyond to the north of the city. The pedestal was constructed in the States but the statue itself was made in France. When you visit it, you will _____[6] the amount it moves in the wind and its _____[7] size. It is not only a _____[8] for the entrance to New York Harbour, but also for what it represents in American history.

4 Choose the best word to complete these explanations.

1 _____ is when you are so hot that you lose liquid through your skin.
2 _____ is when you are so cold that parts of your body shake.
3 _____ occur when you are cold and you get little lumps on your skin.
4 _____ is when your skin goes very red and sore because you haven't used suncream.
5 People suffer from _____ when they have to stay outside in temperatures that are too hot or too cold.
6 If you don't drink enough water, especially in the heat, then you become _____ .
7 Many people get _____ in strong winds or when the air pressure is high.
8 It's very easy to become _____ in hot weather because the heat makes you feel tired.

Eye witness

witness

surveillance

petty crime

Unit 09

Introduction

1 Which of these jobs can you see in the pictures?

> police officer   security guard   judge   traffic warden
> prison officer   legal secretary   private detective   lawyer
> passport control officer   CCTV control officer

2 Which of the jobs in Exercise 1 would you most and least like to have? Why?

3 What is the difference between these pairs of phrases?
crime wave – petty crime
serious offence – serious offender
do community service – face a custodial sentence

4 Discuss these questions with another student.
1 What crime can you see being committed in picture d? Would you consider this to be a petty crime or a serious offence?
2 What sort of punishment do you think the offender should be given? Why?

Listening

1 Work in pairs. Check you understand the meaning of the words and phrases in the box. Use a dictionary if necessary.

> closed-circuit television cameras (CCTV)
> identity card   identity theft   computer hacking
> fingerprint   tracking technology   tagging criminals
> surveillance   personal security   crime prevention

2 R.27 ▶ Listen to part of a radio interview in which an expert, Chris, is talking about surveillance, personal security and personal freedom. Which of the topics in the box in Exercise 1 are not mentioned?

3 Look at the questions and options, which focus on six detailed parts of the interview. Underline the words and phrases you need to listen out for in order to concentrate on those parts.

LISTENING SKILLS

Identifying what to focus on

Try to identify which parts of the recording to focus on, using information from the questions and options. This will help you concentrate on the essential parts and make it easier to pick out the answers.

1   Which of these things is not mentioned as something you can do with the Malaysian ID card?
    A   go through immigration
    B   be in charge of a vehicle
    C   get appropriate medical care
    D   get money out of your bank account

2   According to Chris, how do many people feel about ID cards?
    A   They should just be used for people who have broken the law.
    B   They should be available for anyone who wants one.
    C   It should be easier to get one when you lose it.
    D   You should have more control over the information on them.

3   What warning does Chris give about using the Internet?
    A   Your address and phone number could be made public.
    B   You could get a lot of unwanted electronic advertising.
    C   People could use your wireless Internet connection for themselves.
    D   People could use your bank account details to buy things for themselves.

4   What statistics does Chris give about CCTV cameras in the UK?
    A   There are four times as many cameras than people.
    B   There are fourteen times as many people than cameras.
    C   There are over fourteen million cameras covering the whole of the UK.
    D   There are 300 times as many cameras in London as elsewhere in the UK.

5   What connection does Chris make between CCTV cameras and crime?
    A   CCTV cameras are a great help in solving crimes.
    B   CCTV cameras are just a small part in the process of solving crimes.
    C   CCTV cameras have reduced the crime rate considerably.
    D   CCTV will be used more and more in the future to prevent crime.

6   According to Chris, what kinds of things do the 'speaking' cameras do?
    A   They warn people not to break the law.
    B   They tell the public what someone has done.
    C   They tell someone to put right what they've done wrong.
    D   They give out names of people who have committed minor offences.

4 R.27 ▶ Listen again and for each question decide which answer A, B, C or D best fits according to what you hear.

5 Discuss these questions with other students.

1   Do you think that a 'surveillance society' is a good description of modern life? Why/Why not?
2   How is the situation in your country the same as or different from that described on the programme in relation to identity cards and CCTV cameras?

premium plus   35 ▶

Grammar | passives

1 Answer these questions for each sentence pair A and B.

1 Which verb is active and which is passive?
2 Why would you be more likely to use the passive sentence in each case?

1 A We *are watched* constantly by an extremely sophisticated network of cameras, in the street, in shops, in the workplace, in schools, even in people's homes.
   B An extremely sophisticated network of cameras, in the street, in shops, in the workplace, in schools, even in people's homes *watches* us constantly.

2 A They *are introducing* ID cards for a number of reasons.
   B ID cards *are being introduced* for a number of reasons.

3 A *People feel* that these ID cards are taking away our personal freedom.
   B *It is felt* that these ID cards are taking away our personal freedom.

4 A I think people *should take* the problem of identity theft seriously.
   B Identity theft is a problem which *should be taken* seriously.

5 A *Being watched* constantly is something we'll have to get used to.
   B *Having cameras watching* us constantly is something we'll have to get used to.

6 A They *need to do* more research into identity theft.
   B More research *needs to be done* into identity theft.

•• see grammar reference: page 179 ••

Grammar note | *past passive forms*

1 Change the passive verbs in *italics* in these sentences into the past.

   1 The thief *must be seen* by at least one camera.
   2 She started running, *being filmed* by CCTV cameras.
   3 Six cameras *are to be installed* by the end of the month.

2 Explain how the meaning changes in each case.

2 Read this text quickly. Say what experiment was carried out and what the possible implications are.

I'm watching you!

People believe[1] that people act more honestly if they feel *someone is watching them*[2]. This appears to be true, even if the eyes are not real, according to some research which *a team at Newcastle University has done*[3].

The team monitored[4] the amount of money put in a canteen 'honesty box' when buying a drink. Over the course of ten weeks, *they placed a poster*[5] at eye level above the honesty box. *The poster featured*[6] a list of the drinks available and different images of either flowers or a pair of eyes looking directly at the customer.

At the end of every week, *someone counted the total amount of money*[7] and the team worked out *the amount of drink people had consumed*[8]. The results revealed that people paid 2.76 times more money when the 'eyes' poster was on the wall, as opposed to the image of flowers.

The feeling of *someone observing you*[9], it seems, really does make people act more honestly. The fact that the eyes are not real doesn't seem to matter. People's brains are set up to process faces and eyes, and *someone watching us*[10] has a direct effect on our brains, whether the eyes are real or not.

The scientists believe[11] that their findings may have applications in schemes to crack down on anti-social behaviour and on law enforcement. *Someone could put up pictures of eyes*[12] next to CCTV and speed cameras and it is likely that they would be even more effective.

3 Where possible, rewrite the parts of the text in *italics*, changing them into a passive form.

4 Are you surprised by the findings of the 'honesty box' experiment? How successful do you think putting a picture of eyes next to speed cameras would be? Why?

premium plus 36 ▶

Vocabulary | multi-word verbs – crime

1 Work in pairs. Try to explain in your own words what the multi-word verbs in *italics* in these sentences mean. Use the context of each sentence to help you.

1 The camera operator *tells* the offender *off* and asks them to put the litter in the bin.
2 They think they've *got away* with it, and then a voice lets them know that someone has seen them.
3 It could be something more serious too, like someone *breaking into* a building.
4 Someone *tipped off* the police about where the thieves were hiding.
5 Two armed men *held up* the bank on the high street yesterday.
6 He was robbed and *beaten up* on his way home from work.
7 The police decided not to arrest him but just to *let* him *off* with a warning.
8 Thieves *walked off* with thousands of pounds' worth of electronic equipment.
9 After he left college, he *got mixed up* in drugs and petty crime.
10 The government has announced plans to *crack down* on violent crime.

2 Check your answers in the Exam Reviser.

exam reviser   p11 | 9.1

3 Work with a partner and answer these questions.
1 Which, if any, of these sentences are incorrect? Why? Look at the Exam Reviser if necessary.
   A The camera operator *tells the offender off.*
   B The camera operator *tells off the offender.*
   C The camera operator *tells off him.*
   D The camera operator *tells him off.*
2 Which of the multi-word verbs in Exercise 1 can be 'separated' and which cannot? Use the Exam Reviser to help you if necessary.

exam reviser   p30

4 You can make compound nouns from some multi-word verbs. Look at these nouns and say what each one means.

> a get-away   a break-in   a hold-up
> a tip-off   a crack-down

5 Look again at the verbs in Exercise 1 and the nouns in Exercise 4 and <u>underline</u> the stress on each one. Use a dictionary to help you if necessary.

6 Choose two of these headlines. Write a short paragraph explaining what happened for each one. Use at least three multi-word verbs from Exercise 1 in each paragraph.

Crack-down on litter bugs

Tip-off leads to three arrests

Quick get-away on bikes

Tenth break-in at college

Hold-up at bank – £1m stolen

7 Compare your paragraphs with another student.

Speaking

1 R.28 ▶ Listen to two people discussing one of these questions. Which question are they discussing?

1 Do you think it is a good thing that there are so many CCTV cameras now (including the 'speaking cameras') in the street, in the workplace, on buses, etc.? Why/Why not?

2 Do you think that having to have an ID card which contains a lot of personal information affects your right to personal freedom or is it a very good way of cracking down on crime? Give reasons.

3 Are you worried about computer hackers gaining access to your bank account and other personal details and becoming a victim of identity theft? Why/Why not?

2 R.28 ▶ Read the sentences in the box. Then listen again and complete sentences 2–5 with two words in each gap.

Thinking aloud

1 That's an interesting question which we should consider carefully.

2 Well, that's not something I've _____ much before.

3 I think this is a _____ with many different and valid points of view.

Staying on topic

4 That's true, but perhaps we should _____ to what we were saying about …

5 I think we're _____ the point a bit here.

6 That's an interesting idea, but I don't think it's entirely relevant to the question of …

3 Check your answers in the Exam Reviser.

exam reviser p23 | 10,11 ▶

4 You are going to discuss one of the questions in Exercise 1. First remind yourself of some useful language by looking at the Exam Reviser.

exam reviser p20 | 1,3 ▶

5 In groups of three, choose one of the questions in Exercise 1 to discuss. Use the language in Exercise 2 if necessary.

Watching and listening

You can improve your English by taking as many opportunities to listen to spoken English as you can.

1 Which of these do you do often, sometimes and never?

2 Choose one of them to decide to do it more often. Tell your partner which one you chose and why.

- watch/listen to the news online, on TV or on the radio
- watch/listen to programmes online, on TV or on the radio
- watch films on DVD, online or at the cinema with and without subtitles
- listen to English songs with and without the lyrics
- listen to the recordings in this book at home

learning tip

CAE close-up | Reading Themed texts (Paper 1, part 1)

Exam information

In this part of the exam, you read three texts on one theme from a range of sources. Each text has two multiple-choice (A, B, C or D) questions. These questions may test your understanding of specific information in the text, text organisation features, text structure, attitude, tone, opinion, main ideas and implications.

Approach

1 Read the rubric to the task. It will tell you the theme of the three texts, which will help you with overall understanding.

2 Read the first text quite quickly to get a general idea of what it is about.

3 Look at each question but *not* the options (A, B, C, D). Underline the key words. Then, mark the part of the text each question refers to.

4 Now read the text carefully. When you come to a part you have marked, read through the relevant question and the options (A, B, C, D). Choose the option that best matches what the text says. Make sure you read *all* the options before you make a decision. Look for words and phrases with similar meanings in the options and the text.

5 Repeat steps 2, 3 and 4 for the other two texts.

Practice task

You are going to read three extracts which are all concerned in different ways with crime and punishment. For questions **1–6**, choose the answer (**A**, **B**, **C** or **D**) which you think fits best according to the text.

Crime and punishment gone mad?

With crime rates and the cost of policing increasing in many parts of Europe and the US, the general public is entitled to feel somewhat dismayed about stories about various punishments that have been appearing in the news lately.

Last year, police in the US arrested a twelve-year-old boy for opening his Christmas presents early. The boy's mother, Brandi Ervin, from South Carolina, called the police after discovering Brandon had taken his new Nintendo Game Boy from under the tree and unwrapped it. He was handcuffed and taken to the station for questioning. 'He's been going through life doing stuff and getting away with it,' said Mrs Ervin. 'It's impossible to control him and I've had enough.'

And almost as unbelievable, a teenager from Manchester in the north of England, was fined recently for leaving an ice-lolly stick on a wall. Sorrell Walsh, sixteen, started crying when she was ordered to pay up even though she then offered to put it in a bin. Neither the offer nor her tears changed anything, however, with the council warden telling her, 'It's nice of you to offer … but it's too late, you've got yourself a £75 fine.'

One story in the news told a slightly different story … of the law cracking down on itself. Police Chief Richard Knoebel of Wisconsin, USA is nothing if not conscientious. He was driving to work one day when he absent-mindedly overtook a school bus that was waiting at a bus shelter, flashing its 'stop' lights. As soon as he realised what he'd done, he issued himself a $235 ticket and four points on his licence. 'The law states you should stop for a flashing school bus,' he said 'and I shouldn't be any different.'

---

1 What is the writer's attitude to the crimes involving a boy in the US and a girl in England?

   A He is amazed that they weren't punished more.

   B He is surprised at the harshness of the punishments.

   C He is astonished that the stories have been reported.

   D He is concerned that the punishments don't stop them committing crimes.

2 What happened to the Police Chief in Wisconsin?

   A He punished himself for committing a crime.

   B He committed a crime on purpose to see what would happen.

   C He punished someone else for making him commit a crime.

   D He accidentally punished the wrong person for committing a crime.

The Runaway Jury by John Grisham

Set in Biloxi, Mississippi, *The Runaway Jury* follows a landmark trial against a tobacco company with hundreds of millions of dollars at stake, which begins routinely, then swerves mysteriously off course. The jury is acting strangely, and a least one juror is convinced he's being watched. Soon, they have to be isolated and kept away from the public eye. Then, a tip-off from an anonymous young woman suggests she is able to predict the jurors' increasingly odd demeanour. Is the jury somehow being manipulated, or even controlled? If so, by whom? And, more importantly, why?

I have to admit that I have been mildly disappointed with some of Grisham's work recently, but not so here. It seems that he has redeemed himself with his latest thriller. *The Runaway Jury* is certainly one of his best works to date, with just the right combination of drama, action and insight into the ugliness of the legal process. A classic Grisham courtroom drama, it is extremely well-written, without any of the repetition that sometimes characterises Grisham's books. The main thrust of the book rails against the evils of cigarettes and their manufacturers, who will go to any lengths to avoid responsibility for the harm their products cause. Grisham manages to use his skill in taking an otherwise dull trial and turning it into something fast-paced and exciting. Right to the end you do not know why the jury is being manipulated, nor can you be sure in which direction things will go.

3 What is the main focus of *The Runaway Jury?*

    A The unusual behaviour of the jury during a trial.

    B The mysterious disappearance of millions of dollars during a trial.

    C The kidnapping of a woman member of the jury during a trial.

    D The use of CCTV cameras to watch members of the jury during a trial.

4 What does the writer say about Grisham's style in this book?

    A He is very insightful about the main characters in the book.

    B He is good at getting the details of the court process exactly right.

    C He is skilful in creating interest in a potentially boring subject.

    D He is very clear about where the plot is going throughout the book.

Security Guard – Job description
Mallinson's Department Store

Responsibilities

You will be responsible for patrolling the store day and night (on a shift system).

When the store is open, you will need to monitor and authorise the entrance and departure of employees, customers and other persons to guard against theft and maintain the security of the premises. When the store is closed, you will need to prevent and detect any signs of intrusion and ensure the security of doors, windows and gates.

You will also be required to answer alarms and investigate disturbances, calling the police or other relevant services in cases of emergency, such as fire or the presence of unauthorised persons. You may also need to warn people against rule breaking, and apprehend or evict them from the premises, using force where necessary.

Personal Qualities and Experience

The suitable candidate will be an exceptionally honest and trustworthy professional, who understands that disregarding rules or ignoring protocol ultimately endangers everyone. You will need to be diligent and able to constantly assess the situation, with excellent powers of recall and attention to detail.

An effective security guard must also have a level of personal presence that commands respect and shows definite leadership qualities. This is not necessarily dependent on age or height, but on an intangible trait which our trained interviewers will be able to assess at the interview stage.

Specific experience as a Security Guard is not absolutely necessary but impeccable references from at least two previous employers is essential.

5 If an intruder breaks into the premises, the security guard

    A should never talk to the intruder.

    B may be required to hold the intruder to prevent them escaping.

    C must not use physical force in any circumstances.

    D should call the police before approaching the intruder.

6 What does the advertisement say about leadership?

    A It is not necessary to have strong leadership skills.

    B They will give leadership training during the interview process.

    C They will look for leadership skills when they meet the candidates.

    D Age and physical presence are more important than leadership skills.

Vocabulary | breaking the law

1 Put the words and phrases in the box into the correct column in the table.

> juror   identity theft   vandalism   traffic warden
> speeding   young offender   witness
> computer hacking   driving offence   hardened criminal
> allowing a child to play truant   suspect

Crimes	People
identity theft	*juror*

2 Check your answers in the Exam Reviser. Then write at least four more words or phrases in each column. Compare your ideas with other students.

> exam reviser   p11 | 9.2

3 Work in two groups A and B. Student As should look at column A and student Bs at column B. For each verb phrase, find the meaning, the pronunciation and an example sentence.

A	B
be arrested for	be sentenced to
be accused of	be released from
be charged with	be acquitted of
be convicted of	be punished for
admit to	be taken into custody
do community service	face a custodial sentence
go on probation	get a suspended sentence
pay a (heavy) fine	be cautioned
plead (not) guilty	act as a deterrent
be found (not) guilty of	get a fair trial
get a criminal record	be tried (in court)

4 Work in A/B pairs and tell each other what you found about each of your verb phrases.

5 Choose two of the verb phrases and write an example sentence for each in the Exam Reviser.

> exam reviser   p12 | 9.3

> premium plus   37

6 Work in small groups. Choose three of these questions to discuss.

1 Do you think that a £75 (€110) fine for dropping litter is too harsh? If not, why not? If so, why, and what do you think would be a more suitable punishment?
2 Do you think parents should be responsible for their children playing truant? What do you think should be done to punish the children or the parents? Why?
3 For what types of crimes do you think the criminal should always face a custodial sentence? Why?

4 How do you think the public could help in preventing crime and in catching criminals?
5 What would you think of a scheme in which criminals were forced to face the consequences of their actions by having to meet and talk to their victims?

7 Which question was most interesting? What conclusions did you reach and did you all agree?

Grammar | introductory *it*

1 What is grammatically the same about all these sentences?

1 It's impossible to control him.
2 It seems that his latest thriller is better than the rest.
3 It is said that CCTV cameras help with crime detection.
4 It's pointless applying for the job – I'm too old.
5 It was raining and really dark and I couldn't see his face.
6 It frightens me that there is so much crime in big cities today.

2 Match each sentence from Exercise 1 with the correct rule A to F in the box.

> **We can use *it* as an introductory subject in these cases:**
>
> A When *it* refers forward to a noun clause (starting with *to*-infinitive, -*ing*, a *that* clause or a *wh*-clause). This structure is used to emphasise the adjective.
> B To talk about the weather and the time.
> C To avoid using noun clauses in a subject position (at the beginning of the sentence), which sounds too formal.
> D With reporting verbs used in the passive.
> E With the structure *it + (would) seem/appear + that* when reporting events.
> F With some common set phrases, e.g. *it's no use ..., it doesn't matter*, etc.

•• see grammar reference: page 180 ••

3 For each question, complete the second sentence so that it has a similar meaning to the first sentence, using the word given. Do not change the word given. You must use between three and six words, including the word given.

1 Being punctual is vital and you really must understand that.
   essential
   It _____ is vital.

2 It looks as if someone broke into the flat last night.
   appears
   It _____ into last night.

3 What is the truth about your car being vandalised?
   true
   Is _____ your car?

4 The arrival time isn't really important.
   matter
   It _____ you arrive.

5 They think that cracking down on speeding will reduce accidents.
   thought
   It _____ reduced if there is a crackdown on speeding.

6 Someone will probably vandalise your car if you leave it there.
   likely
   It _____ vandalised if you leave it there.

7 Will obtaining the CCTV images of the intruders be possible?
   possible
   Will _____ the CCTV images of the intruders?

8 Crying about your bag now it's gone is useless.
   use
   It _____ your bag now it's gone.

4 With a partner, choose two of these statements to discuss. How far do you agree with each other? Give reasons.

- It doesn't matter if you sometimes go on a bus without paying.
- It's pointless trying to stop people dropping litter.
- It's vital that people put security software on their computers.
- It's interesting how far some people will go to protect their own property.
- It's frightening to think about how so many young people get involved in crime.

Writing | information sheet

1 Discuss these questions with another student.
- How safe do you think your school/college/workplace is in terms of: a) intruders/burglary, b) pickpockets, c) graffiti/vandalism?
- What measures are in place to prevent some of these crimes? What else could or should be done?

2 Look at the writing task. How many things must you include in your answer? What are they?

> **Writing task**
>
> You are a member of the students' committee at your college. There have been some intruders in the buildings recently, and a number of small incidents of theft have occurred.
>
> You have been asked to write an information sheet entitled *Keep Safe!* which:
>
> - informs students about which crimes they could be vulnerable to at the college
> - encourages students to report any information which may be relevant
> - gives students advice about how to keep their belongings safe and watch out for intruders

3 Tick the features in the box which you would expect to find in an information sheet.

WRITING SKILLS
Thinking about format and layout
- text divided into sections ☐
- headings ☐
- sub-headings ☐
- bullet points ☐
- a chatty, conversational style ☐
- a direct, more impersonal tone ☐
- advice ☐
- information ☐
- recommendations ☐
- idiomatic language ☐
- complex sentences ☐
- passive forms ☐

4 Check your ideas in the Writing Reference.
•• see writing reference: **page 202** ••

5 Work in pairs. Plan your information sheet for the task in Exercise 2. Think about format and layout, and plan your ideas for each paragraph.

6 Write your information sheet using 220–260 words.
premium plus 38

Grammar

1 There are mistakes in six of these sentences. Find the mistakes and correct them.

1 More should been done to secure the empty property.
2 Victims of crime need to be given more support.
3 The thieves were been filmed smashing the window of the jewellery shop.
4 Being arrest was a very traumatic experience for the young man concerned.
5 Research has done into the effects of various different types of punishment.
6 The security systems are being monitored very closely.
7 It felt that installing CCTV cameras would be too expensive.
8 The broken locks are be replaced by the end of the day.

2 There are eight mistakes with phrases related to the introductory *it* in this text. Find the mistakes and correct them.

1984 by George Orwell

In some ways, amazes me that George Orwell's novel *1984* is still such a popular classic. It was written in 1949 about a frightening future world set in 1984. It had appear, however, that although that year is now in the past, the messages are still very relevant for the present and future.

Various people had recommended the book to me, and when I finally read it, turned out that all the hype was true. Was incredible to read such a well-known book and not be disappointed in the least. It strikes that the reason I was so moved by *1984* is the fact that it works on so many levels. First and foremost, the book is a political warning about a power-crazy minority. However, it is interested that the story is what makes it even more powerful. There seems to me that the empathy created by the personal story of the central character, Winston, is what really hooks the reader in.

I would definitely recommend this book. That doesn't matter how old you are or how much you know about the subject already, I'm sure you won't be disappointed.

Vocabulary

3 Read the text and decide which answer A, B, C or D best fits each gap.

LAPTOP USER ARRESTED

A man who was seen using his laptop in the street has been arrested _____[1] illegally logging on to a wireless (Wi-Fi) broadband connection. Two officers saw the thirty-nine-year-old man sitting on a garden wall outside a home in West London. When questioned, he _____[2] to using the homeowner's unsecured broadband connection from his position on the wall. He was _____[3] into custody and the case was passed to the Metropolitan Police Computer Crime Unit.

He has been released _____[4] custody until October when he will be _____[5] in court. If he _____[6] guilty to the charge, he is likely to either have to pay a _____[7] or to _____[8] a custodial sentence of six months, or both. The arresting officer said that he hoped the sentence would act _____[9] a deterrent.

The first time someone was convicted _____[10] this offence was in 2005 when Gregory Straszkiewicz from London was _____[11] guilty of dishonestly obtaining an electronic communication service. He was fined £500 and given a twelve-month _____[12] sentence.

1	A by	B for	C from	D with
2	A admitted	B accused	C acquitted	D arrested
3	A held	B got	C taken	D sent
4	A to	B for	C with	D from
5	A tried	B trialled	C tracked	D tied
6	A finds	B answers	C pleads	D pays
7	A fine	B fare	C fee	D fund
8	A take	B spend	C find	D face
9	A as	B for	C with	D to
10	A with	B for	C as	D of
11	A made	B held	C found	D taken
12	A criminal	B probation	C suspended	D community

4 Complete each sentence with the correct part of the multi-word verb.

1 Our house was broken _____ while we were away on holiday.
2 At school, I was always getting told _____ for chatting.
3 Police were tipped _____ about the names of three suspects.
4 Young people shouldn't be allowed to get away _____ cheating in exams.
5 The police are helping banks and other financial institutions to crack down _____ identity theft.
6 He walked off _____ a computer and a lot of software.
7 I left the bank just minutes before it was held _____ by an armed gang.
8 Two men were beaten _____ as they tried to stop a burglary.
9 He was caught speeding but let _____ with just a warning.
10 I don't want my children to get mixed up _____ drugs.

Recycle, restyle

Premium | Unit 10

awareness

eco-friendly

celebrity

Unit 10

Introduction

1 Look at the pictures and discuss these questions with another student.

1 Who is the celebrity in picture a? What is she doing? Why?
2 Why do you think the animal in picture b is in danger of becoming extinct? What other animals are in similar danger? Why?
3 What can you see in picture c? What other sources of energy do you know about?
4 Who is the famous vegetarian in picture d? Do you know any other famous vegetarians?
5 What is the environmental significance of picture e?

2 Which of these statements are true for you? Discuss with other students, giving reasons.

- Personally, I waste resources on a huge scale every day.
- I only eat organic produce and I'm considering becoming a vegetarian.
- I think the effects of global warming are mostly exaggerated.

Grammar: participle clauses; reported speech | Vocabulary: environment; dependent prepositions | Writing: essay

Unit 10

CAE close-up | Listening Unrelated extracts (Paper 4, part 1)

Exam information

In this part of the exam you hear three short extracts from conversations between two people talking in different situations, e.g. friends chatting, part of a radio programme, someone buying something by phone. There are two multiple-choice questions on each extract, with three options, A B or C. You hear each extract twice. The questions will be on a range of different things, including:

- the purpose of the conversation;
- the opinions being expressed;
- the feelings and attitudes of the speakers;
- general and detailed understanding.

Approach

1 Read the rubric, the questions and the options for the first extract before you listen for the first time. Underline the key words to help you focus as you listen.

2 Listen to the first extract and choose the answers you think are correct.

3 The second time you listen, check that the other options are wrong. Also, listen out for key words or phrases that justify your choice.

4 Repeat the same steps for the second and the third extracts.

5 Always put something for each question – you do not lose marks for a wrong answer.

Practice task

R.29 You will hear three different extracts. For questions **1–6**, choose the answer (**A**, **B** or **C**) which fits best according to what you hear. There are two questions for each extract.

Extract One
You hear a woman on a radio programme being interviewed about the role of celebrities in ecological issues.

1 What does the woman think about events like 'Live Earth'?
   A that celebrities just use them to get more publicity for themselves
   B that using celebrities to educate people in this way is beneficial
   C that they should have had much larger audiences than they did

2 What does she say about celebrities on environmental programmes on TV?
   A They are learning about something at the same time as the viewer.
   B Their personalities are more interesting than those of environmental experts.
   C The topics they talk about are generally more engaging.

Extract Two
You hear two friends discussing vegetarianism.

3 The man decided to become a vegetarian when
   A he was a teenager and his friends were doing the same.
   B he realised the impact on the environment of the meat industry.
   C he saw a Joaquin Phoenix film based on the topic of cruelty to animals.

4 The man says that the singer Russell Simmons chose to be a vegetarian
   A for his own health reasons.
   B in order to encourage other people to do the same.
   C because he didn't like the way animals were treated.

Extract Three
You hear two people discussing an experiment that the British journalist, Nicky Taylor, took part in.

5 During the experiment Nicky decided not to
   A use any products or any water.
   B use any products except toothpaste.
   C use any water but she did use products like soap.

6 According to the woman, why did Nicky feel free?
   A because she didn't have to go to a wedding and other events
   B because she didn't have to go shopping and buy products so much
   C because she didn't have to wear make-up and other products

Go to www.iTests.com or your CD-ROM for interactive exam practice

Grammar | participle clauses

1 Work in pairs. Look at sentences A and B and discuss the questions.

A She decided to cut down on how much water she used because she had done the experiment.

B Having done the experiment, she decided to cut down on how much water she used.

1 What is different about the grammatical structure of the sentences?

2 Why might we choose to use sentence B instead of sentence A?

2 Look at the participle clauses in *italics* in sentences 1–8. Match each sentence with the correct rule A or B. Look at the Grammar Reference to help you.

> **Participle clauses**
>
> A can be used after nouns, in a similar way to relative clauses (adding information about the noun).
>
> B can be used in a similar way to adverbial clauses, (expressing condition, reason, time relations, result, etc.).

1 There was a fair amount of controversy *surrounding that event*.

2 The issues *highlighted by 'Live Earth'* were brought to a much larger audience.

3 TV programmes featuring celebrities *talking about saving tigers* are a good thing.

4 She was upset about her hair *looking rather strange*.

5 *Concerned about what all these products do to us*, she wanted to bring these issues to the public's attention.

6 She felt much freer *being completely natural*.

7 *Having heard Joaquin Phoenix talking about the link* between being a vegetarian and saving the planet, I decided to give up meat.

8 *Having done the experiment*, she would use far less of both in the future.

•• see grammar reference: **page 180** ••

3 Rewrite these sentences using participle clauses.

1 Anyone who wants to know more about climate change should see the film *An Inconvenient Truth*.

2 There are still some people who are not prepared to change their wasteful lifestyles.

3 After I saw 'Live Earth', I was inspired to do some voluntary work abroad.

4 It rained extremely hard for two days so that our whole village was flooded.

5 Once I'd found out about battery farming, I became a vegetarian immediately.

6 Some celebrities are very happy to use their time to help less fortunate people because they want to give something back.

4 Read the text and answer these questions.

1 What 'environmental experiment' is described?

2 How do you think you would feel about taking part in an experiment like this?

A s we got nearer still, I could see a queue of rubbish trucks which were entering the site. And the number of trucks which were arriving served as a good reminder that we don't actually throw our rubbish away. It just gets taken somewhere else. And it fills up huge areas of land.

I had answered an advert to take part in an 'environmental experiment', and I had presumed I'd be off to the Amazon jungle. When I found out what the experiment actually was, I nearly left. The ten people who were chosen were going to spend ten days living on a rubbish dump.

The TV company who were making the programme brought us food, but otherwise everything we needed came from the dump itself. First, we all searched the dump for useful materials, as we realised that we quickly needed to make a shelter, a shower and some sort of kitchen. It worked surprisingly well, and we even had hot water, which we heated using solar power.

Once we got over the initial shock, we all got used to it and even started to enjoy the challenge of coping. When we found things, we were excited about what we could do with them and we made some really useful and creative things. Now that I've had that experience, my whole way of looking at 'rubbish' has changed.

5 Using a range of different sentence structures, like participle clauses, can make your writing more interesting. Rewrite the text using participle clauses where appropriate.

6 Compare your rewritten text with another student. Do you think you could have used more participle clauses?

premium plus **39**

Vocabulary | environmental issues

1 Complete the phrases in the Causes column of the table using the words in the box. Check your answers in the Exam Reviser.

> chemicals emissions fishing fuels fumes
> layer farming sewage spills sprays

Problems	Causes	Effects
Air pollution	1 car exhaust _____ 2 factory _____ 3 burning fossil _____	A *breathing problems* B _____
Water pollution	4 untreated _____ 5 oil _____ 6 agricultural _____	C _____ D _____
Global warming	7 deforestation 8 using aerosol _____ 9 depletion of the ozone _____	E _____ F _____
Animal cruelty/ extinction	10 battery _____ 11 over-hunting 12 over-_____	G _____ H _____

exam reviser p12 | 10.1

2 With a partner write down some ideas in the Effects column in the table. Use your own ideas and those in the box to help you. Check your answers in the Exam Reviser.

> breathing problems   loss of plant, animal and marine species
> increased risk of skin cancer   rise in Earth's temperature
> lower quality of food produce   destruction of coral reefs

exam reviser p12 | 10.1

3 Look again at the table in Exercise 1. Which do you think is the biggest problem where you live and for the world as a whole? Why?

premium plus 40

Recycling your vocabulary

In order to remember new vocabulary, you need to recycle it frequently and make sure you use it.

1 Which of the following do you do?
  - Write a selection of new words and phrases on a card and put it in your pocket. Use each one at least once during that week.
  - Remind yourself of the words and phrases you can include in your writing by looking in your Exam Reviser.
  - Try to remember as many words and phrases as you can connected with a topic. Talk to another student about that topic using some of the vocabulary.

2 Can you add two more suggestions to the list?

Speaking

1 Look at the sentences in the box and choose the correct alternative for each one from the list 1–10.

> **Talking about effects and influences**
>
> **A**
> 1 Celebrities can *have an enormous _____ on* people's opinions.
> 2 Increased pollution has already *had a profound _____* on climate change.
> 3 The success of this campaign could *have important _____ for* the future.
> 4 This campaign could *make a big _____ to* the long-term future of the environment.
>
> **B**
> 5 We need to _____ *the public's awareness about* environmental issues.
> 6 An effective publicity campaign needs to _____ *the public's attention.*
> 7 People often *don't _____ much notice of* environmental issues outside their own area.
> 8 People would _____ *more attention to* campaigns led by celebrities.

1 influence/difference
2 impact/implication
3 influences/implications
4 difference/effect
5 raise/grab
6 take/grab
7 pay/take
8 pay/raise

2 R.30 Listen to the sentences and check your answers.

3 Complete the sentences in the Exam Reviser in your own words. Then compare your sentences with another student.

exam reviser p24 | 12

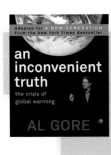

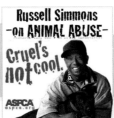

4 A national environmental charity is planning a campaign to raise awareness about environmental issues. There are some ideas they are considering and they would like your opinion.

Look at the pictures and discuss these questions in pairs or small groups. Use the language in Exercise 1 for talking about effects and influences.

1 Do you think that the campaign would be more effective using celebrities (who the public recognise) or experts (who the public don't recognise) on its posters? Why?

2 Which of the celebrities in the pictures do you think would be most influential in getting the public to think about the environment? Why?

3 What slogan or message could you add to the picture to increase the impact of the campaign? Why do you think the message you've chosen would be effective?

5 Compare the ideas and opinions you discussed with students from other groups. How far did you all agree?

Writing | essay

1 Look at the writing task. Discuss these questions with another student.

1 Can you outline the problem stated in the task in your own words?

2 Why do you think this has become such a major problem?

3 What two solutions can you think of that would start to solve this problem?

Writing task

A local English-speaking environmental group has asked you to write an essay for their magazine giving your opinion about the problem outlined in this statement.

The 'celebrity culture' is a major problem for the world today as many people are far more interested in the lives of celebrities than in serious issues like the environment.

Explaining a problem and suggesting solutions

Outlining a problem:
Nowadays it seems that ...
Anyone who has ... will know that ...
Over recent years, people have become concerned that ...

Explaining a problem:
There are a number of reasons for this.
One of the causes of ... is ...
This is largely due to ...
This has led to ...
This means that ...

Suggesting solutions:
It is essential that we ...
There are many ways which we could ...
If we ..., we will be able to ...
One possible solution would be ...
The most obvious solution is to ...

2 Look at this paragraph plan and the two in the Writing Reference. Decide which paragraph plan is the most appropriate for your essay.

Paragraph 1: Introduction: Outline the problem. You could also explain more about the problem, give some background information or some reasons why we should be interested.

Paragraph 2: Suggest a possible solution. You should then discuss the benefits of this solution, and also some of the difficulties involved.

Paragraph 3: Suggest another possible solution. You should then discuss the benefits of this solution, and also some of the difficulties involved.

Paragraph 4: Conclusion: State your opinion about which solution you consider the best, summarising the reasons.

•• see writing reference: page **194** ••

3 Use your chosen paragraph plan and the language in the box to make brief notes about what you're going to write.

4 Write your essay in 220–260 words using your chosen paragraph plan and your notes. Look at the Exam Reviser for appropriate language.

exam reviser   24 | 13

Reading

1 Do this mini-survey with other students.

How much energy do you use?

1 Which electrical items do you have in a) your living room, b) your kitchen and c) your bedroom?

2 Do you leave your TV on 'stand-by' when you're not watching it?

3 Do you turn off the light when you leave a room?

4 Do you unplug your phone charger when it is not in use?

5 Do you use a machine to dry your clothes?

6 How often do you have the heating/air-conditioning on?

7 What kind of lightbulbs do you use?

8 Do you have an open fireplace?

2 How wasteful do you think you and the other students in your class are?

3 Read the article and number the mini-summaries A–G in order according to where they come in the text. Ignore the gaps at this stage.

A The coach worries about insulation

B Some 'green' buildings already exist

C The coach can help you save electricity

D The coach advises about heating

E People want to be 'green'

F The coach assesses your house

G A carbon coach can help you be 'green'

READING SKILLS

Understanding the flow of a text

It is a good idea to read a text quickly first and try to get an understanding of the flow of the main points. This will help you understand the logical ordering of information. You could write a short sentence for each paragraph to summarise the main idea.

The carbon coach

I invited Simon McGill into my home to tell me just how wasteful I am!

A few years ago, 'going green' was a relatively new issue. Now, in a surprisingly short time, nobody can argue about its importance. Trying to live an environmentally-friendly life is something that we should all aspire to. But many people are unsure about what actually to do. Many people ask: 'What difference can I make?'

1

He started the service in the 1990s when there was a lot of talk of eco-issues, but, as Simon says, there wasn't much actual advice given 'on the ground'. The problem was that some people, however keen they were to make a difference, didn't have a clear understanding of what they could realistically do. He felt that, for the ordinary person, a 'home carbon audit' could be the answer.

2

Once the calculations are done, Simon looks around the client's house and points out any electrical equipment that uses a lot of energy. He will then suggest ways in which your carbon footprint could be reduced and you can become 'carbon-balanced'. In many cases, the possible reductions are huge, depending on the original lifestyle of the client.

3

The monitor is also able to show how much carbon dioxide the energy being used translates into, and how much the electricity is costing you per gadget. Simon told me that some of his clients were shocked when they saw their results. It's not only how much things cost which was shocking,

4 Six paragraphs have been removed from the text. Read it again and choose from the paragraphs A–G the one which fits each gap 1–6. There is one extra paragraph which you do not need to use.

A

I asked Simon what the least energy efficient thing he'd seen in people's homes was, and I was genuinely surprised by his answer – the lightbulb. People don't know that although they are very cheap, they are incredibly inefficient, with up to 90% of the energy that the bulb uses being lost as heat. He advised anyone with these old-fashioned types of lightbulbs to smash them up!

B

After Simon's visit, I was keen to get on with all the changes he had advised me about. As I did so, I began to wonder how far we could go with all these things. Why stop with just knowing the size of your carbon footprint and then trying to cut down on it? Shouldn't we all be seriously thinking about becoming completely carbon neutral? These thoughts set me wondering what was being done already to this end.

C

That was a question that I put to Simon McGill, an eco-makeover consultant, who came to check out my home. He told me that if people put their minds to it, and make even small changes in their lives, the cumulative difference can be enormous. Seeing that many people wanted to make a difference but didn't know what to do, Simon decided to help by offering a 'home carbon audit' service.

D

When he came to my house, I was interested in finding out how exactly he would work out the energy consumption of each appliance. The first thing he did was to switch off all the gadgets around the house. He then clipped a special 'carbon meter' onto the electricity meter which registered how much electricity was passing through. By turning on each piece of electrical equipment one at a time, you could then see how much electricity each one was using.

E

He works with individuals, families and businesses, both large and small, and even some celebrities. One of his celebrity clients was a band who wanted to become 'carbon balanced' by minimising their impact while touring and also cutting the amount of carbon produced when making a CD.

F

This involves coming into someone's home and working out their 'carbon footprint'. He does this by finding out about the client's lifestyle. He needs to work out how much carbon dioxide (CO_2) they have generated over the last year by looking at their bills, finding out how much waste they throw away, how much they use the car, and so on. The total carbon footprint in tonnes of CO_2 is then calculated.

G

While up on my roof, Simon had some other suggestions for me. Fitting a solar hot water system, for example, which connects up to solar panels on the roof, means no more bills for heating or hot water. He estimated that in most cases, although it is a bit expensive to install, it would generally pay for itself in about five years.

but also the waste involved and the energy inefficiency.

4

Another of Simon's major concerns about waste is lack of insulation. In many homes, there is no insulation at all, with all the heat going straight out through the roof. People don't realise the negative impact that this has on the environment, or how easy and cheap it is to solve. He suggested asking the government for a grant to install insulation if you have difficulties in paying.

5

Other ways of cutting down on heating bills that he suggested were replacing the fireplace, which loses an unbelievable 90% of its heat up the chimney, with a wood-burning stove. Secondly, he advised me to replace my carpets with ceramic floor tiles. This is especially beneficial in large, sunny rooms as stone retains the heat much better than other materials.

6

I phoned Simon to discuss my afterthought and again he surprised me. Various organisations are already working on introducing a really green type of home into the UK, he told me. Buildings are now being built that create their own energy, heat and cool themselves, harvest their own water and deal with their own waste. Not only that, but they are also completely built using waste materials. Suddenly my small changes seemed very small. But as Simon said, 'we've all got to start somewhere.'

5 Discuss these questions.

1 Would you like to get a carbon coach to come and check out your house for you? Why/Why not?
2 If you only made one of the changes mentioned in the article, which would it be? Why?

Vocabulary | dependent prepositions with verbs and nouns

1 Look at the verbs and nouns in *italics* in these sentences. Complete the sentences with the correct prepositions in the box.

> on (×2)   in   to   of   about

Verbs

1 Nobody can *argue* _____ the importance of green issues.

2 An environmentally-friendly life is something that we should all *aspire* _____.

3 The possible reductions are huge, *depending* _____ the original lifestyle of the client.

Nouns

4 Another of Simon's major concerns about waste is *lack* _____ insulation.

5 People don't realise the negative *impact* that this has _____ the environment.

6 He suggested asking the government for a grant to install insulation if you have *difficulties* _____ paying.

2 Check your answers in the article on pages 104–105.

3 Write the dependent prepositions in the Exam Reviser. Choose five items from each column and test your partner on the correct preposition.

> **exam reviser**   p13 | 10.2 ▶

4 Complete these statements in your own words.

1 Environmentally, I think people should focus …

2 It would be good if more people aspired …

3 Reducing your carbon footprint can result …

4 A lot of waste is due to a lack …

5 To become 'carbon-neutral' you need to acquire a taste …

6 To cut down on car usage, people need better access …

5 Discuss your statements with another student.

Grammar | reported speech

1 Which sentence is correct, A, B or both? Why? Look at the words in the Grammar Reference.

Direct speech:

'I only buy energy-saving lightbulbs,' he said.

Reported speech:

A *He said he only buys energy-saving lightbulbs.*

B *He said he only bought energy-saving lightbulbs.*

•• see grammar reference: **page 181** ••

2 Complete the sentences using the correct form of the verb in brackets and adding any other words as necessary, e.g. *me, she, him.*

1 verb + object + infinitive
   He *encouraged* _____ about how to save energy. (think)

2 verb + object (+ *that*) + clause
   She *told* _____ as much paper as possible. (recycle)

3 verb (+ *that*) + clause
   I *explained* _____ old-fashioned lightbulbs were so wasteful. (not know)

4 verb + *-ing* form
   They *admitted* _____ the heating up too high. (turn)

5 verb + infinitive
   She *refused* _____ that she was wasting energy. (accept)

6 verb + (object) + preposition + *-ing* form
   He *apologised* _____ so many plastic carrier bags. (waste)

3 Put these reporting verbs in the correct groups 1–6 in Exercise 2. Some verbs can be used in more than one group. Use the Grammar Reference to help you.

> decide   insist   admit   say   persuade   invite
> recommend   claim   discourage   advise   offer   remind

•• see grammar reference: **page 181** ••

4 **R.31** ▶ Listen to an interviewer asking five people about what they do to help save the environment. Make brief notes about what each person says.

5 Write sentences about what each person said starting with the verbs given. Use your notes to help you.

Person 1

1 She claimed …   2 She also said …

Person 2

3 He admitted …   4 He explained …

Person 3

5 She refused …   6 She told …

Person 4

7 He recommended …   8 He suggested …

Person 5

9 She asked …   10 She also asked …

> **premium plus**   42 ▶

CAE close-up | Writing Report (Paper 2, part1)

Exam information

Part 1 of the Writing paper consists of one question that all candidates must answer – it is compulsory. You are required to read some input material (e.g. an advertisement, an extract from an article). You then write a report, an article, a proposal or a letter based on what you have read. The focus of the task is generally on evaluating, expressing opinions or persuading. You will be asked to write between 180 and 220 words.

A *report* is generally written for a boss, a teacher, some colleagues or other club members. It usually requires you to give some factual information (based on what you read) and then make some suggestions and recommendations of your own.

Approach

1 Read the rubric to the task and all the input material carefully. Underline the key parts.

2 Make a plan of what you are going to write before you start writing. Organise your points into logical paragraphs and make sure you use the correct format and layout for what you are writing.

3 Include everything the rubric and the task ask you to do. Also, be careful not to include irrelevant information which is not asked for.

4 Do not copy large phrases or sentences from the input material – you need to use your own words. Also, think about the appropriate style of your writing.

5 A *report* should be clearly organised and may include headings, sub-headings and bullet points. You should also use more formal language in a report, including more formal grammatical constructions (passive forms, formal linking phrases, nominalisation, introductory *it*, etc.).

6 When you have finished writing, take some time to check what you have written, including format, layout, paragraphs, style, completion of the task, mistakes (grammar, vocabulary, spelling, punctuation) and correct number of words.

Practice task

You are on the student committee at an international college. The committee has done a survey about environmental problems in the college. The school's director has asked you to write a report about the results of the survey.

Read the extract from the survey results below, on which you have made some notes. Then, **using the information appropriately**, write the report, outlining the results of the survey, suggesting how students can be encouraged to improve the situation and recommending which area should be highlighted to students first.

Survey results

make one person responsible?

own water bottles?

use recycling bins

available in school shop!

Problem	Student replies
Turning off lights	95% said they never did
Waste paper and empty drinks cans	97% said they throw them in bin
Plastic cups (for water)	65% said they use more than four cups a day
Waste paper	88% said they don't buy recycled paper

Now write your **report** for the director of the school (**180–220** words). You should use your own words as far as possible.

Go to www.iTests.com or your CD-ROM for interactive exam practice

Vocabulary

1 Complete the text using the words in the box. Three of the words cannot be used.

> environmental sewage warming wasting
> polluted pollution emissions emitted away
> fuels cruelty depletion deforestation

Too many bags

Plastic bags, like all plastic products, are made from petroleum. Globally, the problem is huge, with over 380 billion plastic bags a year being produced in the US alone, effectively throwing _____¹ millions of barrels of oil. _____² oil is not the only problem. There is also a negative effect in terms of air _____³, caused by a huge amount of factory _____⁴ being produced during the manufacturing process, as is the case with the burning of all fossil _____⁵. Many plastic bags are reused, but the majority end up becoming litter – posing a huge threat to animals. Activists against animal _____⁶, for example, estimate that 100,000 marine animals are killed annually by plastic bags.

Though many of us do not realise it, the manufacture of paper bags has an even worse _____⁷ impact than that of plastic ones. 70% more gases which cause global _____⁸ are emitted while making a paper bag than a plastic bag, and water in rivers and seas is fifty times more _____⁹ during the process. Making paper bags also contributes to climate change through _____¹⁰ – it has been reported that in 1999, Americans used ten billion paper shopping bags, consuming fourteen million trees. Paper bags are also unlikely to be re-used in the same way as plastic ones, with 80% of them ending up in landfills.

2 Choose the correct prepositions.

Grammar

3 Complete these sentences with participle clauses using the verb in brackets.

1 Even cars _____ for short journeys create a lot of pollution. (use)
2 _____ so close, shouldn't you start walking to work? (live)
3 _____ a bit more time now, I'm going to try to use my car less. (have)
4 _____ well enough, the environmental conference should be a great success. (organise)

4 Complete the second sentence so that it has a similar meaning to the first sentence, using the word given. Do not change the word given. You must use between three and six words, including the word given.

1 'I'm so sorry about my late arrival,' she said.
   apologised
   She _____ late.
2 'Are you going to the demonstration?' he asked me.
   asked
   He _____ going to the demonstration.
3 She said I should get some more information before deciding.
   suggested
   She _____ I had some more information.
4 'They'll fine you if you drop any litter,' he told us.
   warned
   He _____ fined for dropping litter.
5 'Food is wasted on a daily basis in our house,' she said.
   admitted
   She _____ day in her house.
6 'I'll definitely bring it tomorrow,' he said.
   promised
   He _____ day.

THE 'FAB TREE HAB'

If your problem is a lack *of/with*¹ affordable housing, then grow your own! For the past few years, US architect Mitchell Joachim and his team have been working *by/on*² a project to create sustainable housing. The purpose *about/of*³ the project was to design a living space which is totally environmentally-friendly, and their hard work has resulted *with/in*⁴ a creation called the 'Fab Tree Hab'. The team has succeeded *in/on*⁵ creating a house which actually makes a positive impact *on/to*⁶ the environment, because it is made totally of trees and other plants. The frame consists *with/of*⁷ young tree trunks bound together and then branches and vines support the clay and straw walls. How long it takes to grow your house will depend *of/on*⁸ where you live – a few years in tropical countries, longer elsewhere.

Progress Check 2 Units 6–10

1 Choose the correct alternative in these sentences.

1 *Suppose/I suppose* he's feeling cross that he didn't work harder.
2 The company expanded too quickly. *Hence/Though* it ran into difficulties.
3 He *looks like/looks as if* trouble to me!
4 He left early *so as/so* to be sure of catching the flight.
5 *Doing/Having done* all the work, he was annoyed his boss didn't acknowledge the fact.
6 I walk to work so I *used to exercise/I'm used to exercising* every day.
7 They can spend what they want on holidays, *nevertheless/whereas* we need to be careful with our resources.
8 *In any case/Owing to* his lack of funds, he decided to travel round the States by bus.

2 Complete these dialogues with the correct form of the verb in brackets.

1 A: Do you think she's happy in her job.
  B: No, she _____ (be) because she's always complaining.
2 A: I don't envy Jo that journey to Hong Kong. It'll take ages.
  B: Yes, he _____ (sit) on the plane for ten hours now!
3 A: Did he enjoy himself?
  B: He _____ (do), but he looked a bit grumpy to me!
4 A: Have they done that report yet?
  B: No, they promised they _____ (get) it done by Friday.
5 A: Can you come over for dinner tonight?
  B: No, sorry. I _____ (travel) to London this evening.
6 A: Oh, no I've lost all my data!
  B: _____ (see) what happened last time, I would have thought you'd remember to save it.
7 A: Do you like flying?
  B: Not really. I've found that _____ (travel) slowly, like on the train, you get to see more.
8 A: Did you see the way she shouted at him?
  B: Yes! He _____ (be) really angry, don't you think? I know I would be!

3 Read these reviews and complete the gaps with the correct word. You have been given the first letter of each word.

An Inconvenient Truth

I don't know if you have managed to see *An Inconvenient Truth* yet but, if you haven't, you should. It is a truly incredible film that accurately outlines the state of the planet – explaining in detail the disastrous results of things like factory e_____¹, burning f_____ f_____² and the depletion of the o_____ l_____³ but in an interesting and engaging way. It not only shows the damage to our environment, but also outlines other effects, such as the fact that severely polluted air can cause b_____ p_____⁴ for many people. It really makes you think and can even change the way you live.

The Delights of Buenos Aires

Somewhere which had long been in my dreams as a place to visit is Buenos Aires in Argentina. Finally I managed to visit it last month and I was enchanted. It is a hi_____⁵ port city with im_____⁶ architecture along wide open streets, but there are also g_____⁷ glass skyscrapers in this most cosmopolitan of places. From these you can get a b_____⁸ view across the city skyline. I would strongly recommend you visit this diverse city as soon as you can.

Changing attitudes to crime

This book describes new research which shows that our attitudes to crime are changing. It seems that as it has been shown that violent crimes usually occur between people who know each other, we now see crimes like i_____ t_____⁹ as much more likely to affect us. On top of that it is hard to find the criminals, as these are crimes with victims but no w_____¹⁰! The other worrying thing is that it is hard to think of what could act as a d_____¹¹ as, if convicted, these criminals sometimes only get a s_____ s_____¹². It appears that all of this is feeding into new levels of concern regarding these crimes.

4 For each group of sentences 1–4, think of one word which can be used appropriately in all three sentences. The first one has been done for you.

1 They tried to get a __shot__ of him as he stepped off the train but it was too dark.
  I asked her to wait but she __shot__ off for some reason.
  He took a __shot__ at the bird as it was flying over but missed, thankfully.
2 He's been asked to _____ up a special group to investigate the problem.
  I don't know how she gets anything done as she's always got her _____ in the clouds.
  You _____ off now and we'll catch you up.
3 I've been racking my _____ for ages trying to remember her name.
  He's very clever – he's definitely the _____ behind the outfit.
  Some of our best _____ leave the country every year to get better jobs.
4 You need to _____ the sauce before you put it on the pasta.
  It was a decision he made in the _____ of the moment.
  In the running competition, he came first in his _____.

Progress Check 2 Units 6–10

5 Complete the text with one word in each gap.

At the movies

What do we expect from films we see at the cinema nowadays? Is it more and more thrills or shock? More convincing or elaborate special effects? The moguls in Hollywood who decide _____¹ the next blockbuster will be need to have a good understanding _____² the type of entertainment that the public is likely to _____³ in for in the future. _____⁴ invested in our computers and TV screens, what can possibly entice us into the cinema? _____⁵ many people are wondering _____⁶ the cinema can go nowadays, the producers are spending their time debating key questions. Why do we go and see films? Is it for the story, the thrills or the actors? Certain films, such as the Bond brand, seem to have no difficulty _____⁷ attracting audiences, even though the plots are very similar. And then there are the odd 'hard' or art films that prove to be surprisingly popular _____⁸ limited funding and an unknown cast. It seems that two themes prevail – either we like to be taken out of ourselves, to escape from our reality, _____⁹ we like to see a reflection of our lives, the issues and problems that beset us and _____¹⁰ the characters in the film handle these problems. Films that fall into either of these categories are ones that either excite us or move us. Which do you prefer to watch?

6 Complete the second sentence so that it has a similar meaning to the first sentence, using the word given. Do not change the word given. You must use between three and six words, including the word given.

1 I lost my keys so I stayed at his house.
   have
   If I hadn't lost my keys _____ at his house.
2 Trucks take the coffee away.
   by
   _____ trucks.
3 'This boy is very lazy,' she said.
   about
   She _____ of the boy
4 If you're not sure what to do, you should ask the supervisor.
   doubt
   You should ask the supervisor _____ what to do.

5 We were surprised the room was empty.
   surprising
   _____ the room empty.
6 I think you should have asked him first.
   better
   _____ if you had asked him first.
7 I imagine she was very upset by her aunt's illness.
   have
   She _____ by her aunt's illness.
8 They ate their meal and then walked round the square.
   having
   _____ walked round the square.

7 Use the word given in capitals at the end of some of the lines of this text to form a word that fits in the gap in the same line.

Someone's lying

There are lots of things you can learn to increase your effectiveness. One of these is to learn how to tell when other people are lying to you. Not only can this improve your (1) _____ of others, but you can **UNDERSTAND** also discover signs that you are giving out which you may be (2) _____ of. Classic **AWARE** signs of lying include bringing the hand up to the face. The speaker makes these (3) _____ almost to hide the words **MOVE** coming out of his mouth. You should also look at people's eyes. Generally, if people are thinking of (4) _____ information **VISION** to answer a question, then their eyes move up. This is how we retrieve mental pictures – but we do it (5) _____. Most **CONSCIOUS** of us have an (6) _____ to cover up these **ABLE** small telltale signs. Most people imagine we maintain eye contact when we tell the truth and break it when we are being (7) _____. In fact, because they don't need **HONESTY** to retrieve information from their minds, the (8) _____ of people will maintain eye **MAJOR** contact when lying. However, it is not necessarily the case that people who display these types of (9) _____ are lying. What **BEHAVE** you need to watch for is an answer that breaks the rules. Look for patterns – the (10) _____ will be the lie. **EXCEPT**

Progress Check

What's in a name?
Premium | Unit 11

brand new

a

FLIPPER

b

c

COURTHOUSE LODGE

named after

nickname

d

e

Unit 11

Introduction

1 Work in pairs and look at the pictures. Which of these names do you think best fits each picture? Give reasons.

> Tranquillity Dave Buster Ambleside Clearbrite
> Alexandra Dunroamin Trixie Summer Gleam

2 Decide on one more name for each picture. Compare with other students. What were the best names?

3 Discuss these questions with other students. Use the words in the box.
  1 How many different names have you got? Do you like them? Why/Why not?
  2 How do you feel about children being given very unusual names or made-up names? Why?

> first name   middle name   last name/surname/family name
> full name   initials   nickname   username   maiden name
> pen name   stage name   job title

4 Discuss these questions with other students.
  1 What is the difference between *a brand* and *a logo*?
  2 Name three of your favourite brands. Why do you like them?
  3 How far do you agree with this statement? Give reasons.
  Buying branded goods is a total waste of money.

CAE close-up | Reading Multiple matching (Paper 1, part 4)

Exam information

In this part of the exam, you read several short texts or one long text which is divided into sections. There are fifteen prompts and you have to decide which part of the text matches each prompt. (Sometimes more than one part of the text matches a prompt.)

Approach

1 Read the title and sub-headings (if there are any) and skim the texts quickly to get a general idea of what they are about. (Do not read through the prompts at this stage.)

2 Read the prompts carefully. Underline the key words in each one.

3 Go through the texts to find the relevant section of information for each prompt.

4 Underline the part(s) of the text which matches the prompt. Look for words and phrases which mean the same as the words in the prompt. (If you can't find the answer to a particular prompt, leave it until the end.)

5 Always choose an answer. You do not lose marks for a wrong answer.

Practice task

You are going to read an article about a man called Dave Gorman and a project he did with his friend Danny. For questions **1–15**, choose from the sections (**A–E**). The sections may be chosen more than once. When more than one answer is required, these may be given in any order.

In which section(s) are the following mentioned?

the fact that Dave and Danny live together	**1**	
the humorous nature of the book and project	**2**	**3**
the additional projects that happened as a result of their project	**4**	
the different opinions of the two men	**5**	**6**
the writer's opinion of Dave and Danny as people	**7**	
the fact that there is no real reason for doing the project	**8**	**9**
Dave's financial situation	**10**	
whether the story they wrote in the book is true or not	**11**	
the length of their trip	**12**	
the type of people who do similar projects	**13**	
the difficulties one of them had with a girlfriend	**14**	
how the writer understands Dave's interest in the topic	**15**	

Go to www.iTests.com or your CD-ROM for interactive exam practice

112

'Are *you* Dave Gorman?' – a tale of obsession and adventure

A

Different cultures have their own stereotypes and particular characteristics which come through in different ways. One of the idiosyncratic elements of British culture is eccentricity. People do things which may seem odd to people of other countries. Another common characteristic of many British people is that you must be seen to see things through to the bitter end, whether in glorious triumph or in heart-breaking failure.

These characteristics have thrown up some of the more heroic expeditions and projects. We've seen Britons taking on extraordinary challenges; trying to run faster than anyone else across deserts, or to race someone in a boat while facing backwards, or whatever it is, but very occasionally, the cause is not so much nobly pointless, as comically pointless.

B

As it turns out, the project described in the book *Are you Dave Gorman?* by Dave Gorman and his friend Danny Wallace, is clearly the latter, but none the less compelling for that. Not a work of fiction, but very much a work of fact, the story begins when Dave Gorman, newly-arrived in London, finds himself a new flatmate, Danny Wallace. One, now-legendary, night in the pub, the pair had a discussion, which quickly turned into an argument, which then became a full-blown project taking over the next few years of both their lives.

It all started when Dave told his friend about an email that someone had sent him. As Dave says in the book, 'I'd had an email that day, and tucked away in a PS at the bottom was a fact that made me all but forget what the rest of the email was about … Apparently, in the 1970s, East Fife Football Club had had a goalkeeper by the name of Dave Gorman. He was, it went on, still working at the club to this day, now in the capacity of Assistant Manager.'

C

With a curiosity about names myself, I can appreciate that Dave found this news of a Scottish namesake fascinating, unlike Danny, who didn't even believe his friend's story. Danny doubted that any other Dave Gormans existed at all, whereas Dave was sure that there must be hundreds of people in the world who shared his name. The argument continued until they found themselves making a bet on it. And five hours later they were on an overnight train to Scotland, on a mission to meet the Dave Gorman in question.

That first meeting with the Scottish Dave Gorman, heralded the start of an uncontrollable adventure that would take them around the world, finding and meeting complete strangers with only one thing in common – they were all called Dave Gorman. Before continuing, in order to simplify the challenge slightly, they decided to refine their bet. They decided to try to meet fifty-four Dave Gormans. This corresponded, rather arbitrarily, to the number of cards in a pack of playing cards (including the jokers).

D

During their six-month odyssey, Dave and Danny got caught in a tornado in New York, they lost their shoes in Norway and caused a security alert at an Israeli airport. They met booksellers, carpet fitters, police officers, film stars and a semi-retired lighthouse technician. As their project went on, they found themselves becoming interesting news, with people recognising them in the street as they went about their business.

They appeared in a British tabloid newspaper and they were front page news in Denmark. They were even asked to make a TV show about their adventure. With Dave nearly bankrupting himself, and Danny's personal life and relationship nearly in ruins, the result of their travels was a book describing the journeys and adventures of the two friends and their worldwide quest.

E

The book could be as aimless and bizarre as the whole adventure itself, and of course, in a sense, it is. However, it is very well-executed and, to my mind, an amusing and compelling read. They have used an unusual style, in that the book is written by both of them, with the author at the time being identified by the font (Dave in bold text, Danny in plain). Although it may seem confusing and slightly weird to have two sides of the same story in one book, it actually works well and is surprisingly clear, giving two perspectives at the same time.

While they do travel a lot, don't expect this to be a travel book as such. You get no descriptions of the places they have visited – that's clearly not their aim. What you do get, however, is an excellent understanding of the relationship between the two authors and the difficulties that arise when trying to succeed in a ridiculous bet. The book is a lot of fun – I laughed out loud when I read it – and both of the authors are clearly very likeable. What I appreciated most was the unpretentiousness of it all – a project completed by two friends just because they wanted to.

Vocabulary | word formation – suffixes

1 Underline the suffixes in each of these words.

> argu<u>ment</u>   curiosity   obsession
> pointless   uncontrollable   personal
> simplify   modernise   surprisingly

2 What does each suffix tell you about the grammar of the word? Add your underlined suffixes from Exercise 1 to the correct columns in the table.

Suffixes to make nouns	Suffixes to make adjectives	Suffixes to make verbs	Suffixes to make adverbs
-ment			

3 The suffixes -less and -able add meaning to the word as well as telling you about the part of speech. What meaning do they add?

4 Sometimes we can add more than one suffix to a word. Look at the suffixes in the Exam Reviser and make new words by adding one or more of them to these words. The first one has been done for you.

1 commerce: *commercial / commercially / commercialise / commercialisation*
2 forget: _____ / _____ / _____
3 scandal: _____ / _____ / _____
4 scarce: _____ / _____
5 relate: _____ / _____ / _____ / _____
6 outrage: _____ / _____
7 depend: _____ / _____ / _____ / _____
8 deaf: _____ / _____ / _____ / _____

> **exam reviser**   p13 | 11.1

5 Complete these sentences with eight of the new words from Exercise 4.

1 They have started to _____ the whole area and there are far more shops than there used to be.
2 Can you turn that music down? It's _____ loud at the moment.
3 I can't believe the _____ comments he made to his boss.
4 The successful candidate will be totally _____ as well as having good initiative.
5 His memory isn't as good as it was and his _____ has become more and more of a problem.
6 There are _____ few problems with lateness now compared with what there used to be.
7 There were huge crowds of people and I could _____ walk down the pavement.
8 The way he behaved at work _____ the whole company.

6 Complete each gap in the text using the correct form of the words in brackets.

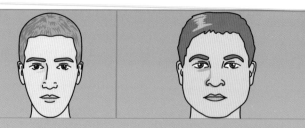

Do you look like a Bob or a Tim?

Do you have trouble remembering some names, but not others? According to a recent study, people tend to associate certain names with certain _____[1] (face) features. For example, for many people, the name Bob has _____[2] (associate) with a larger, rounder face than the name Tim.

To test their theory, researchers _____[3] (specific) fifteen names and, using special software, people were asked to create faces that they felt matched each name. Only white male faces were used in order to _____[4] (simple) the experiment, and to avoid _____[5] (complicate) introduced by different race and gender. The results showed that even with a homogenous set of names, participants still demonstrated that they believed there were _____[6] (stereotype) face types for individual names.

The study also concluded that people find it much more _____[7] (problem) remembering names that go against our preconceived _____[8] (expect) of what someone with a given name should look like.

7 Add six new words from Exercises 4 and 6 to the table in the Exam Reviser.

> **exam reviser**   p13 | 11.1

8 Discuss these questions with other students.

1 What do you think about the research in the text? Do you think it is easier to remember certain names than others? Why?
2 Does Dave Gorman (in the picture) look like you imagined? Why/Why not?
3 How many people do you know with the same name as you? How do you feel about that?
4 What reasons do people have for choosing a particular name for a baby? Why was your name chosen for you?

> **premium plus**   43

Grammar | verb patterns

1 Look at these parts of dictionary definitions from the *Longman Exams Dictionary*. What do the symbols [T] and [I] mean?

be·lieve /bə'liːv/ *v* [T]   **laugh** /lɑːf; læf/ *v* [I]

2 Look at the verbs in *italics* in these sentences. How many objects are there in each sentence: none, one or two? Write the verbs in the correct columns in the table.

1 Danny didn't *believe* his friend's story.
2 Someone had *sent* him an email.
3 I *laughed* out loud when I read it.
4 He *woke up* Dave when they got to Scotland.
5 They *woke up* when they got to Scotland.

transitive	transitive with two objects	intransitive	transitive and intransitive

3 Work in two groups. Group A and Group B look at page 167.

4 Now work in A/B pairs. Tell each other about the patterns of your verbs and add them to your table. Check your answers in the Grammar Reference.

•• see grammar reference: **page 182** ••

Grammar note | *transitive verbs with two objects*

When there are two objects, usually the first object is a person and the second object is a thing. With many of these verbs, we can reverse the order of the objects by using *to* or *for*.

• *I sent **him** an email.*

• *I sent an email **to him**.*

Certain transitive verbs, however, always need a preposition before the person. In this case, the person must come second. Which of these sentences is correct?

1 *He explained the story to them.*
2 *He explained to them the story.*
3 *He explained them the story.*

5 There are mistakes in these sentences. Find the mistakes and correct them.

1 She told her name and I've completely forgotten it.
2 I described the police the man who pulled my bag off my shoulder.
3 I warned him about the time of the train but he still missed.
4 They assured to us of their total commitment to offering value for money.

5 She sent to me a lovely photo of us eating dinner together.
6 I could hardly believe it when they informed of my exam results.

Speaking

1 R.32 ▶ Look at this list of 'pointless projects' similar to the one Dave Gorman did. Listen to part of a conversation between two friends and say which project they decide to do.

1 Find and meet fifty-four people with the same name.
2 Visit thirty-one towns whose name begins with the letter T.
3 Buy a copy of the same book in thirty-eight different towns.
4 Watch twenty-two films with the word **and** in the title.
5 Buy twenty-five products of the same brand in twenty-five different shops.
6 Find forty-seven pairs of words which produce only one result in a Google search.

2 R.32 ▶ Listen again and tick the phrases you hear.

Negotiating
1 *What else do you think is important?* ☐
2 *How would you feel if we decided ...?* ☐
3 *I think it would be far more interesting to ... than ...* ☐
4 *If you really feel strongly about that, then we should ...* ☐

Decision-making
5 *So, have we decided which one ...?* ☐
6 *Shall we check that we agree on ...?* ☐
7 *Anyway, we have to make a decision about ...* ☐
8 *It seems that we both/all agree about that.* ☐
9 *There are more good reasons for ... than for any of the others.* ☐

3 Look at the Exam Reviser and complete the phrases.

exam reviser   p25 | 14 ▶

4 With a partner decide which project in Exercise 1 you would do. You have 3 minutes.

5 Make a group of four with another pair and agree on one project. You have 3 minutes.

6 Make a larger group. Can the whole group come to a decision which everyone agrees on?

premium plus   44 ▶

Listening

1 Discuss what you think is happening in the pictures with another student.

2 Look at these sentences and <u>underline</u> the key words and phrases. Ignore the gaps for the moment.

1 Having the right brands as a teenager made Neil feel that his life wasn't so _____.

2 In his current job as the _____ for a style magazine, he is surrounded by brands all the time.

3 Neil now understands that being so obsessed with brands as an adult is _____.

4 Like Neil, most people use branded goods to give them a sense of belonging and to have something to _____ with.

5 Recently, Neil realised that instead of making him feel good, the brands brought him a feeling of _____.

6 He decided to burn every single branded thing he owned, despite admitting it was a _____ of these things.

7 He found the initial _____ of his experiment very difficult, but then things got better.

8 At the end of the experiment, Neil not only felt happier but he also had more money and lost _____.

3 What synonyms or paraphrases can you think of for each of your underlined words and phrases?

LISTENING SKILLS

Paraphrasing and keeping track

In order to keep track of where you are during a listening, it is useful to listen out for paraphrases and words which are similar to those you are listening for.

Before you listen, look at the questions, <u>underline</u> key words and phrases and briefly note down any similar words and phrases that you think you might hear.

4 **R.33** Listen and tick the paraphrases that you've written down as you hear them. You could also note down any others you hear that you didn't write down.

5 **R.33** Listen again and complete the sentences in Exercise 2.

6 Read these messages about Neil's actions and discuss these questions.

1 Which message is most similar to your opinion? Why?

2 What difference would it make to your life if you stopped buying brands? Give details.

> *A great story and an inspiration! Well done, Neil. I think people spend far too much boosting the profits of all these big companies for no reason at all.* **Marcia, Madrid**
>
> *What a stupid waste – at least take your stuff to a charity shop so that someone else can use them. Instead you've not only wasted them, but also contributed to global warming by burning them!* **Dan, Edinburgh**

7 Tell other students which message is most similar to your opinion and why. Do you mostly agree or disagree?

Vocabulary | words with multiple meanings

1 Work in pairs. Look at the words and phrases in *italics* in these sentences. Explain their meaning.

1 I got some *brand new* Nike trainers for only €50 by shopping online.

2 I had to buy a different *brand* of shampoo this week because they'd run out of my usual one.

3 It's not fair to *brand all teenage boys as hooligans* – many of them are very responsible.

2 The word *brand* has multiple meanings. In pairs, say in which sentence in Exercise 1 *brand* has each of the following:

• a core, basic meaning
• a metaphorical meaning
• a meaning as part of a fixed phrase

3 For each group of sentences 1–4, think of a single word which can be used in all three sentences. In each group, the word is used in its basic meaning, its metaphorical meaning and as part of a fixed phrase (but not necessarily in that order).

1 A The director knows everyone by _____ even though there are over 300 employees.
  B It took a long time to decide on a good _____ for this product.
  C The company got a bad _____ for itself because it kept failing to deliver on time.

2 A Neil made a good _____ about being accepted by your peers.
  B I was on the _____ of giving away some old clothes when I realised I could make a lot of money by selling them.
  C There is no _____ in buying expensive branded goods when unbranded goods are just as good.

3 A There is a small _____ for leaving your coats in the cloakroom.
  B Take care when the doors open as people usually _____ in to grab the best bargains.
  C I would like to insist on speaking to whoever is in _____ of sales please.

4 A She really seemed to come to _____ when she started talking about fashion.
  B This bicycle never does what I want it to do – it seems to have a _____ of its own!
  C I'm sorry I didn't phone you but my _____ is very busy at the moment.

4 Look again at the sentences in Exercise 3 and underline the parts of the sentences containing the key word which are fixed phrases or expressions.

5 Work in two groups, A and B. Within your group, work with a partner to write sentences for each of the meanings of the word in your box. Use a dictionary to help you if necessary.

A	B
root	fire
1 root of a tree	1 a warm fire
2 to root for someone	2 to fire someone from something
3 get to the root of (a problem)	3 fire questions at someone
care	race
1 take care of someone	1 win a race
2 not have a care in the world	2 race around
3 send something care of someone	3 a race against time

6 Now work in A/B pairs and show each other your sentences, explaining the meanings if necessary. Then add the words and phrases to the Exam Reviser.

exam reviser   p14 | 11.2

7 Look at the highlighted sounds in the words in boxes A and B. Write each word in the column with the same sound.

A
> track   fast   group   task
> match   blue

1 brand	2 charge	3 root
track		

B
> race   high   boy   fair   break
> price   where   choice

1 name	2 point	3 life	4 care

8 R.34 Listen and check your answers.

9 Look at the words again and say them with a partner. Which group of words have vowel sounds and which have diphthongs? What is the difference between vowels and diphthongs?

10 Choose four of the words and phrases in this section and write questions to ask other students.

*What is your favourite **brand** of sports clothes?*

*How would you feel if you had **to fire someone from** their job?*

11 Ask your questions to at least three other students.

Expanding your vocabulary

When you learn a new word or phrase, it is a good idea to check in the dictionary for any other phrases or expressions connected with the word. In this way, you can expand your vocabulary further.

For each of these words, find the basic meaning, and two other common phrases or expressions in which it occurs.

> rest   power   case   light

Write a sentence for the basic meaning and each expression you find so that you can learn them in context.

learning tip

Grammar | using noun groups

1 Look at the highlighted parts of these sentences. Which sentence has a noun group, and which has a verb and adjective group?

1 The brands were why he felt so miserable.
2 The brands were the reason for his misery.

2 Which sentence in each pair A and B uses one or more noun groups? <u>Underline</u> the noun groups in each case.

1 A We did an experiment to find out how much people recognised different brands.
  B The aim of the experiment was to test recognition of different brands.

2 A The realisation of his problem led him to take drastic action.
  B When he realised what his problem was, he decided to take drastic action.

3 A Brands occupied all his thoughts: what they look like, what they do, what they mean. This obsession continued into his adult life.
  B Brands occupied all his thoughts: what they look like, what they do, what they mean, and he continued to be obsessed with them into his adult life.

4 A Self-esteem is increased with the right brands.
  B You feel better about yourself if you've got the 'right' brands.

5 A He had a huge obsession with brands and because of this he became involved in a career based on image.
  B His huge obsession with brands led to his involvement in a career based on image.

3 Why do we use noun groups? Match the examples in Exercise 2 with the correct rules A–E in the box. Look at the Grammar Reference to help you if necessary.

We use noun groups:

A to change the emphasis of the sentence (usually making one clause instead of two).
Example: _____

B to make sentences shorter and more concise, (leaving room for new information at the end of the sentence).
Example: _____

C to refer back to phrases already mentioned.
Example: _____

D to make sentences more impersonal.
Example: _____

E often in formal, academic or scientific English.
Example: _____

•• see grammar reference: page 183 ••

4 Complete the second sentence so that it has a similar meaning to the first sentence, using the word given. Do not change the word given. You must use between three and six words, including the word given.

1 Many people have written to complain about how expensive branded goods are.
  price
  We have received a large number of _____ of branded goods.

2 The main reason he is addicted to brands is because he isn't very confident.
  of
  His addiction to brands is largely due _____.

3 Some people feel that you can only measure how successful you are by looking at how wealthy you are.
  measurement
  Some people feel that the _____.

4 Sales have increased hugely because people have responded positively to the advertising campaign.
  meant
  The positive response to the advertising campaign _____ sales.

5 A good advertising executive needs to be imaginative and ambitious.
  essential
  Qualities of _____ for a good advertising executive.

6 Higher interest rates may be a reason why far fewer people are using credit cards.
  use
  The sharp _____ credit cards may be due to higher interest rates.

7 He found he had more money in the bank after he gave up branded goods.
  situation
  Giving up branded goods meant that _____ considerably.

8 Since she became involved in the project, we have produced better work.
  increase
  Her involvement in the project has meant an _____ of our work.

premium plus   45

5 Complete the noun groups in *italics* using the correct form of a word in the box.

> consumer   responsible   sponsor   please   expose

1 *Constant _____ to advertising* via TV, radio, magazines and other media is bad for society.
2 *Large-scale _____* would be reduced hugely if the number and type of adverts on TV were cut, especially those aimed at children.
3 *_____ of popular sports events* (e.g. football and motor-racing) by major companies shouldn't be allowed.
4 *Some of the _____ for reducing debt* should be borne by credit card companies.
5 *Much of the _____ that people get from shopping* stops as soon as they've bought the item.

6 Do you agree or disagree with the statements in Exercise 5? Discuss with other students, giving reasons.

Writing | report

1 Read these questions about consumerism. Before you discuss them, note down any words or phrases that you think will be useful when talking about these topics.
- Which group of consumers do you think spends the most: children, teenagers or adults? Why?
- How far does having lots of possessions contribute to personal happiness?
- Why do you think people become compulsive shoppers?
- What do you think is the aim of a 'Buy Nothing Day'? How do you think people in your country would react to having one?
- What other ways can you think of for reducing consumerism?

2 Compare your words and phrases with other students and write down any more that you think will be useful.

3 Discuss the questions in small groups.

4 Read the writing task and decide which of the paragraph plans A or B is most appropriate and why.

> **Writing task**
>
> An international research group is investigating attitudes to brands, shopping habits and advertising in different parts of the world. You have been asked to write a report on consumerism in your country, describing the main issues connected to shopping and advertising in your country at the moment, and explaining how you would like to see things change in the future.

A
Paragraph 1: Introduction – give an outline of what you're going to write about
Paragraph 2: Give some information about the current situation
Paragraph 3: Make some suggestions/recommendations for the future
Paragraph 4: Conclusion – give your overall opinion about the topic, including a summary of your suggestions

B
Paragraph 1: Introduction – give an outline of what you're going to write about
Paragraph 2: Make a suggestion/a recommendation for the future
Paragraph 3: Make another suggestion/a recommendation for the future
Paragraph 4: Conclusion – give your overall opinion about the topic, stating which suggestion you prefer

5 Paragraph plan B in Exercise 4 would be more appropriate for a proposal than for a report. Work with a partner and discuss these questions, using the Writing Reference if necessary.

1 What are the similarities between a report and a proposal? (Think about purpose, intended reader, organisation, language and giving a personal view.)
2 Which of these describes a report and which describes a proposal?
   A suggesting something that might happen and persuading someone to help or contribute
   B describing something that has already happened and including a brief suggestion at the end

> •• see writing reference: page 190 ••

6 Prepare to write your report by making brief notes using paragraph plan A and some of the ideas from your discussions in Exercises 2 and 3. Look at the Writing Reference again to find any relevant formal language you could use.

7 Write your report in 220–260 words. Don't forget to check your writing for mistakes.

Grammar

1 Look at the verb patterns in this text and find eight extra words which should not be there.

Can I have a refund?

Do you shop things on impulse, and then take the whole lot back later for a refund? If so, you're not alone. Shoppers in the UK receive them a huge £6.2 billion a year in refunds.

Recent research has found it that eight of out ten British shoppers have a non-committal attitude to spending. Nearly 22.8 million Brits use them any excuse they can think of to get their money back; the most common excuse being telling to the shop assistant that the item was an unwanted present.

But why do so many people buy things that they don't actually want? Emma Jackson, a twenty-three-year-old Londoner, explained me that she is a compulsive shopper. 'It's the chase,' she said me. 'I love the whole process of looking at things you want and being able to buy them. Once I've bought something, though, it often loses its appeal, so I take it back. At least I waste it less money that way!'

2 Complete the first sentence so that it is similar in meaning to the second one.

1 _____ led to _____ to study to be a clothes designer.
She loved clothes and fashion and because of this she decided to study to be a clothes designer.

2 _____ are important because often _____ are made.
It is important to try to impress people when you first meet them as they often judge you quickly.

3 _____ was to try to find out _____ on people.
They did some research to try to find out how much people were influenced by advertising.

4 _____ has been affected by _____ .
They haven't started modernising the company yet because the funding has been delayed.

Vocabulary

3 Complete each sentence with the correct form of the word in brackets.

1 You need good _____ qualities to be the director of a large company. (leader)
2 It's _____ that companies think it's worth spending a lot of money on advertising. (understand)
3 They've _____ the shopping centre and it's got loads of new shops now. (modern)
4 I've got a job as a _____ for the summer to make a bit of extra money. (type)
5 It's common for rival companies to show quite a lot of _____ towards each other. (hostile)
6 When I go shopping, I'm very _____ and I make up my mind quickly about what to buy. (decide)
7 You can get fruit drinks which are very _____ and don't contain too much sugar. (nutrient)
8 I'll really need to _____ that skirt because it's far too long at the moment. (short)

4 Complete each pair of sentences with a single word which can be used appropriately in both sentences.

1 A One of the first things you need to do when you're camping is to build yourself a _____ .
  B Throughout the whole interview, all they did was _____ questions at me.

2 A We need to have a meeting and try to get to the _____ of the problem.
  B They had to cut through the main _____ of the tree in order to start the building works.

3 A I'm determined to win the _____ this time as I've done so much training.
  B After the accident, it was a _____ against time to get the doctors to him as quickly as possible.

4 A We'd like to thank all the staff for taking _____ of us so well during our stay.
  B My childhood was a time of great happiness – I really didn't have a _____ in the world at that time.

Be your own boss

Premium | Unit 12

professional

career

Unit 12

Introduction

1 Match the pictures with five of these jobs. Three of them cannot be used. Then put all the jobs into the correct place in the table.

> head chef   newsreader   flight attendant   referee   textile designer
> film director   stockbroker   building site foreman

Entertainment	Fashion	Construction	Tourism	Catering

Financial	Health	Education	Media	Sport

2 Add three more jobs to each category in the table in Exercise 1. Which of the categories above most and least appeals to you to work in? Why?

3 Number these things from 1–8 according to what is most important to you in your job. Discuss your list with a partner.

being your own boss	☐	entertaining people	☐
earning a lot of money	☐	working as a team	☐
feeling happy in your work	☐	working outdoors	☐
helping people	☐	travelling a lot	☐

Listening

1 Look at the pictures and the two lists in Exercise 3. Discuss these questions with another student.

1 Which of the jobs in the Task One list do you think each picture shows? What clues helped you decide?

2 Are there any clues in the Task Two list which helped you decide which picture shows which job?

2 R.35 Listen to five short extracts in which people are talking about different jobs. Look again at the lists in Exercise 3 and at these two questions. As you listen, note down key words which could help you answer them correctly.

1 What kind of job is being described?

2 What is the main point each speaker is making about the job?

LISTENING SKILLS

Building up answers from clues

It is a good idea to try to collect as many clues as you can before and while you listen. Pick out key words from the questions and note down important points during the listening. By building up your answers using various pieces of information in this way, you will be able to understand what you hear more accurately.

3 R.35 Listen again and do these two tasks. Use all your clues to help you.

Task One

For questions 1–5, choose from the list A–H what job is being described.

1 Speaker 1: _____
2 Speaker 2: _____
3 Speaker 3: _____
4 Speaker 4: _____
5 Speaker 5: _____

A a public relations officer
B an art gallery owner
C a product designer
D a music and arts festival organiser
E a cook
F an artist
G a restaurant owner
H a personal assistant

Task Two

For questions 6–10, choose from the list A–H what main point each speaker is making about the job.

6 Speaker 1: _____
7 Speaker 2: _____
8 Speaker 3: _____
9 Speaker 4: _____
10 Speaker 5: _____

A The positive aspects of the job outweigh the negative aspects.
B It's good to be successful doing something you love.
C Having more than one job at the same time is very tiring.
D It doesn't matter about the money if you're achieving your aim in other ways.
E It combines benefit to people and financial success.
F There is very little job security.
G It's very difficult to make a profit because costs are so high.
H It's very well-paid but very hard work.

4 Discuss these questions with other students.

1 Which of the jobs you heard about would you be most interested in doing? Why?

2 If you could have a completely new career or start a completely new business, what would you like to do? Why?

Vocabulary | work

1 Work in two groups, A and B, and look at the Exam Reviser. Group A check the meaning and pronunciation of the words and phrases in columns 1 and 2. Group B check those in columns 3 and 4.

exam reviser ▸ p15 | 12.1 ▸

2 Work in A/B pairs and tell each other about your words/phrases.

3 R.36 Listen to two people playing a game and answer these questions.

1 What is the aim of the game?

2 What do you think the man is going to guess?

4 R.37 Listen and check what the man guessed.

5 Work in A/B pairs and play the game. Follow these instructions.

Student A: Think of a job but don't tell your partner.

Student B: Ask your partner a maximum of twenty Yes/No questions and try to find out what job he or she is thinking of.

premium plus 46

CAE close-up | Use of English Word formation (Paper 3, part 3)

Exam information

This part of the exam consists of a text containing ten gaps. Each gap corresponds to a word. The stems of the missing words are given beside the text and must be changed to form the missing word in the same line.

Approach

1 Read the text quickly before filling in any of the gaps in order to get a general sense of the meaning.

2 Before you fill a gap, decide what part of speech the missing word is, e.g. an adjective (e.g. *ambitious*), an adverb (e.g. *ambitiously*), a noun (e.g. *employee*), etc.

3 Remember that the missing word will sometimes need to be plural (e.g. *businesses*) and will sometimes need

to be negative (e.g. *unemployable*). Read the whole sentence to check.

4 Remember, too, that sometimes the change will not just be adding prefixes (e.g. *un-*) or suffixes (e.g. *-ity*) but that the whole word will need to change (e.g. *strong > strengthen*).

5 For each gap, form words from the word in capitals and see which one you think fits the gap. Check that each word you have written is the right part of speech (noun, verb, etc.) for that sentence and that the whole sentence makes sense. Remember to check that your spelling is correct, too.

6 Remember that in the exam you should always write something in each gap: you do not lose marks for a wrong answer.

Practice task

For questions **1–10**, read the text below. Use the word given in capitals at the end of some of the lines to form a word that fits in the gap **in the same line**. There is an example at the beginning (**0**).

Write your answers IN CAPITAL LETTERS **on the separate answer sheet**.

Example: | 0 | P R O F E S S I O N A L

Footballers dig deep for nurses

The highest-earning **(0)** _____ footballers earn around £150,000 a week, whereas it takes the   **PROFESSION**

average nurse four years to earn that. Struck by the obvious **(1)** _____ of this huge discrepancy,   **FAIR**

Dr Noreena Hertz has set up the 'May Day for Nurses' campaign, creating an unlikely **(2)** _____   **ALLY**

between the two professions.

The idea of the campaign is that top players make **(3)** _____ of a day's salary into a fund, which   **DONATE**

is then redistributed to nurses. Dr Hertz says getting the fund started wasn't easy, because she didn't

know who to ask, but her **(4)** _____ has paid off. In all, 239 players, including stars like Thierry   **PERSIST**

Henry, have now promised their **(5)** _____, as well as whole clubs, such as Tottenham Hotspur.   **EARN**

Almost every nurse is eligible for some money as most struggle to survive **(6)** _____, often doing   **FINANCE**

other jobs as well as nursing to make ends meet. Not only is their pay **(7)** _____, but generally   **ADEQUATE**

nursing is a stressful job with little job **(8)** _____. For some, having access to the fund may well   **SECURE**

make the difference between staying in the profession and **(9)** _____.   **QUIT**

Dr Hertz hopes that the campaign will not only raise money, but will also raise awareness about the

(10) _____ professions and their low status in society.   **CARE**

Go to www.iTests.com or your CD-ROM for interactive exam practice

Grammar | countable and uncountable nouns

1 Look at the way the words *job*, *work* and *business* are used in these sentences. Which sentence is incorrect? Why?

1 I've got a really good job.
2 I wish work wasn't so stressful.
3 I'd like to get a new work.
4 He's a good person to do business with.
5 She's just set up a new business.

2 Look at these words and say which are countable, which are uncountable and which can be both. Look at the Grammar Reference if necessary.

money   wealth   time   space   pressure   advice   weather
rubbish   shelter   glass   information   research   knowledge
experience   accommodation   news   travel   trip   furniture
strength   happiness   iron   hair   coffee   chocolate   bread

• • see grammar reference: page 183 • •

3 Decide if one or both of the verbs in these sentences is/are correct. Then put the highlighted nouns into the correct place in the table on page 168.

1 The news *is/are* generally very depressing.
2 The goods *was/were* despatched to you this morning.
3 That TV series about new businesses *was/were* very interesting.
4 The team *was/were* overjoyed at their success last week.
5 The stairs at work *is/are* very narrow and dangerous.
6 Economics *is/are* important but sometimes a bit boring.
7 The proceeds of the concert *is/are* going to the school.
8 The public *has/have* a right to know how the money will be spent.

4 Work in pairs. Think of two more words for each group, then check your ideas in the Grammar Reference.

• • see grammar reference: page 183 • •

Grammar note | *a piece, a tube, a crowd*, etc.

1 What nouns can collocate with these uncountable nouns to make them countable? e.g. *a tube of toothpaste*

piece   bit   tube   slice   loaf   bar   carton   lump
joint   fit   breath   spot   rumble   gust   stroke
item   state

2 What nouns collocate with these collective nouns to describe groups? e.g. *a crowd of people*

crowd   gang   flock   herd   swarm   shoal   pack
bunch   set   pile   stack   couple

---

5 Look at these extracts and decide if one or both of the alternatives is correct in each case.

Happy hairdressers

I got my first *job/work*[1] as a hairdresser when I was just seventeen. That means I've got fifteen years' experience/experiences[2] of cutting the *hair/hairs*[3] of hundreds of different clients. With my *knowledge/knowledges*[4] of the business, I wasn't surprised to hear that hairdressers came top in a survey on job satisfaction.

Happy Denmark

Recent news *reveals/reveal*[5] that the USA is the twenty-third happiest country in the world. Research done at a university in England *shows/show*[6] that Denmark is the happiest country. The research team *say/says*[7] they asked people about their satisfaction relating to work, personal life and environment.

Gross National Happiness

On a recent *trip/travel*[8] to Bhutan, actress Cameron Diaz found it hard to believe that the country's wealth *was/were*[9] not measured in money terms. The happiness of their citizens *is/are*[10] what the Bhutanese value more than anything else, measured on a scale of Gross National Happiness (GNH).

Happy doctors?

That new drama series *is/are*[11] guaranteed to put you off becoming a doctor – that's for sure. The staff at the hospital *is/are*[12] overworked and stressed, and the whole place seems to be in a continuous *state/spot*[13] of emergency. Take my *advice/advices*[14] – 'Switch it off and relax!'

6 Discuss these questions with another student.

1 Which jobs do you think would come top and bottom in a survey on job satisfaction? Why?
2 Where do you think your country would be in a survey of happiness? Why?

Speaking

1 R.38 ▶ Listen to three extracts of a student talking about these statements. Which statement does she talk about in the least interesting way? Why is that?

1 People in the caring professions like nurses should be paid as much as professional footballers.
2 Working from home is more desirable than working in an office.
3 Financial success is more important than job satisfaction.

2 Work in pairs. Choose one of the statements in Exercise 1 to discuss. Before you start speaking:

1 Think about how far you agree with the statement and briefly note down some examples to justify your opinion.
2 Look at the Exam Reviser to remind yourself of useful language.

exam reviser p20 | 3 p22 | 7 ▶

SPEAKING SKILLS
Giving extended responses

When you are speaking, you need to give extended responses to a question or a discussion topic. Your speaking will be much more interesting for the listener if you include reasons and examples to justify your opinions.

3 Discuss the statement with your partner, making sure you give an extended, interesting response with reasons and examples.

4 Work with a different partner and choose a different statement. Prepare your speaking first in the same way as above. Then discuss the statement together.

premium plus 48 ▶

CAE close-up | Writing Essay (Paper 2, part 2)

Exam information

In part 2 of the Writing exam, you may have the choice of writing an essay. The main purpose of an essay is to develop an argument and/or to discuss issues surrounding a certain topic. The intended reader is usually a teacher, as a follow-up to a class discussion. You will be expected to give reasons for your opinions. Your answer should be written in an appropriately formal/neutral style in between 220 and 260 words.

Approach

1 Underline the key words in the task and check you know what kind of essay is required; whether it asks you a) to give your opinion, b) to give both sides of an argument or c) to outline a problem and suggest a solution.

2 Spend some time thinking of all the ideas and arguments to support your opinion and against your opinion. Then organise these ideas and write a paragraph plan, including an introduction, clear development and an appropriate conclusion.

3 It is important only to write about the statement in the question. Be careful not to include irrelevant information which is not asked for.

4 When you have finished writing your essay, check your writing. Make sure you have:

- organised your essay into paragraphs;
- used an appropriate style;
- responded to the statement in the question and nothing else;
- checked any mistakes with grammar and vocabulary;
- checked any mistakes with spelling and punctuation;
- written approximately the correct number of words.

Practice task

Your teacher has asked you to write an essay saying how far you agree with the following statement.

Job satisfaction is more important than financial success. How far do you agree?

Write your **essay** in **220–260** words.

Go to www.iTests.com or your CD-ROM for interactive exam practice

Improving your English for work

In many jobs, you may need to use English for something (e.g. to write an email, to socialise at a work party or to give a presentation). What other things might you have to do in English for work?

Look at these tips for how to improve your English for work. Which three do you think are the most useful? Can you add any other tips?

- Do a course specifically designed for Business English, English for Tourism, English for Lawyers, etc.
- Read professional journals, newspaper articles and relevant books to expand your specific vocabulary.
- Watch documentaries, news stories and other programmes relevant to the field you work in.
- Go out and socialise with other English speakers to improve your social English.

Reading

1 Look at the pictures and discuss these questions with other students.

1 What clothes and accessories can you see in the pictures?
2 In what work situations do you think the clothes and accessories in the pictures would not be acceptable? Why?

2 Read the article quickly and number the things A–E in the order they are referred to.

A uniforms ☐
B tattoos ☐
C colour of clothes ☐
D perfume and aftershave ☐
E jewellery and accessories ☐

What not to wear at work

Recent research suggests that 55% of the impact you make at work depends on how you look, and only 7% on what you say.

Yes – 55%. That's a huge figure, and although John T Molloy, in his classic book *Dress for Success,* declares that 'The first rule of dress is common sense', many of us it seems, do not have the required common sense. He claims that we commit all sorts of suicidal errors when it comes to the image we project in the workplace. Personally, I believe that some people may have a natural ability to dress appropriately at work. For many, however, usually those who are not totally convinced that appearance counts, it takes a more concerted effort and some well-informed professional advice.

So, let's start by talking about colour – an area where without guidance, people can, and do, go badly wrong. The results of a recent survey of American company directors about their preferred suit colour revealed no surprises. 53% said they favoured blue or dark blue, and 39% opted for grey or dark grey. For both men and women, dark suits spell formality and authority, and although fashions may change, this rule has remained firm, applying to ties as well as suits. Shirts, on the other hand, should be a contrasting white. Even in the less formal settings, beware of bright colours. Hot

colours are not good for the office; red can be particularly intimidating. Some softer colours are to be avoided, too. To add authority, women should be especially careful to steer clear of pink, baby blue or other colours reminiscent of nurseries. Green, however, is said to be soothing and to show commitment.

These ideas about colour may of course be turned upside down depending on the job you're doing. Research into the uniforms worn by various different professions has meant that some sectors have begun to think about changing away from dark colours towards the pastels. Immigration officers in the UK may soon be following in the footsteps of traffic wardens and wearing softer uniforms in softer colours including soft grey, a sand colour, a pale blue and perhaps even pink. The researchers say that the public would be less intimidated by these people if they were in more approachable colours. One design consultant, however, offers a word of caution that 'smart-casual' is very difficult to pull off, and they may just end up losing their authority.

It is not just where colour is concerned that the rules are largely conservative; and this goes for both men and women. Generally speaking,

employers are more willing to trust conservative dressers. There may be the occasional 'Dress-down Friday', but most of the talk about relaxing the conservative rules is more fashion fantasy than business fact. The truth is that business styles change very little, and there is no point in risking a promotion by gambling on a passing trend. Similarly with jewellery and accessories – there's little authority to be gained from dangly earrings or a cheap digital watch. Keep it simple and classy and if in doubt, leave it out.

So, you're getting the idea now. Make a note of the basic rules and you can't go far wrong. But what else is a no-no? There are a few obvious taboos, such as messy shoes and unironed clothes. Excessive perfume or aftershave is to be avoided, as well as, for women, skirts which are too short and/or too tight, and for men, white socks and bow ties. Other taboos may be less obvious, but no less important for that. Shirts, for example; we know the colour is important but what about the sleeves? Take note: wearing short sleeves to work comes across as far too casual and will completely destroy your professional image, even in hot weather.

There are other things, too, which you may not immediately associate with clothes, but nonetheless contribute to your overall image. Tattoos are becoming more common and prominent; in the US, for example, while only 1% of the population had a tattoo thirty years ago, by 2006 the number had jumped to 24%. Their popularity, however, doesn't mean they are any more accepted in the workplace. Visible body art is often seen as unprofessional and undesirable by co-workers as well as employers. So, if you're keen on expressing yourself through body art, do it at home but cover up at work.

Whether you like it or not, then, a person's success or failure at work depends, to a large extent, on how one dresses. There is one overriding concept that every employee must constantly keep in mind: the way you dress is the single biggest non-verbal message you send about yourself. I can't say that this is necessarily fair, just or moral and I don't expect you to like it. But just remember, in order to get where you want professionally, you want to be known for your talents and energy, not for that pink skirt or those white socks, that cheap jewellery or those trendy tattoos.

3 Look at these sentences from the text and discuss the questions.

A We commit all sorts of suicidal errors when it comes to the image we project in the workplace.

B Women should be especially careful to steer clear of pink, baby blue or other colours reminiscent of nurseries.

1 What does sentence A (from paragraph 1) tell you about the writer's attitude to the type of mistakes people make?

2 What does sentence B (from paragraph 2) tell you about the reasons the writer gives for avoiding these colours?

READING SKILLS
Inferring underlying meaning

When you read a text, it is not always completely obvious what the writer means. Sometimes you need to try to infer the underlying meaning from the actual words, phrases and sentences the writer uses. Think about why the writer chose particular words or phrases and what effect he or she hoped they would have on the reader.

4 For each question 1–7, choose the answer A, B, C or D which you think fits best according to the text.

1 In the first paragraph, the writer suggests that
   A many people don't believe that physical appearance is very important.
   B you shouldn't rely on your common sense alone when choosing your clothes.
   C your professional image and your personal image are likely to be different.
   D dressing appropriately for work does not need a great deal of effort.

2 What is one of the most important rules about colour?
   A You can wear brighter clothes in less formal job situations.
   B As long as you wear a dark suit, you can wear a brighter coloured tie.
   C Ties and suits should be dark but you should wear a lighter shirt.
   D Softer colours are only suitable for women.

3 According to the writer, what is the advantage of softer colour uniforms?
   A They look more fashionable.
   B They promote better relationships.
   C They make the person wearing them feel happier.
   D They make it easier to identify different jobs.

4 What does the writer say about the relationship between fashion and business?

A that the business world is becoming more fashionable

B that the bigger your promotion, the more fashionable you can be

C that it is advisable to largely ignore trends when dressing for business

D that you should never wear jewellery if you want to be taken seriously in business

5 What does the writer think about short-sleeved shirts?

A Short sleeves are fine in more casual jobs.

B Short sleeves are acceptable if it's very hot.

C The length of sleeves is less important than the colour.

D Long sleeves are far more professional than short sleeves.

6 According to the writer, tattoos are

A unlikely to affect your image if they are discreet.

B a good way of expressing yourself in certain jobs.

C acceptable in non-professional jobs.

D becoming increasingly popular at work.

7 What is the writer's message in the last paragraph about the rules for what not to wear at work?

A Wearing the wrong clothes may not matter if you are very talented.

B Although you may not always approve of the rules, they are essential.

C Most people like their professional image in the end, even if they don't expect to at first.

D Being known for breaking the rules can sometimes get you where you want professionally.

5 Discuss these questions with another student.

1 How far do you agree with this quote from the article? Why?
A person's success or failure at work depends, to a large extent, on how one dresses.

2 Which of the rules in the article surprises you most, and which do you disagree with most strongly? Why?

Grammar | question forms

1 There are mistakes in seven of these questions. Find the mistakes and correct them. Use the Grammar Reference to help you if necessary.

1 What you think about wearing bright colours at work?

2 Do you know if you're allowed to wear short sleeves?

3 Tell me what do you usually wear to work?

4 Who did tell you to cover up your tattoos?

5 You've bought some new shoes again, haven't you?

6 Didn't you wear those earrings at your interview, did you?

7 Are you going to wear the white shirt, aren't you?

8 About which earrings are you talking?

9 Cover up those tattoos, would you?

10 Hardly anybody wears a suit where we work, don't they?

• • see grammar reference: page 184 • •

2 R.39 ▶ Listen and check your answers.

3 You are going to do a class survey about clothes. First with a partner, choose a topic for your survey, (e.g. Clothes at work, Uniforms, Things you would never wear, etc.) by using your own ideas or looking at the ideas below.

- most/least favourite colours at work/out of work
- colours you would never wear
- most/least favourite styles at work/out of work
- styles you would never wear
- attitudes to bright colours/dark colours/pastel colours
- uniforms (work and school) – preferences, advantages and disadvantages
- formal/informal clothes – work, leisure, social occasions, etc.
- 'Dress-down Fridays' – advantages and disadvantages
- tattoos, piercings, hairstyles, etc.
- cultural differences in clothes and appearance
- TV shows about 'what (not) to wear', 'makeovers', etc.

4 In pairs, write six questions about your topic to ask other students. Use a variety of question types.

5 Ask your questions to other students, making brief notes of the answers.

6 Report back to the class on the most interesting thing you found out.

Vocabulary | using precise vocabulary

1 Find the two verbs used in the article on pages 126–127 instead of the verbs highlighted in these sentences. What do the verbs in the article give you that these verbs do not? Why?

Although John T Molloy, in his classic book *Dress for Success*, says that 'The first rule of dress is common sense,' many of us it seems, do not have the required common sense. He says that we commit all sorts of suicidal errors when it comes to the image we project in the workplace.

2 Using more precise vocabulary in your writing, rather than repeating the main verb, makes it more interesting. Look at the verbs in the table and write the main verb for each one.

A: _____	B: _____	C: _____
declare	flick	scrawl
claim	browse	scribble
mumble	skim	jot down
stutter	scan	make a note of
gossip	pore	fill in
chat	plough	print

3 Check the meanings in the Exam Reviser. Then choose three of the verbs that you'd like to remember and write an example sentence for each.

exam reviser p15 | 12.2

4 Now write your sentences from the Exam Reviser leaving a gap for the verbs (and prepositions if necessary). Test other students.

I waited ages in the hairdresser's and spent the time _____ a fashion magazine really slowly.

premium plus 49

Writing | letter

1 Read the writing task and answer these questions.

1 Who is the intended reader of your letter?
2 What is the main aim of your letter, a) to give information and your opinion, or b) to outline a problem and suggest solutions?

Writing task

Last month you went on a training course for work. The Director of Training in your company has written to you asking about it. Read the extract from his letter and from your diary below. Then, using the information appropriately, write a letter to the Director of Training saying whether or not you would recommend this course to other people in your company and giving your reasons.

> I'd like to know about some of the things you did and if you learned anything new. Basically, I need to know if it's worth paying for other people to take this course.
>
> Thanks for your help.
> *Director of Training*

Day 1: Working in a team		
a.m.	Team-building	*Good ideas – fun and relevant*
p.m.	Negotiating skills	*Interesting but nothing new*
Day 2: Being a leader		
a.m.	Public speaking	*Gaining confidence – very useful*
p.m.	Socialising at work	*Small talk, etc. – very good*

2 Work in pairs and follow these instructions.

1 Underline all the parts in the task which ask you to give information in your letter. Underline all the parts which provide information for you to include.
2 Circle all the parts in the task which ask you to give your opinion and to give reasons for your opinion. Circle all the parts which provide clues about your opinion and your reasons.
3 Write some brief notes to help you extend the points you need to include, with reasons and examples to support what you are saying.

WRITING SKILLS
Expanding and developing notes

It is important to be able to expand and develop the notes you are given in order to include all the relevant details in your writing.

- identify which notes refer to which parts of the task
- put them together in an appropriate order
- add your own ideas (reasons, examples, etc.) to support and extend your answer

3 Write a paragraph plan for your letter, making notes about which parts of the task you will include in each paragraph. Look at the model in the Writing Reference to help you.

•• see writing reference: **page 205** ••

4 Write your letter in 180–220 words, using your plan and your notes. Make sure you expand and develop the notes from the task appropriately.

5 Check your writing, especially for correct use of punctuation and use of a range of vocabulary.

Grammar

1 There are mistakes in five of these sentences. Find the mistakes and correct them.

1 Your advices were very helpful and I'd be grateful for any more information you could give me.
2 Today's news are full of speculation about the new team which is playing in the final on Saturday.
3 In the distance, he heard a rumble of thunder and then a sudden stroke of wind made him shiver.
4 I thought the cast of that new musical was brilliant but apparently the audience weren't impressed.
5 I've done some researches on the Internet to find some cheap accommodation in Paris, where I'm staying next weekend.
6 Aerobics are one of my favourite ways of keeping fit and I've bought some great new leggings to wear.

2 For each direct question, write an indirect question starting with the words given.

1 Where were you when I called yesterday evening?
   I'd like to know _____?
2 Are you going to wear that lovely new dress you bought?
   Can you tell me _____?
3 What happened to the minutes of the meeting?
   Do you know _____?
4 Did he pay back that money he owed you?
   Would you mind telling me _____?
5 Who told you about my promotion?
   I want to know _____?

3 Add appropriate question tags to these sentences.

1 He's got that new job, _____?
2 She can't play the violin as well as she says, _____?
3 Don't let him upset you, _____?
4 Nobody knows what happened, _____?
5 Let's go shopping at the weekend, _____?

Vocabulary

4 Complete the text using words and phrases in the box. Four of them cannot be used.

> works from home   work nine-to-five   work overtime
> work shifts   on duty   employee   commuters   colleagues
> trainee   job satisfaction   job security   perks   unsocial hours
> work-related stress   understaffed   overcrowded

Welcome, I'm your virtual receptionist

When Anna Morris of Silicon Valley, Northern California was a regular _____[1], working as a hotel receptionist, she suffered from _____[2]. With guests often arriving during the night, she couldn't just _____[3] but had to _____[4] – often getting up at three in the morning. By 4.30 a.m. she would join the other _____[5] battling across the city on _____[6] roads by whichever means they could.

Sixteen hours later, she would arrive back home, completely exhausted, hardly seeing her family at all. Although Anna enjoyed her work, having to work such _____[7] meant that she had little _____[8]. Then one day, she found out about video-conferencing systems; one thing led to another and now, instead of the daily 130-kilometre drive, Anna _____[9], taking just a few steps to her workplace – a bedroom in her own house.

Guests still go up to the reception desk as usual but instead of the flesh and blood version, they can talk to Anna via a giant TV screen. As the world's first virtual hotel receptionist, she is still often _____[10] at all hours of the night, and she misses seeing her _____[11] at the hotel every day. However, she feels the _____[12] of working in this way make her the luckiest person on earth. 'I am thankful I have this chance to work and enjoy my children and home,' she says.

5 Choose the correct alternatives.

1 I spent ages slowly *browsing/flicking/ploughing* through the magazines in the dentist's waiting room.
2 He *scribbled down/jotted down/printed* his address clearly at the top of the application form.
3 He *claims/declares/stutters* to have proved the existence of life on Mars but there is no concrete evidence for his theories.
4 I quickly *skimmed/scanned/pored over* the notice board to see which platform my train was leaving from.
5 You should *make a note of/fill in/scrawl down* my phone number in case you need it later.
6 It's upsetting when people spend all their time *gossiping/chatting/mumbling* about other people.

New science, old beliefs

luck

science fiction

technology

Unit 13

Introduction

1 Discuss these questions with other students.

1 How are the things in pictures a and b connected with luck? What other symbols of luck do you know?

2 How far do you think luck is:
- completely beyond our control?
- down to individual skill or hard work?
- explainable scientifically?

2 Picture c shows some of the characters in the science fiction TV series *Heroes*. Discuss these questions with another student.

1 Are you interested in science fiction and stories/films which are beyond real human experience? Why/Why not?

2 What science fiction (TV, films, books) is popular in your country? Have you got a favourite?

3 Look at pictures d and e and discuss these questions.

1 What branches of science do the pictures represent? Can you name two other branches of science? Check your ideas in the Exam Reviser.

2 Which two branches of science listed in the Exam Reviser are you most interested in? Why?

exam reviser p17 | 13.1

CAE close-up | Listening Multiple matching (Paper 4, part 4)

Exam information

In this part of the exam, you hear five short monologues which are all related to the same theme. Each lasts about 30 seconds. You need to complete two different tasks, both of which require you to select the correct options for each speaker from a list of eight. You listen to the recording twice. You have 5 minutes at the end to transfer your answers to an answer sheet.

Approach

1 Read the information about the recording and the rubrics and lists in both Task One and Task Two. Read the lists in both tasks very carefully and try to think about what words/phrases you might hear. This will help you

focus on what to listen for and can help lead you to the answers.

2 As you listen the first time, try to complete both tasks at the same time.

3 When you listen for the second time, check the answers you put the first time and try to complete any you missed.

4 Check your answers and make sure you've written something for each one. Remember you cannot lose marks for an incorrect answer.

5 At the end of the Listening test, make sure you transfer your answers to your answer sheet very carefully. Check you have the right answer by the correct number.

Practice task

R.40 ▶ You will hear five short extracts in which people are talking about the superpowers that different characters in the TV series *Heroes* have.

While you listen you must complete both tasks.

TASK ONE

For questions **1–5**, choose from the list **A–H** the ability each person has.

A to become invisible

B to predict the future

C to heal oneself very quickly

D to fly like a bird

E to stretch one's body

F to move in space and time

G to read people's minds

H to influence technology

Speaker 1: ☐ **1**

Speaker 2: ☐ **2**

Speaker 3: ☐ **3**

Speaker 4: ☐ **4**

Speaker 5: ☐ **5**

TASK TWO

For questions **6–10**, choose from the list **A–H** what the speaker says about how the power might work in real life.

A some people say they've done it but it is unproven

B evidence about animals shows it is impossible

C evidence from humans and animals shows it might be possible

D it's clear even to ordinary people that it is not possible

E some people have shown that they have similar abilities

F evidence about humans shows only a tiny part can be achieved

G it's likely that it will be possible in the near future

H what scientists say they can do is different from the actual power

Speaker 1: ☐ **6**

Speaker 2: ☐ **7**

Speaker 3: ☐ **8**

Speaker 4: ☐ **9**

Speaker 5: ☐ **10**

Go to www.iTests.com or your CD-ROM for interactive exam practice

Speaking

1 With a partner discuss which two superpowers in Task One in the listening would you most like to have? Give reasons.

2 You are going to listen to two students talking about these pictures and questions. Write three adjectives for each picture which you think you might hear.

- What different aspects of scientific invention or discovery do they show?
- How might the people be feeling?

3 R.41 ▶ Listen and tick your adjectives as you hear them. Make a note of any others you hear.

4 Put these ways of describing contrasting pictures and ideas into the correct places in the skills box.

1 Add an intensifier to the same adjective/idea
2 Refer to a previous similar idea
3 Add a negative to the same adjective/idea
4 Say in what ways the idea is different

SPEAKING SKILLS
Ways of contrasting pictures and ideas

A _____

… these new legs which must have changed his life.
Computers have also changed our lives.

B _____

Computers have also changed our lives …
but I think we take computers for granted in our lives these days.

C _____

This is an amazing scientific invention.
The computer is also absolutely amazing.

D _____

He's feeling very pleased with himself.
The man at the computer doesn't look so cheerful!

5 Check your answers in the Exam Reviser.

exam reviser ▶ p25 | 15

6 Work in pairs. Follow these instructions and take turns to be A and B.

Student A: Choose two of the pictures on this page to compare. Answer the questions and compare the pictures, using the strategies in the skills box.
Student B: Listen and note down which of the strategies Student A uses.

premium plus ▶ 50

Vocabulary | verb + noun collocations

1 Choose the correct verbs in the box to complete the collocations in *italics* in these sentences.

> make do pay have lose give take break

1 He _____ *the impression* of being a very proud and determined person.
2 I think it _____ *sense* to say that the computer is the most important invention.

2 Look at the table of verb + noun collocations in the Exam Reviser and put each of the verbs in Exercise 1 into the correct place.

exam reviser ▶ p17 | 13.2

3 <u>Underline</u> any collocations in the table in the Exam Reviser which you are unsure about the meaning of. Work with a partner and check you both understand all of them. Use a dictionary if necessary.

4 Choose the correct alternatives.

1 I didn't *give/make/pay* much attention to my science lessons at school.
2 I'd like to *take/have/do* a go at inventing a new computer game.
3 I *lost/broke/took* interest in computer games ages ago.
4 I've never used voice technology before but I'd like to *make/take/give* it a try.
5 I'd like to *do/make/take* research into some aspect of medical science.
6 I don't think anyone will ever *break/make/do* the record for running 100 metres in less than 9.77 seconds.
7 I disagree with genetic engineering as I think we are *having/taking/making* too many risks with our health.
8 I don't like science fiction films because you need to *make/give/pay* too much effort to understand them.

5 Which of the sentences in Exercise 4 are true for you? Which are false? Explain why to your partner.

premium plus ▶ 51

Grammar | quantifiers – phrases

1 Underline all the grammatically possible alternatives in each sentence. Use the Grammar Reference if necessary.

1 *Both/All/Neither/Either/None/No* of them claim to be able to read people's minds.

2 In the TV series *Heroes*, *each/every/one/another/ other/one another/each other* person has an amazing superpower.

3 There is *much/many/a lot of/few/a few/little/a little/most* evidence to prove that life exists on other planets.

4 If I had a superpower, I'd like to be able to fly *any/some/ anywhere/somewhere/nowhere* I wanted.

•• see grammar reference: **page 185** ••

Grammar note | *verb agreement*

Look at the verbs in *italics* and say which are incorrect and why.

1 Both of them *studies* molecular biology at university.

2 Neither of the films I got *are* science fiction.

3 None of them *have* ever seen the TV series *Heroes*.

4 Everybody I've spoken to *wants* to be able to fly.

5 Each superpower *has* its own benefits.

6 Someone *have* taken my science homework.

2 Complete the sentences with the most appropriate phrase in the box.

> every single time   every last   each and every one
> one by one   all too often   every so often
> every reason   no reason why   nothing less than
> nowhere near   not much of a   by any means

1 He's a brilliant scientist, but he's _____ teacher.

2 There is _____ you shouldn't pass your physics exam.

3 _____ you come across a new invention which sounds too good to be true.

4 I'd like to thank _____ of you for helping us finish the project on time.

5 We have _____ to believe that he will go on to become a famous scientist.

6 We're expecting _____ the best from you all.

7 _____ people say they can't do something, when actually they're really capable.

8 She's quite good at her subject but she's not _____ an expert.

9 The evidence we've got at the moment is _____ enough to prove the sceptics wrong.

10 _____ I meet him, he tells me about his new invention.

11 Even when the teacher went through the answers _____, I still didn't understand.

12 I searched through _____ cupboard before I found my iPod.

3 R.42 ▶ Listen to the sentences and check your answers.

4 Work in pairs. Check you understand the meaning of the phrases in Exercise 2 by saying each sentence in your own words.

5 Look at the highlighted syllables in the sentences on page 166. Think about the pronunciation and say what you think they have in common.

6 R.42 ▶ Listen to the sentences again. Check your answers and mark any other weak forms that you hear. Repeat the sentences with correct pronunciation.

7 Read the text and think of a word which best fits each gap. Use only one word in each gap.

THE 'MAGIC WARDROBE'

How do you feel about clothes shopping? _____[1] too often, it becomes a chore – something that we begin to dread. We hate _____[2] single thing in the wardrobe, nothing fits or matches. If that's you, the 'Magic Wardrobe' could be the answer. Every _____[3] often, something comes onto the market which changes your life – and there's _____[4] reason to believe that this could be it!

Designers in the US have come up with some new technology which could transform your wardrobe into _____[5] less than your own personal shopper. You could soon be cataloguing all your clothes, one _____[6] one, with a special tag. The 'Magic Wardrobe' would then know all about _____[7] and every one of your pieces of clothing, including its colour, size and brand. There is then _____[8] reason why the system couldn't check every new purchase you make against your old stuff, and make sure you were buying the right thing. It could also suggest clothes combinations you could try or inform you when you need to buy something new. According to the designers, it is _____[9] near as complicated as it sounds, and anyone can use it.

And the system doesn't, by _____[10] means, have to be restricted to clothes. Perhaps you're not _____[11] of a cook? A 'Magic Kitchen' could keep track of _____[12] last bit of food in your cupboards and suggest recipes based on what you've bought, or help you to maintain a healthy diet. The possibilities are endless!

8 Discuss these questions with another student.

1 What do you think about the idea of having a 'magic wardrobe' or a 'magic kitchen'? Why?

2 Can you think of anything else this technology could be used for?

premium plus   52 ▶

134

Writing | proposal

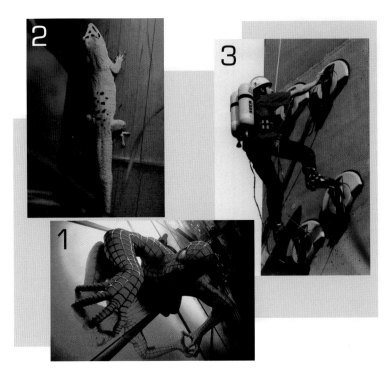

1 Look at the pictures and discuss these questions with other students.

1 What powers does Spiderman (in picture 1) have? Can you name two other superheroes and their superpowers?

2 What powers do geckos (in picture 2) have? Can you think of two other animals with 'special powers'?

3 Scientists sometimes get ideas for new inventions from their imagination (e.g. from superheroes) or from looking at animals (e.g. the gecko). The man in picture 3 is using a new invention called a Gekkomat. How do you think it works? What uses do you think it could have?

4 What other inventions do you think scientists could come up with based on superheroes or animals?

2 Look at the writing task. What three things do you need to include in your proposal?

3 Work in pairs. Brainstorm some ideas for your proposal and decide on a topic for each paragraph. Write them in this plan. Look at the model in the Writing Reference to remind you about planning a proposal.

Paragraph 1
Topic: *Introduction – say the purpose of the proposal*
Topic sentence: *The purpose of this proposal is to explain why the college should subsidise a student visit to a science exhibition.*

Paragraph 2
Topic:
Topic sentence:

Paragraph 3
Topic:
Topic sentence:

Paragraph 4
Topic:
Topic sentence:

•• see writing reference: page 192 ••

4 Now write a topic sentence for each paragraph, which clearly states the main point of that paragraph.

WRITING SKILLS
Topic sentences

It is important to think about topic sentences at the planning stage of your writing. Writing a topic sentence for each paragraph in your plan will help you organise your writing in a logical way and make sure that the reader knows what each paragraph is about.

5 Write your proposal in 220–260 words using your paragraph plan and topic sentences. Remember that you need to persuade the reader of your point of view.

Writing task

You are studying at a college in the UK. A science exhibition is on in a nearby city and you and some fellow students would like to visit it as part of your course.

Talks good for my English.

Read the advert for the exhibition and some comments from other students. Then using the information appropriately write a proposal to the principal of your college outlining what the exhibition is about, explaining how you and the other students would benefit from visiting the exhibition and persuading the principal to contribute to the costs of the visit.

Superheroes Exhibition

Look, no hands!
Have a go at 'cranial gaming' – video games using just your brain.

The bionic man!
Try out new household robots.

Climb like a gecko!
Talks on new inventions – including the 'Gekkomat'.

Opportunity to meet people interested in science.

Need to find out about latest video games.

Reading

1 Look at this quote. What point do you think Jefferson is making, 1, 2 or 3?

I'm a great believer in luck, and I find the harder I work, the more I have of it.
Thomas Jefferson

1 If you work hard you will be lucky.
2 There is no such thing as luck.
3 Hard work enables you to make the most of luck.

2 Why is giving an example or illustrating an idea more effective than just giving an opinion?

3 You are going to read three texts that are all connected in some way with the topic of luck. For questions 1–6, choose the answer A, B, C or D that fits best with what you read.

Do you feel lucky?

Believe it or not, the way that you answer that question is a predictor of your level of success and joy in life. Dr Richard Wiseman, a psychologist at the University of Hertfordshire, has proved scientifically that luck isn't a coincidence. Lucky people think and act with specific behaviours that open the way for good things to happen. Wiseman has investigated the science of luck and found four scientific principles of luck, which he claims could 'quite simply, change your luck and your life'.

Wiseman discovered that the first principle of luck is to maximise opportunities. Everyone is estimated to know about 300 people, so chatting to someone on the train could open up hundreds of doors. Lucky people also tend to have a relaxed attitude to life, allowing them to notice opportunities around them. Secondly, listening to lucky hunches needs trust and an ability to act on intuition. Wiseman proved that boosting intuition – for example, through techniques such as meditation – can also improve luck. Thirdly, lucky people's expectations about the future help them fulfil their dreams and ambitions. Lucky people tend to persevere more in the face of failure and let their more positive attitude about the future motivate them to achieve their goals. The final principle involves turning bad luck into good fortune by refusing to dwell on ill fortune. Lucky people learn from their bad experiences and take constructive steps to prevent more bad luck in the future.

1 Why does the writer use the example of chatting to people on a train?
   A to show how easy it is to talk to people
   B to illustrate where people can make contact with each other
   C to demonstrate how many people you can speak to in this situation
   D to show how a chance encounter can lead to something important

2 What does the author say about lucky people?
   A They refuse to acknowledge that bad luck exists.
   B They see bad luck as an opportunity to learn something.
   C They try to prevent bad luck affecting their lives.
   D They are able to prevent bad luck happening to them.

4 Discuss these questions with other students.
   1 Do you think some people are just lucky? Why/Why not?
   2 Can you think of anything 'lucky' that happened to you which has a more logical explanation?
   3 Would you be prepared to make random decisions like Luke Reinhardt? Why/Why not?

My lucky day

I am living proof that luck is more than chance. I have now met over 100,000 people and I am sure this is the reason I now earn a six-figure income! The income is from my books and public speaking and other people constantly comment on how lucky I am, but luck has got nothing to do with it. My luck came about from hard work. I spent five years working all hours, doing night jobs while I was writing and earning no money. A few years ago I hit on the novel idea of wearing a nametag 24/7 to encourage people to talk to me. This taps into one of the key elements of luck, which is networking.

At first, I seemed to be getting nowhere. Then, one day I was sitting on a bus and this guy started talking to me about the book I was writing. He gave me his business card and said he would buy me a drink when my book came out. I never heard from him again. However, the next day the editor of my local paper phoned me about my book and ended up doing a news article about it that was syndicated nationwide, so my book sold loads on the back of that. Only much later did I realise that this editor was the girlfriend of the guy on the bus!

3 The writer implies other people think he is lucky because
A he has a career as a writer and public speaker.
B he seems to have achieved his success easily.
C he has had the opportunity to meet so many people.
D he managed to hit on an interesting and novel idea.

4 The writer mentions his meeting on the bus to illustrate that the most important feature of luck is
A approachability.
B networking.
C expertise.
D commitment.

THE DICE MAN

5 How does the writer suggest the main character in *The Dice Man* feels about his dice life?
A He is worried about where his dice life will lead.
B He is concerned about the decisions he is making.
C He becomes confident that living by the dice is the best way.
D He is happier taking risks than living safely.

6 The author of *The Dice Man* experimented with living his life by the dice in order to
A improve his academic scores.
B construct a new personality.
C get out of a routine.
D change the way he taught his classes.

Imagine that every decision you made in life was governed by chance, specifically the role of a die. That is just what the hero of Luke Reinhardt's *The Dice Man* does. The main character is a world-weary psychologist who, inspired by an intriguing happenstance, one day makes a decision. He lists half a dozen options, then rolls the die to decide which one he should follow. The result pushes his boundaries and opens up a new set of experiences. Bit by bit, he hands his life over to decisions made by a roll of the die. The result is a hilarious rampage of a novel as he infects others with his ideas and injects a pattern of chaos into the order of his urbane, successful world.

It contrasts with the author's own dicing lifestyle – he says he started rolling dice to break down his shyness and stuffiness as an academically-inclined teenager. He saw rolling a die as a means to break away from habit and reformulate himself. The author insists that life is too precious to just allow it to drift, to allow habit to dictate, making the same decision again and again. But, not until he was teaching psychology did he pose the question to one of his classes, asking them whether the ultimate freedom lay in making all decisions randomly, by the throw of the die. Thus were sown the seeds of *The Dice Man*. This novel will outrage some, it will intrigue others, it might inspire ... you might even find yourself looking in the toy cupboard for a set of dice.

Grammar | emphasis with inversion

1 Complete these sentences. Use the texts on pages 136–137 to help you.

1 Not until he was teaching psychology _____ pose the question to one of his classes.

2 Only much later _____ realise that this editor was the girlfriend of the guy on the bus.

2 Work in pairs. For each sentence in Exercise 1 decide:

• which verb is inverted;

• what aspect of meaning is emphasised;

• the effect of changing the order of information in this way.

3 Complete these sentences. Use the pronoun and the correct form of the verb in brackets and any other words that are necessary. Use the Grammar Reference to help you.

1 Not only _____ (I/be) interested in the exhibits, _____ I found the lectures very interesting as well.

2 Hardly _____ (she/finish) the game, _____ she saw there was another level.

3 No sooner _____ (they/develop) the vaccine _____ a new strain of the virus occurred.

4 Only _____ (he/see) the film _____ (realise) how clever the special effects were.

5 Little _____ (I/ realise) the problems the experiment would cause.

6 Never before _____ (she/conduct) such difficult research.

7 At no time _____ (he/feel) confident in the data he was using.

8 In no circumstances _____ (you/leave) the lab unlocked.

•• see grammar reference: **page 186** ••

4 Look at the completed sentences in Exercise 3 and decide which information is emphasised in each one.

5 R.43 Listen to three people telling stories about strange coincidences. Underline the words which are stressed in these sentences.

1 Not until they turned up at the house was I aware I knew them both!

2 Only then did I realise how strange this was.

3 But little did they imagine how attached the house was to them!

6 Do you think there is a more scientific explanation to any of these stories, or are they just 'coincidences'? Give reasons.

7 Follow these instructions.

1 Write a short story about a strange coincidence you know. This may have happened to you or to somebody else. Use one of the structures in Exercise 3 in your story.

2 Read your story to a partner. Remember to use stress in your sentences to make it sound dramatic.

premium plus 53–▶

Improving your pronunciation

Which do you think is the most important aspect of English pronunciation? Why?

1 individual sounds

2 stress

3 intonation

Need help?

• Make sure you know which sounds are difficult for a speaker of your language, e.g. /θ/, the difference between /r/ and /l/ or /ʃ/ and /s/. Practise these sounds.

• Remember to stress the important words or new information in a sentence.

• Underline the stressed syllable when you record new words.

• In a conversation, think carefully about your intonation at the end of your turn.

learning tip

Vocabulary | multi-word verbs – science and research

1 Look at the multi-word verbs in these sentences and decide what they mean. Use the Exam Reviser to help you.

1 He *set about* proving that luck could be explained scientifically.

2 The explosion *set off* a series of smaller bangs.

3 We had to abandon the research because the money *dried up*.

4 The team *set out* to develop a new way of creating special effects in films.

5 The research *brought about* a change in the way cars were tested for safety.

6 The idea *fizzled out* because it didn't have much support.

exam reviser p17 | 13.3 ▶

2 For each multi-word verb in Exercise 1, underline the particular verb or noun it goes with in the sentence.

3 Each of the multi-word verbs can collocate with other particular verbs or nouns. Match each multi-word verb in Exercise 1 with the groups of words A–F that they typically collocate with. Some may come before the verb.

A to achieve, to prove, to demonstrate, to show, to discover
B enthusiasm, conversation, interest
C doing, showing, demonstrating, developing
D funding, resources, supply, work, orders
E improvements, advances
F a crisis, a debate

4 Choose three verbs and write sentences of your own using their collocations in Exercise 3. Compare your sentences with a partner.

5 Work in two groups, A and B, and look at your box. Find out the meaning of these verbs in a scientific context. Use a good dictionary, such as the *Longman Dictionary of Phrasal Verbs*, to help you.

A | set up   spark off   finish off

B | start off   stir up   wind down

6 Work in A/B pairs and teach your verbs to your partner. Then add them to the Exam Reviser.

exam reviser   p17 | 13.3

7 Complete the text with the correct form of the verbs from Exercises 1 and 5.

The science of positive thinking

Lucky people expect success, moving beyond the 'glass-half-full' power of positive thinking. They are skilled at noticing things and this alone ____1 new possibilities. An American psychologist measured this facility when he ____2 an experiment asking 400 subjects (people who thought of themselves as lucky and unlucky) to count the number of photographs in a newspaper. Everybody ____3 to try to show they were the most accurate, so they started counting very carefully. At the third page was a large advertisement that boldly declared: STOP COUNTING! THERE ARE FORTY-THREE PHOTOGRAPHS IN THIS NEWSPAPER. Lucky people noticed, stopped counting, laughed and asked if they should keep going. Yes, they were told, keep counting. This ____4 a competitive streak in the 'unlucky' group who saw the others had stopped and thought that they were ahead of the game. Further along there was another advertisement that read: STOP COUNTING! TELL THE EXPERIMENTOR YOU'VE SEEN THIS AND WIN £150. Once again, the people who considered themselves lucky consistently noticed the advertisement. In contrast, the 'unlucky' ones flipped right past it. So the so-called lucky group actually ____5 their own luck!

8 Discuss with another student what you think you would have done in this experiment and why.

CAE close-up | Writing Contribution (Paper 2, part 2)

Exam information

In part 2 of the Writing exam, you may be given the choice of writing a contribution. This will normally be a contribution to a larger piece of writing, such as a guidebook, a research project or a book.

Approach

1 Read the question and think carefully about whether you know enough information to answer it. A contribution often asks you to refer to your own country, so make sure you do this if required.

2 Think about what your piece of writing is a contribution to and how that will affect the tone and style of your writing. For example, a guidebook entry may be more informal than a contribution to a research project.

3 Make a list of points you need to include and plan your answer.

4 Remember to use topic sentences to guide your reader.

5 Make sure you write within the number of words given.

Practice task

A friend of yours is doing a research project on attitudes to science in different countries. The friend has asked you to write a contribution to the project saying how popular science is as a subject in your country, explaining why it is popular or unpopular and saying whether you think attitudes will remain the same in the future.

Write your **contribution** to the project. Write **220–260** words.

Go to www.iTests.com or your CD-ROM for interactive exam practice

Grammar

1 There are mistakes in these sentences. Find the mistakes and correct them.

1 This homework was anywhere near as difficult as last week's.
2 All very often you don't get a proper explanation from the doctors.
3 Congratulations on your research paper which was nothing much than brilliant!
4 She is not for any means the most hard-working student in the class.
5 You have each reason to feel proud of your fantastic achievements this term.
6 There's any reason why science can't be made accessible to young people.
7 Every too often someone comes round and checks the safety equipment.
8 It's really annoying because each single time I phone him he's out.

2 Rewrite these sentences using the words given.

1 He thought the experiment would work until he got the initial results.
   Only ...
2 As soon as they arrived at the exhibition they realised they had forgotten their notebooks.
   No sooner ...
3 She didn't realise how difficult it was to use the equipment.
   Little ...
4 I have never seen such an amazing gadget before!
   Never ...
5 He has been successful but he is lucky as well.
   Not only ...
6 I had only just started networking when I was offered a job.
   Hardly ...

Vocabulary

3 Complete the text by writing one verb in each gap.

Are computer games good for you?
Almost every newspaper you read these days will _____[1] you the impression that video games are ruining today's youth. It has been reported that they are _____[2] a negative effect on the brain development of young people, as well as making them fat and unhealthy. To my mind, however, people have _____[3] sight of many of the advantages of gaming.

In my opinion, gaming is good for you and more parents should let their children _____[4] advantage of the benefits it offers. Cognitive scientists in New York have _____[5] research that concludes gaming improves your concentration, attention span and hand–eye coordination. What's more, many of the games are directly educational and some children, who _____[6] problems retaining information in the more conventional way, _____[7] far more interest when it is presented via a video game.

Of course, I _____[8] the point that games played to excess are not healthy. The same is true of most things done to excess. But it clearly _____[9] sense to say that many different cognitive functions are required for these games. They require children to _____[10] attention for an extended time, as well as needing puzzle-solving abilities and lateral thinking. It's time to think again about computer games.

4 Complete the sentences by using the correct form of one of the multi-word verbs in box A together with a word in box B that it collocates with.

A	B
fizzle out	improvements
spark off	funding
dry up	strong feelings
bring about	a debate
stir up	to prove
set out	enthusiasm

1 We wanted to continue our research but the _____ _____ so we had to abandon it.
2 Technological changes have _____ huge _____ in the way we work.
3 Some genetic research has _____ _____ about how far we should allow this research to continue.
4 Recent research into animal cloning has _____ _____ among many sections of the public.
5 At first my tutor was interested in my project but then his _____ _____ so I lost interest, too.
6 We were _____ _____ that luck was explainable scientifically.

A different perspective

identity

rat race

culture shock

Unit 14

Grammar: complex sentences; causative *have* and *get* | Vocabulary: word pairs; fixed phrases with *change* | Writing: set text

Introduction

1 Find out what these expressions mean and match them to the most suitable pictures. Explain your choices.

> culture shock   get out of the rat race   a fish out of water
> selling up, moving on   you haven't lived

2 Have you ever experienced culture shock? If so, when and why?

3 Look at these aspects of change people may have to deal with when they arrive in a new culture. Which would you find the most difficult and the least difficult to deal with? Compare and discuss your answers with a partner, giving reasons.

- language
- daily life
- culture and customs
- weather and location

4 Discuss these questions with another student.

1 What situation do you think the man in picture c is in? Why?
2 Why do you think people may want to change the way they live?
3 How do you think living in a different way might change you?

Unit 14

CAE close-up | Reading Gapped text (Paper 1, part 2)

Exam information

This part of the exam consists of a text in which there are six gaps. You complete the gaps with the paragraphs which follow the text. There is one extra paragraph which does not fit any of the gaps.

Approach

1 Read the whole text through, including the title, to get the general idea of what the text is about and a feeling for the flow of the text.

2 Read all the extracted paragraphs to get a sense of the subject of each one.

3 Look at each gap in the text and what comes before and after it. If you are sure about what should go in any of the gaps, make a note of your ideas.

4 Look carefully at the remaining gaps. Look for clues to help you decide which paragraphs complete them. Are there any referring words such as *that, him, the problem* which refer to something or someone in the previous paragraph? Are there any synonyms of words in the previous paragraph? Also think carefully about the logical ordering of the text.

5 Decide on one paragraph for each gap. Read the complete text through with the completed gaps. Does it all make sense?

6 Make sure you have filled all the gaps and have not used any paragraph more than once.

Practice task

You are going to read a newspaper article about a man who made a television programme about hidden tribes. Six paragraphs have been removed from the article. Choose from the paragraphs A–G the one which fits each gap (1–6). There is one extra paragraph which you do not need to use.

The Tribesman

Bruce Parry has been living with tribal communities for his television programme, Tribe.

Parry is the *Tribe* guy; he goes and lives with tribal communities around the world – in Africa, in South America, in the frozen wastes of Greenland, the Himalayas and in the steamy jungles of south-east Asia – for the successful BBC programme of the same name.

But it also raises issues to do with the global environmental and cultural threats that we know exist but that we don't know what best to do about. Although recognised to some extent, traditional tribal wisdom is still not valued enough, so the programme challenges our view of commercialism and perceptions of our individual, materialistic world.

For his programme, Bruce went and actually lived among each tribe he visited; living as they live. And he came away with a deep respect for the way they work with nature not against it and for their cultural traditions, which while sometimes strange for him, were explained by the environment in which each tribe lives.

Cultural identity is also evident in the different methods of child-rearing and family organisation. For instance, Inuit children are believed to be the incarnations of elders and are given the respect and freedom to evolve, slowly learning from the world around them. Other cultures are more rule-bound and many have strict divisions between genders and age groups.

Change is more difficult. Parry says, 'Of course we change them a little bit, but we have to ask whether change is good or not, and that's a big old issue in its own right. As long as it's done correctly and they are aware of what's going to happen to them, then there's nothing wrong with that either.'

A The hot debate is about whether programmes like *Tribe* exploit these tribal people, or worse, permanently alter their way of life. Parry is adamant they exploit no one. The programme makers pay their way and the tribes, satisfied with their side of the bargain, are certainly not complaining.

B Bruce says, 'First and foremost, *Tribe* is about looking at the way other people live and asking questions about the way we live. It's about family values, free time, gender, health and sustainable living. It's about everything that we talk about down the pub. Not just me and you, but everyone. All our lives.'

C Is there anything in tribal life that Parry would like to follow and introduce into his own life? 'I've learnt so much from tribal communities. Mostly it's a philosophy for a way to live rather than any particular trait, object or ritual. These lessons have come about from looking at our own culture through fresh eyes.'

D The thought of a non-anthropologist who doesn't speak the language going in and living with tribal communities for a month was abhorrent to the anthropology world. After seeing it, many softened.

Some of the anthropologists still don't like it, but there's quite a lot of discussion about the pros and cons now.

E He continues, 'I've realised the danger in this and the way that these views can be used by others to gain power and control over our lives. I'm no angel, but I try to question everything now and see all sides of the argument where I can.'

F His visits also highlighted the many facets that make up a culture. Language, for example, is what gives an individual their identity and confirms their links with their family, community and culture. More fundamentally, for tribal people who believe that plants and objects in the world around them have souls, there is a magical connection between a word and the object or person it names.

G This knowledge held by indigenous people is informed by a profound understanding of their ancestral territories. Every tribal culture has its own rules and rituals for the treatment of animals and plants, which ensure selective harvesting and sustainable forms of land and wildlife management. Instead of trying to change the world, these traditional cultures seek to know it.

5

'I feel that it's very important to question all of one's own preconceptions. So much of what many of us say and believe in strongly is nothing more than a belief instilled in us from our parents or our peers or our society and yet we have no actual personal experience or true knowledge of that belief or view.'

6

This show is not just about tribal communities, says Parry, it is also a reflection of our own. 'To me, it's all about society – looking at other ways we can live our lives, where we got it right and where we went awry.'

Go to www.iTests.com or your CD-ROM for interactive exam practice

Speaking

1 Look at the pictures. Would you like to experience living in one of these places for a short period? Why/Why not?

2 R.44 ▶ Listen to two people discussing this statement. Decide how certain each speaker is about what they say. Tick the phrases in the box as you hear them.

The knowledge that tribes have about sustained farming can be applied worldwide.

Expressing uncertainty	
As far as I know ...	☐
From what I know ...	☐
I might be wrong but ...	☐
I'm not sure but I've read that ...	☐
I don't know very much about it, but ...	☐
I wonder if that's true ...	☐

3 Look at these statements. Decide how certain you are about the truth of each one.

- Language is the most important feature of our cultural identity.
- Children are children and should be raised the same wherever you live.
- Individual cultures will not survive in the future.

4 Discuss the statements in groups of three or four. Use the Exam Reviser to help you.

eHam reviser   p25 | 16 ▶

5 Compare your opinions with another group. Discuss which statement you were most certain about and which one you were least certain about.

premium plus   55 ▶

Grammar | complex sentences

1 Your writing will be more effective if you use complex sentences. Look at the techniques used in complex sentences A–F. Match them with sentences 1–6. Look at the Grammar Reference to help you.

A a shortened relative clause (Unit 5)
B the use of *It* at the beginning (Unit 9)
C a participle clause (Unit 10)
D inverting a clause for emphasis (Unit 13)
E a very long object
F a clause inside a clause

1 The tribes, satisfied with their side of the bargain, are certainly not complaining.
2 The cameraman, after he had filmed the villagers working in the fields, took a boat down river to film the fishermen.
3 He invited all the tribespeople who had been so kind and hospitable to him to a party in the village hall.
4 It concerned him that people thought he was exploiting the tribes.
5 Little did they realise how much they would miss their homes.
6 Having no means of preserving food, they eat fresh meat only when they hunt and kill an animal.

•• see grammar reference: **page 187** ••

2 Combine these pairs of sentences into one sentence, using the structures from Exercise 1 in brackets. Compare your sentences with a partner.

1 In the remotest parts of the world food is obtained by hunting and gathering. It might need a lot of preparation to make it edible. (C)
2 If you wish to improve your life, *Tribe* taught me that there is a way. This is by paying more attention to those around you. (E)
3 The visitors experienced the warmth of the Nenet people and saw them living in extremely cold surroundings. They realised that this couldn't have been more different. (F)

4 We hadn't been in contact with the outside world for three months. This worried me. (B)

5 I realised that family was more important than material things. I realised this after living with the Adi tribe for a while. (D)

6 The Matis are a tribe who were once devastated by western disease. They are determined to preserve their culture. (A)

3 Decide how each of these techniques can improve your writing.
- by avoiding unnecessary repetition
- by presenting ideas or events concisely
- by emphasising an idea or event

4 Read this extract from *The Enigma of Arrival* by V S Naipaul. How many different types of complex sentences can you find?

It is the 1950s and the author has just arrived from a small island in the Caribbean to live in the UK.

And coming back night after night – after my tourist excursions through London – to this bare house, I was infected by its mood. I took this mood to what I saw. I had no eye for architecture; there had been nothing at home to train my eye. In London I saw pavements, shops, shop blinds, shop signs, undifferentiated buildings. On my tourist excursions I went looking for size. It was one of the things I had travelled to find, coming from my small island. I found size, power in the area around Holborn Viaduct, the Embankment, Trafalgar Square. And after this grandeur there was the boarding house in Earl's Court. So I grew to feel that the grandeur belonged to the past; that I had come to England at the wrong time; that I had come too late to find the England, the heart of empire, which, like a provincial, from a far corner of the empire, I had created in my fantasy. Such a big judgement about a city I had just arrived in.

5 Discuss these questions with another student.

1 Do you like this piece of writing? Why/Why not? What effect do you think is created by using a variety of complex structures?

2 What sort of things do you think we can be disappointed by when we go to another place?

3 Think of a city you would like to visit. What expectations do you have about that city? Why?

6 Choose one of these subjects for a short piece of writing, then follow the instructions 1–3.

A how you think someone arriving in your country for the first time would see your country

B how you might feel arriving somewhere you had always wanted to travel to

1 Make notes on what you want to include.

2 Write a short paragraph using some of the complex sentence structures from Exercise 1.

3 Read your paragraph to a partner and ask for their views.

premium plus 56

Vocabulary | word pairs

1 Look at the article on pages 142–143 and complete these word pairs. Which one expresses emphasis? Which expresses opposite ideas?

first and _____ (paragraph B)
pros and _____ (paragraph D)

2 Complete these pairs with the words in the box. Use the form and meaning of the word to help you.

quiet   times   swim   fro   outs   choose

1 pick and _____
2 to and _____
3 sink or _____
4 peace and _____
5 life and _____
6 ins and _____

3 Put each word pair into the best column in the Exam Reviser.

exam reviser p18 | 14.1

4 Complete these sentences with word pairs from Exercise 2.

1 I'm reading a book about the _____ of Christopher Columbus.

2 I don't know the _____ of the problem but I hope they solve it.

3 She went for a walk in the countryside to get some _____.

4 He hasn't prepared his presentation so he'll have to either _____.

5 _____, they managed to win the public's approval.

6 You'll have to take what you're offered – you can't _____ like that!

7 The tribes move _____ across the valley with the seasons.

5 Ask questions to as many other students as possible, and find someone who:

- likes to pick and choose activities at the weekend, rather than just going along with what their friends are doing
- doesn't mind if they sink or swim when trying something new
- needs at least one hour's peace and quiet a day
- likes to know the ins and outs of their friends lives
- always weighs up the pros and cons before making a decision

premium plus 57

Listening

1 If you lived abroad for a period, what do you think you would find difficult when you returned home? Why?

2 Look at this extract from an interview. <u>Underline</u> the words that have a similar meaning to the highlighted words in the two summary sentences below.

'The weather's a bit of a problem for me, because I can't stand the sun. Today has been horrifically hot. If I ever feel fed up, though, all I have to do is think about Finsbury Park tube station. That's my absolute benchmark of misery. Living in Australia feels brighter, more open, less crowded. I still can't get over our luck just being here.'

1 The speaker doesn't like the weather when it is very _____.
2 He prefers Australia because it is not so _____ as the UK.

3 Which of these words goes in each gap in the sentences in Exercise 2? Why?

1 sunny/hot/horrific
2 bright/open/crowded

LISTENING SKILLS

Writing what you hear

When you have to complete some notes:

- don't repeat what is already on the page
- only write the word(s) you hear, not a paraphrase
- make sure what you write fits the sense and grammar of what is on the page

4 R.45 ▶ You are going to listen to Philip Breech talking about his return to the UK after living abroad. For questions 1–8, complete the sentences.

1 Philip felt that he had learnt a lot from his period of _____.

2 Philip immediately noticed the _____ in the way of life in the UK.

3 Philip was surprised that the UK felt _____.

4 Shortly after his return, Philip participated again in his _____.

5 Philip warns that your friends may not be interested in your _____.

6 When Philip was in Santiago he had felt fairly _____.

7 In the UK, Philip felt disturbed by other people's _____.

8 Philip says that your adventures may be met with _____ by other people.

5 R.45 ▶ Listen again and check your answers.

6 Discuss these questions with other students.

1 Did the speaker find the same things difficult as you predicted in Exercise 1?
2 In the UK, many people who have lived abroad say that if they could change one thing about the UK it would be the food. What feature of your country do you think you would change? Why?
3 Is change always a good thing? Why/Why not?

Vocabulary | fixed phrases with *change*

1 Read these sentences, which use expressions of *change*. Discuss with another student what the expressions might mean.

1 He was going to go and live in Australia but he's had *a change of heart*.
2 At first, he wasn't interested, but he soon *changed his tune* when I told him what he would be paid.
3 If you want me to help you, you'll have to *change your ways*.
4 Bored with your home? Then *ring the changes* by moving your furniture around!
5 Going to live in the countryside meant a complete *change of pace*.
6 The visitors may have everything they need materially, but the tribesmen wouldn't dream of *changing places* with them.
7 If you don't *change with the times*, you'll get left behind.

8 I suggested she *changed tack* and tried to get him to agree by being nice to him.

9 You can't keep *chopping and changing* your mind about the wedding; it's not fair on other people.

2 Replace the words in *italics* in each question with the correct form of an expression from Exercise 1.

Do you like change?

1 Do you ever alter your hairstyle just to *make it more interesting*?
   A Yes, frequently.
   B No, never.

2 Do you like *to do something differently* when you are on holiday?
   A Yes, I like to be more active.
   B Yes, I just like to relax.

3 Do you ever *alter your attitude* about something?
   A Yes, sometimes events can change things.
   B No, I usually keep the same attitude.

4 Do people who keep *altering what they plan to do* irritate you?
   A No, everyone can change their mind.
   B Yes, it's not fair on other people.

5 Do you think it is essential for us all to *accept and use new ways*?
   A Yes, otherwise we will get left behind.
   B No, you should stick with what you know.

6 Would you find it hard to *improve the way you behave*?
   A No, I constantly try to.
   B Yes, I am as I am.

3 Do the quiz. Check your answers on page 166. Compare your answers with another student and discuss reasons for the answers you gave.

4 Put each expression from Exercise 1 into the correct column in the Exam Reviser according to what aspect of change it refers to. Some may go in more than one column.

exam reviser   p18 | 14.2

5 Choose one expression from each of your completed columns. Think of an example to illustrate each expression.

to say you want to go out, then that you don't, then that you do again
= chop and change

6 Read your example to a partner. Can they guess which expression you were illustrating?

premium plus   58

Grammar | causative *have* and *get*

1 Match each sentence 1–4 with its meaning A–D.

1 I was far more likely to have my wallet stolen here at home.
2 Even having my hair cut cost six times more than it did in Brazil.
3 I got my suitcase closed even though it was very full.
4 Get your dirty clothes off the floor now.

A an experience or something unpleasant that happens to someone
B an order or imperative
C a service performed for us by someone else
D something difficult that we succeeded in doing

2 What is the difference between *have* and *get* in these sentences?

1 A I had my car repaired yesterday.
   B I got my car repaired yesterday.

2 A The presenter had us laughing from the first sentence.
   B She got us all to help her with her luggage.

3 Complete the text with the correct form of *have* or *get* and the verb in brackets.

_____ Unexpected pleasures _____

When I went to live in Canada I expected it to be similar to the UK but it wasn't all quite as I had expected. For example, it was really hard _____ our house _____[1] (decorate) because there was a shortage of skilled tradesmen. On the other hand, it was easy to _____ your car _____[2] (clean) as this service was offered at every gas station. Also it was much safer – we have never _____ anything _____[3] (steal). We bought a farm when were out there and the first summer was awful. We only managed _____ the harvesting _____[4] (do) on time by _____ all our neighbours _____[5] (come) round and help. I have never known such kindness. Not only did they agree to help but we _____ all our meals _____[6] (cook) for us each evening. It helped us carry on through a difficult period. We became great friends with the son of one of the local farmers who _____ us all _____[7] (laugh) as we worked with his quirky sense of humour. It cemented our relationships with the community and now it really feels like home.

4 What sort of things do you think might be difficult to arrange when you go to live in a new country?

5 What kind of things can you get people to do for you? Compare your list with another student. Say how often you get each thing done.

•• see grammar reference: page 187 ••

CAE close-up | Use of English Gapped sentences (Paper 3, part 4)

Exam information

This part of the exam consists of five sets of sentences (plus an example). One word has been removed from each sentence. You have to fill the gap with a word that is appropriate in all three sentences in the set. The focus of this part is vocabulary. The missing word will not necessarily have the same meaning in all three sentences. Metaphorical meaning, phrasal verbs and fixed phrases are also tested.

Approach

1 Read all three sentences in each set carefully. Make a note of any ideas you have for each sentence.

2 Look carefully at the words before and after the gap. A preposition before the gap may mean you are looking for a word in a fixed phrase. A preposition after the gap may mean you are looking for a word that is part of a phrasal verb.

3 Remember the meaning in each sentence will not necessarily be the core meaning of the word. It may have a metaphorical meaning.

4 You will probably find that you can think of a word for at least one of the sentences in each set. However, you need to check it fits the grammar and sense of the other sentences.

5 Read all three sentences again to make sure they make sense with your chosen word.

6 Write something in each gap. You do not lose marks for a wrong answer.

Practice task

For questions **1–5**, think of one word only which can be used appropriately in all three sentences. Here is an example (**0**).

Example:

0 My grandfather walks with a _____.
 I tried to explain but he got the wrong end of the _____.
 I know snowboarding is hard, but you should _____ with it until you have mastered it.

Example: **0** | S | T | I | C | K |

1 I couldn't use the parking machine as I didn't have the right _____.
 Maybe you should think about going away as they do say that a _____ is as good as a rest.
 She was going to leave her job but I think she's had a _____ of heart.

2 I think booking early for the concert was very _____.
 He made some _____ remark about why people like me couldn't understand the problem.
 You're looking very _____ today! Have you got an interview?

3 I really think that the islands off the coast are _____ a visit.
 He ran the race for all he was _____ but he just missed first place.
 We agreed to help him on Monday and he promised to make it _____ our while.

4 He was _____ out when he lied about what time he left the building.
 You look like you've _____ the sun on the back of your neck as it's all red.
 The film _____ the atmosphere of the book perfectly.

5 It's just a rough and _____ calculation so I wouldn't rely on it.
 I can't pay for it now as I'm short of _____ cash.
 Make sure you have your ticket at the _____ for the inspectors to see.

Go to www.iTests.com or your CD-ROM for interactive exam practice

Writing | set text question

1 Think of a book you have read recently and make notes on the following:

Plot: Was it exciting or slow? Did it have a moral to it?

Characters: Were they interesting? Funny? Unlikeable? Did they learn anything or change in any way?

Events: Was there an important event that affected the outcome of the story?

Setting: Was the geographical or historical setting different from or similar to what you know?

2 Read these set text questions and choose one to answer. In these questions you can choose any book, but in the CAE exam, you have to write about one of two specific books you have studied.

A Your teacher has asked you to write a review of a book you have read that would be suitable for the class to read. In your review say what was unusual about the book you read, what you learnt from reading it and why you would recommend it to the class.

B You see this announcement in a book magazine.

> We are inviting our readers to send in articles on books they have read recently. Choose a book you have read and write an article for our magazine saying how the title of the book connects to the story, explaining which was the most important aspect of the book and whether you would recommend it to our readers.

C Your teacher has asked you to write the following essay:

Main characters are always good people who have a happy ending. How far do you agree?

Write your essay based on a book you know.

3 Which of these statements is true? Use the Writing Reference to help you.

1 When answering an exam question on a set text, you should only include a brief description of the story or characters. Most of your answer should be giving your opinion together with reasons for your opinion.

2 When answering an exam question on a set text, you should include a detailed account of the story and, if possible, include quotes from the book.

•• see writing reference: **page 207** ••

4 Write a plan for your chosen question. Use your notes from Exercise 1 to help you and think carefully about the answer to Exercise 5.

5 Write an answer to your chosen question in 220–260 words. Make sure you use a variety of language and do not repeat yourself. Use the Exam Reviser to help you.

exam reviser   p26 | 17

WRITING SKILLS

Avoiding repetition

- use parallel structures, e.g. *It is better than ... , It is not as good as ...*
- use more precise vocabulary, e.g. *hard = tough, challenging, daunting*
- give a range of reasons for or examples of your point of view

6 Check your writing. Show your writing to another student and ask them to check the points in the skills box.

WRITING SKILLS

Checking your work

- Have you covered all the necessary content points for the task you are doing?
- Have you organised your writing into clear paragraphs?
- Is your grammar accurate?
- Have you chosen the right words in the right context?
- Is your spelling and punctuation correct?

Understanding varieties in pronunciation

English is pronounced in different ways depending on the region where it is spoken, but it can be hard to understand all these different varieties.

1 R.46 ▶ Listen. Can you hear the differences in the pronunciation of these words?

bath   butter   lovely

2 R.47 ▶ Listen to these words spoken by two different people. Can you tell which one is US English and which one is UK English?

can't	1 _____	2 _____
schedule	5 _____	6 _____
thorough	7 _____	8 _____

3 R.48 ▶ Listen and underline the syllable which is stressed in UK and US English.

UK	US
garage	*garage*
advertisement	*advertisement*
margarine	*margarine*

Look at how you can help yourself become more sensitive to the differences. Can you add your own idea?

1 Listening to cable or satellite TV programmes from different countries.

2 Listen to the English version on any DVDs you watch.

3 Listen to the BBC World Service on the radio or online at www.bbc.co.uk/worldservice.

learning tip

Grammar

1 Rewrite each sentence using the structure given in brackets.

1 When immigrants arrive in a strange country, they can take a long time to adjust to their new life. (a shortened relative clause)

2 After Paul had been living in India a month he started to feel comfortable with the language. (a clause inside a clause)

3 A woman greeted him on his arrival and he asked her where he could stay for the night. (a very long object/subject)

4 He found it hard to meet people and this made him worried. (the use of *It* at the beginning)

5 He had hardly ever seen such beautiful buildings. (inverting a clause for emphasis)

6 He decided to copy other people when he saw how they behaved. (a participle clause)

2 Complete the second sentence so that it has a similar meaning to the first sentence, using the word given. Do not change the word given. You must use between three and six words.

1 We all had to show our passports to the official.
got
The official _____ our passports.

2 The return to the UK made us all depressed.
had
The return to the UK _____ depressed.

3 My watch is being repaired at the moment.
having
I'm _____ repaired at the moment.

4 My car was broken into when I was living in London.
had
When I was living in London _____.

5 Can you fix my computer?
get
Can you _____ for me?

6 Something strange happened to me when I was living in Canada.
had
I _____ when I was living in Canada.

Vocabulary

3 Complete the sentences with one word in each gap.

1 It's only a rough and _____ solution; we'll have to look at it again later.

2 I shut myself in the study for a bit of peace and _____.

3 I think we should look carefully at the pros and _____ before we decide.

4 You deserve a bit of rest and _____ after all that hard work.

5 The argument is not black and _____; there are shades of grey in between!

6 We haven't got time for all the activities, so you are going to have to pick and _____ the ones you want to do.

7 He spent ages going into all the ins and _____ but I still didn't understand.

8 They're making a film on the life and _____ of Charles Dickens.

4 Complete the crossword using the clues.

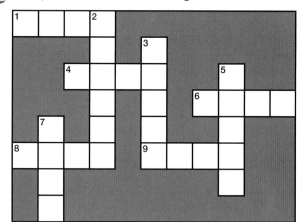

Across
1 to _____ and change (behaviour)
4 a change of _____ (lifestyle)
6 _____ the changes (lifestyle)
8 change your _____ (behaviour)
9 change your _____ (opinion)

Down
2 to change _____ (lifestyle)
3 a change of _____ (opinion)
5 change with the _____ (lifestyle/opinion)
7 to change _____ (behaviour)

graduate

concentration

knowledge

Unit 15

Introduction

1 Look at the pictures and answer these questions.
- What type of learning does each one represent?
- Which is the most effective type of learning. Why?
- In which of the situations do you think people have to do exams?

2 What is the difference between the words in the box? Tell another student how each of the words relates to you.

> a degree   a skill   a certificate   a licence

3 Discuss these questions with other students.
1 How important do you think exams are?
2 How do you revise? (e.g. with diagrams, lists, another student, etc.)
3 What do you think is the worst thing you can do in an exam?
4 What advice can you think of for people preparing for exams? Have a class vote for the best piece of advice.

Reading

1 Discuss these questions with other students.

1 What do you think is the most common difficulty for people doing exams?
- running out of time
- not reading the instructions carefully enough
- panicking

2 If you have to do four reading tasks in 75 minutes, how much time should you allow for each task?

3 How many minutes would you allow for each part of a task listed in the exam skills box?

EXAM SKILLS

Timing a reading task

- scan the reading text
- underline key points in the questions
- do the task
- check your answers

2 Look at this question and underline the three key words.

Which sentence mentions regret at having failed in an ambition?

3 Which of these sentences answers the question in Exercise 2? Why are the other sentences wrong?

1 Although I wasn't that keen on doing it, in retrospect I wish I had managed to get on to the MA course.

2 If only I had worked harder, then I would have achieved what I wanted.

3 I'd rather have failed the course and done it again than got such a mediocre result.

READING SKILLS

Finding a paraphrase of the whole question

- Underline key words in the question.
- Make sure the answer you choose reflects all the key words in the question, not just a part of the question.

4 You are going to read an article where different people give their views on preparing for an exam. For questions 1–15, choose from the extracts A–E. The extracts may be chosen more than once. Time limit: 20 minutes.

In which extract are the following mentioned?

a desire for something to change   1 _____
a problem of over-confidence   2 _____
the consequences of passing an exam   3 _____
students' failure to consider an issue   4 _____ 5 _____
success in tackling a problem   6 _____
the impact of external factors, like work   7 _____
being given some help to prepare   8 _____
a mistaken belief about doing something right   9 _____ 10 _____
a feeling of being overwhelmed   11 _____
being let down by something   12 _____
a wish to change something that happened   13 _____ 14 _____ 15 _____

5 Discuss these questions with other students. First close your books.

- Can you remember all the advice?
- Which advice would you be most likely to follow? Why?

premium plus 59

Taking an exam?
Some advice on how to prepare

A

Most people worry so much about the actual exam that they don't necessarily think about what happens in the time leading up to the exam. Take Martin, for instance. He has had a series of important exams for his medical studies. 'I was given a week off from hospital work just before my exams, so naturally I set aside this time for revision and didn't even attempt to think about it before then as it was hard to work and study. I realised too late that what I should have been doing was starting to use weekends to start revision. Now, of course, I regret not sitting down and working out what I had to do and exactly how long it would take me. Had I done this, I would have been able to prioritise my time and plan a more effective timetable.' Martin's experience shows how important it is to manage your time. The message here is think ahead!

B

A key factor in taking exams, and one which we tend just to accept without doing anything about, is stress. Obviously we have a certain level of nerves and tension before an exam – and this can be a good thing as it gets our adrenaline going and can help us perform well. The problem is when stress levels rise too far and start to have a negative impact. This is what happened to Keira. 'My exam would boost my prospects in my company so I got very worried and tense. This meant I couldn't concentrate when I was revising and I couldn't think clearly in the exam. With hindsight I realised I should have made some time to relax, especially doing something physical like swimming or walking, to clear my head. I wish I had known this at the time!' So make sure you take time out from your revision and do something completely different.

C

A more tricky situation – but a very common one – is when someone taking an exam thinks 'Well, I've done the course and been to all the lessons so I'll be OK.' This is not always the case! Yes, we may have studied the course, but we store information in a variety of ways and, in the exam, we may not always be able to retrieve this information if we have not gone over it enough times. Going back over work definitely improves your retention so is essential before you tackle an exam. An examiner explained, 'I mark French exams and, as the students are often using the language every day, they don't bother to revise. Then, in the exam they forget key vocabulary and grammar. I wish more people realised just how important it is to revise – even if you think you know it.' Take his advice – don't rely on your long-term memory; it may let you down!

D

Students taking an exam often overlook the need to find out what is expected of them. You can do practice tests before an exam so you know what kind of tasks you will have to complete, but it is more than that. Make sure you know how, for example, essays will be marked or, if you have to speak, what you will be assessed on. In other words, what is the examiner looking for? This allows you to target your revision and, in the exam, to produce what you know will get you marks. Jarek, a student of economics, says, 'I was asked to talk about a topic in the exam and I gave lots of facts and figures and didn't realise they were marking me on how well I presented my argument. If only I could go back in and do it again!' What happened to Jarek shows it is essential to find out what the marking criteria are.

E

We all know what revision is, but sometimes it can seem like a mountain to go back over everything. And going back over absolutely everything is not always productive. What most of us should do is targeted revision. In other words, find out where your weak areas are and spend your revision time improving those. Antonia, a law student, did just this. 'I had a big exam to do and it was just too much stuff to remember – I was drowning. I wish they wouldn't give you such enormous tests; it's ridiculous. But they do – so I did a practice test and decided to spend more time on the things that I got wrong. It really worked as I felt much more confident going into the exam, which helped me to perform better anyway, plus the work seemed more manageable and less scary.' So make sure you find out your weak areas and target them!

Grammar | hypothetical meaning

1 Look at sentences 1–5. Which of them expresses:

A annoyance or criticism about attitude or behaviour in the present?

B a desire for a change in a present or future situation?

C a desire to change something in the past?

1 I regret not sitting down and working out what I had to do.

2 I wish more people realised just how important it is to revise.

3 If only I could go back in and do it again!

4 I wish I had known this at the time!

5 I wish they wouldn't give you such enormous tests.

2 Which, if any, of the sentences in Exercise 1 describes a situation that is likely or possible?

3 Discuss any differences between these sentence pairs with another student. Think about the time they refer to and whether or not the situations are possible or impossible.

1 A I wish I could study medicine but I don't like blood!

  B I hope I get accepted at university to study medicine.

2 A She regrets doing so little work for her exams.

  B She regrets having done so little work for her exams.

3 A Come on – it's time to go.

  B Come on – it's time we went.

4 A Supposing you could study abroad, would you?

  B I suppose you could study abroad if you wanted to.

5 A I regret saying I would help him with his maths.

  B I regret to say there are no more places left on this course.

6 A I wish to tell you that your application has been successful.

  B I wish telling you about my failure hadn't affected my chances.

4 Complete this report with the correct form of the word in brackets.

Non-stop education?

New research shows that more and more of us are continuing to learn after we leave school and college. Why is it that so many of us are now doing this? The government has decided that it is time this situation _____1 (investigate). It has commissioned a study which shows that a large proportion of adult students regret _____2 (not + work) hard in school and are now trying to rectify this. In addition, it seems many of us wish _____3 (acquire) skills we can use in a wide variety of jobs. However, 65% of those who study at home say they wish their family _____4 (not interrupt) them while they are studying. A large group, who have no access to further education, claim they wish _____5 (learn) something more useful for their work. Supposing this group _____6 (have) access to courses, they say they would be prepared study up to twenty hours a week as well as working. So it seems we are all very keen to better ourselves.

---

5 What do you wish you could study more of? Why?

6 Think of an event or situation in your current life that you would like to change. Write three sentences using *wish*, *if only* and *supposing*.

7 Think of an event or situation in your past life that you would like to change. Write two sentences using *wish* and *regret*.

8 Say your sentences to other students. Find someone who feels the same as you.

•• see grammar reference: page 188 ••

premium plus 60

Vocabulary | further education

1 Work in groups of four, A, B, C and D. Check you know the meaning and pronunciation of the expressions in your box. Use the extracts on page 153 and a dictionary to help you.

> A What you acquire from education:
> *ability to articulate*
> *improved retention*
> *confidence in yourself*

> B Why you might want to study:
> *to boost your prospects*
> *to give you an academic grounding in a subject*
> *for intellectual/creative fulfilment*

> C What might be difficult:
> *juggling work and study*
> *striking a balance*
> *making sacrifices*
> *prioritising time*

> D What you might have to do when you study:
> *write assignments*
> *have one-to-one tuition*
> *attend evening classes*
> *do vocational training*
> *distance learning*

2 In your groups, tell each other the meaning and pronunciation of the expressions in your list.

3 Complete the Exam Reviser with additional points for each list.

exam reviser p19 | 15.1

4 Read this advertisement and complete the gaps with a suitable phrase from Exercise 1.

STUDY HARD AND GET PROMOTED

Do you want to _____¹ at work so you can get that all-important promotion? We offer courses in a variety of management skills, which will help you do just that. We give you a good _____² as well as showing you the practical applications. The course will give you _____³ and your abilities to manage a variety of projects; it also provides you with _____⁴, drawing as it does on recent theories in business studies. We recognise that you will be working while you do this course and so we offer introductory sessions on _____⁵ between work and study and _____⁶ so that everything gets done. These are also useful skills in any management post. The one-year course consists of _____⁷ of two hours a week, on Thursdays from 7.00–9.00 p.m., plus two sessions of _____⁸ with your personal tutor per term. We also ask you to _____⁹ at the end of every term, which, together with your tutor's grade and an exam, contribute towards your assessment. And don't worry – the cost of the course will be offset by your increased salary!

5 Discuss these questions with other students.

1 Do you think doing extra courses is always useful if you want promotion at work? Why/Why not?

2 What do you think is the main reason from the list in box B in Exercise 1 that people do further education?

3 What sort of learning from the list in box D would you find most appealing? Why?

Speaking

1 Discuss these questions with other students.

1 After we have explained our views, why can it be useful to summarise what we have said?

2 In what situations do we need to summarise our views?

2 R.49 ▶ Listen to four people summarising their views. Match each speaker with a situation A–D.

Speaker 1 _____   Speaker 2 _____

Speaker 3 _____   Speaker 4 _____

A talking to a friend

B giving a presentation at work

C making a joint decision in a speaking exam

D the end of a lecture

3 Compare your answers with another student, giving reasons for your decisions.

4 Answer these questions.

1 Which phrases in the box did the speakers use?

2 Which phrases are formal and which are informal?

> Summarising your views
> *To sum up ...*
> *Let's summarise briefly ...*
> *To conclude ...*
> *In conclusion ...*
> *To recap what I've said ...*
> *Let's go over ...*
> *If I can just remind you of the main points ...*
> *OK, what did we say?*
> *Look, let me go through it again ...*
> *In short, ...*

5 Look at the pictures, which show different things you can achieve through education. What do you think each one represents?

6 Work in pairs and decide which is the most useful achievement and which is the least useful. Make sure you reach a decision even if you disagree.

7 With another pair follow these instructions.

1 Take turns to explain your arguments and summarise your views.

2 Reach a decision as a group of four.

3 Explain your group decision to the rest of the class.

exam reviser   p26 | 18 ▶

CAE close-up | Writing Proposal (Paper 2, part 1)

Exam information

Look at the Exam Information on page 6. In part 1 of the Writing paper, you may be asked to write a proposal.

A proposal is generally written for a boss, a teacher, some colleagues or other club members. It requires you to explain a plan or idea you would like to be put into action. You will have to give some factual information (based on what you read) and give details about a suggestion or recommendation.

Approach

1 Read the rubric for the task and all the input material carefully. <u>Underline</u> the key parts.

2 Make a plan of what you are going to write before you start writing. Organise your points into logical paragraphs and make sure you use the correct format and layout for what you are writing.

3 Include everything the rubric and the task ask you to do. Also, be careful not to include irrelevant information which is not asked for.

4 Do not copy large phrases or sentences from the input material – you need to use your own words. Also, think about the appropriate style of your writing.

5 A proposal should be clearly organised and may include headings, sub-headings and bullet points. You should also use more formal language in a proposal, including more formal grammatical constructions (passive forms, formal linking phrases, introductory *it*, etc.).

6 When you have finished writing, take some time to check what you have written, including format, layout, paragraphs, style, completion of the task, mistakes (grammar, vocabulary, spelling, punctuation) and correct number of words.

Practice task

Write your answer in **180–220** words in an appropriate style.

You are studying English at a college in Canada and you, together with some of the other students, would like to attend classes in the evening in different subjects.

Read the suggestions from the other students, on which you have made some notes. Then, **using the information appropriately**, write a proposal for the principal of the college saying what type of classes you would like, explaining how the scheme could be paid for and giving reasons why the principal should set up the classes.

> **Possible classes – suggestions:**
> painting and drawing — *good for relaxing?*
> another language e.g. Chinese — *needed for work because ...*
> presentation skills
> statistics
> marketing techniques — *useful in most jobs!*
> use other students as teachers? (cheaper)
> classrooms empty after 6 p.m.
> will attract more students to college?
> students pay small fee, e.g. ...

Write your **proposal**. You should use your own words as far as possible.

Go to www.iTests.com or your CD-ROM for interactive exam practice

Listening

1 Discuss with another student what kind of things you normally have to listen to at work or when you study and why. Use the ideas in the box to help you.

> lectures   people on the phone   presentations
> instructions from someone   casual conversations

2 Work in pairs and follow these instructions.

1 Look at this list of things which can make listening difficult. Put them in order of how much they affect your ability to understand. Then compare your list with your partner.

- unknown words
- the speed of delivery
- ability to concentrate
- a complex topic

2 How long do you think you can listen for without 'switching off'?

3 R.50 ▶ You are going to listen to part of a talk on how to listen effectively. Complete sentences 1–8.

HOW TO IMPROVE YOUR LISTENING

In lectures, people sometimes _____¹ to indicate they have understood even if they haven't.

Concentration can be affected by information in our _____².

Your ability to listen can improve if you _____³ of what you are thinking about.

Start by listening to things for a _____⁴ of time and gradually increase this.

Practise listening to things where the speaker does not take a _____⁵.

Also practise by listening to a _____⁶ as it is harder to stay focused.

As you improve, you will notice that your mind begins to _____⁷.

When you have increased the time you can concentrate for, you are ready for a real-world _____⁸.

4 R.50 ▶ Listen again and check your answers.

5 Work in pairs and follow these instructions.

1 What was the most useful advice and why?
2 Choose one of these tasks, A or B. Take turns to give information to your partner and listen carefully
  A Explain a hobby, giving lots of information.
  B Talk about an event that happened to you, giving lots of details.
3 Take turns to say how much you can remember accurately from your partner's information.

Vocabulary | dependent prepositions with adjectives

1 Look at the adjectives in *italics* in these sentences. Complete the sentences with the correct prepositions in the box.

> about   at   for   of   with

1 This is *essential* _____ any kind of listening.
2 You will be *amazed* _____ how you can improve.
3 You need to be *aware* _____ your thoughts, but they can be both your ally and your enemy.
4 You can become more *optimistic* _____ your ability to really understand people.
5 Once you become *familiar* _____ this process, you might want to vary the speeches.

2 R.51 ▶ Listen and check your answers.

3 Look at the table in the Exam Reviser and put these adjectives with their prepositions into the correct column. Some can go in more than one column.

> useless   busy   fond   worried   responsible   clever
> proud   short   disgusted   satisfied   anxious
> famous   curious   sorry   angry

exam reviser p19 | 15.2 ▶

4 Work in pairs and follow these instructions.

1 Choose ten adjectives from different columns in the Exam Reviser and test your partner on the correct preposition.
2 Find three more adjectives to put in each column. Use a good dictionary, such as the *Longman Exams Dictionary*, to help you.

exam reviser p19 | 15.2 ▶

5 Complete these statements with your own ideas. Make sure you use the correct preposition following the adjective.

1 I feel very sorry …
2 The thing I am most proud …
3 I am very curious …
4 I think people should be satisfied …
5 I find I get very anxious …
6 I'm extremely fond …
7 I would like to be famous …
8 I was amazed …

6 Compare and discuss your statements with another student.

premium plus 61 ▶

Grammar | punctuation

1 Work in pairs and find examples in the text on page 155 of each of these punctuation features.
fullstop (.) comma (,) apostrophe (') semicolon (;)

2 Discuss with your partner any rules you know about when to use each punctuation mark. Look at the Grammar Reference and check you have remembered all the rules.

•• see grammar reference: page 189 ••

3 There are mistakes in these sentences. Find the mistakes and correct them.

> **Checking what you have learnt**
> 1 I am confident I know most of the grammar vocabulary and pronunciation.
> 2 In writing I am able to use complex sentence's.
> 3 I can vary my writing, when necessary to take account of the genre and the target reader.
> 4 I can understand a variety of listening texts. Usually in a variety of accents and speeds.
> 5 I have managed to remember many words, with their collocations.
> 6 I can usually guess a words' pronunciation.
> 7 I can perform a variety of functions in the language including the following: persuasion justifying my views summarising.
> 8 I know how to skim a text quickly and understand it's organisation.

4 Look at the checklist in Exercise 3 and decide on a scale of 1–5 (1 = not at all true; 5 = very true) how true each statement is for you. Compare your decisions with another student.

5 Look at a piece of writing that you've done recently. Check it carefully for any punctuation mistakes, using these questions to help you.
- Can you find any sentences which are too long?
- Are there any mistakes with your use of commas?
- Are there any mistakes with your use of apostrophes?
- Could you have used a semicolon anywhere?
- Could you have used a colon anywhere?

6 Tell another student how you have improved the punctuation in your writing.

•• see grammar reference: page 189 ••

premium plus   62 ▶

Writing | competition entry

1 Discuss these questions with another student.
1 What do you think are the advantages of studying in another country?
2 If you could study in another country, what would you study, where and why?

2 Read the writing task and, with a partner, decide what the focus of a competition entry is.
- to describe
- to explain
- to persuade
- to justify

> **Writing task**
> You see this announcement on a website:
>
> ○●○
>
> **Broaden your horizons**
> We are running a competition where we are offering one lucky person the chance to study the course of their choice in another country for six months. If you want to enter, write and say what you would like to study and where, explain why you want to study this subject and suggest how you think your studies will help any company you work for in the future.

3 Look at the sample task and model answer in the Writing Reference and discuss these questions with another student.
1 How many reasons does the writer give for each point in the task?
2 What is the focus of the final paragraph?

•• see writing reference: page 198 ••

4 Write a plan for the competition entry in Exercise 2. Make sure you give a variety of reasons for the points in the question.

5 Write your competition entry in 220–260 words. Use the Exam Reviser to help you.

exam reviser p23 | 9 ▶

6 When you have finished your competition entry, check your writing. Show your entry to another student and ask them to check it against the criteria in the skills box.

WRITING SKILLS
Awareness of marking criteria

In the exam your writing will be marked according to how well you fulfil the following criteria:

- Content: Does the entry include all the points in the question? Has each point been expanded?
- Organisation: Are there clear paragraphs? Are linking words used appropriately?
- Register: Is the tone and style of the writing appropriate to the target reader? Is the tone and style consistent?
- Accuracy: Are the structures and choice of vocabulary accurate? Is the spelling and punctuation correct?
- Range: Is there a variety of advanced structures and vocabulary?
- Target reader: Would the target reader be informed or confused?

Preparing for the exam and planning your revision

1 Add two or three more ways to prepare:
- Revise grammar and vocabulary. Use the Exam Reviser to help you.
- Time yourself doing Reading, Writing and Use of English tasks.
- Check the functional language section of the Exam Reviser to help you with Writing and Speaking.

_____

_____

2 Decide on the advantages and disadvantages of the following revision plans:
- Do 30 minutes each day on a variety of skills.
- Do 1 hour a day, concentrating on a single paper.
- Do revision only at weekends.

CAE close-up | Speaking Collaborative discussion (Paper 5, part 4)

Exam information
In part 4 of the Speaking exam, you, the other candidate and the examiner discuss your opinions about a topic connected to the task you did in part 3. In this part of the exam, you are expected to discuss a topic in depth. You will not be assessed on your ideas but you do have to produce enough language for the examiner to assess you.

Part 4 lasts about 4 minutes.

Approach
- Make sure you have revised the language of:
- giving and justifying opinions
- evaluating
- expressing uncertainty
(See Exam Reviser pages 20, 22 and 25.)

2 Remember to give extended answers and reasons for your views.

3 Try to use a range of structures and vocabulary.

4 Don't hesitate too much. Try to keep a natural flow to your response.

Practice task
R.52 ▶ Work in pairs, listen to the recording and follow the instructions.

Go to www.iTests.com or your CD-ROM for interactive exam practice

Grammar

1 Rewrite these sentences using the words given.

1 Why didn't I realise that I needed to take that course!
If only …

2 What would you do if you couldn't get into university?
Supposing …

3 I'm sorry but we can't come to the graduation ceremony.
I regret …

4 We should start revising – it's only two weeks before the exam.
It's time …

5 He wishes he hadn't left school when he was so young.
He regrets …

6 I hate the way the college give us tests all the time!
I wish …

2 Punctuate this text correctly, using capital letters, fullstops, commas, apostrophes, semicolons and colons.

HOW TO DO YOUR BEST IN AN EXAM

- make sure you know where and when the exam is and how long it is

- listen to your tutor he or she will give you valuable hints

- dont forget to look at previous years papers

- do revision well in advance and plan how you are going to do the work

- remember the following don't revise for too long set targets have breaks

- have some sleep it is impossible to do well in an examination with no sleep the night before

- dont work all the time have some relaxation or you will be stale

---

Vocabulary

3 Complete the text with the correct form of the word in brackets.

Your brilliant career
There are many reasons why you might choose to continue studying or get extra _____[1] (qualify) while you are working. Some people do it because their work demands it, but some do so for the extra skills they gain that they can apply at work, such as improved _____[2] (retain) of information or better writing. There is no doubt that to keep studying does give you extra _____[3] (confident) in yourself, which has a knock-on effect in the workplace. But it's not only for work – not only can these courses give you a good academic _____[4] (ground) in a subject, but they also generally give you a level of _____[5] (intellect) or even creative _____[6] (fulfil) that you may not actually get from your job. The difficulty can be that in order to do these extra courses you need to be good at _____[7] (juggle) work and study. This is where you may have to consider different types of learning, such as _____[8] (distant) if you are going to pack it all in. There is no doubt though that if you are prepared to make sacrifices, it will all pay off.

4 Complete this article with the correct prepositions.

My view of the future
I think in the future we will each have to be responsible _____[1] our own learning. It will no longer be any good simply to be clever _____[2] maths or science. Other skills will be demanded, such as being familiar _____[3] computers in a way that allows you to use them effectively or knowing several languages or being aware _____[4] what is happening in other parts of the world. I know a lot of people are very worried _____[5] the changes that are happening, but this is because they are dissatisfied _____[6] the opportunities they have and cannot see a way forward. The only thing, instead of being worried _____[7] the future, is for everyone to make sure they study something that is essential _____[8] their own fulfilment. In that way, they will be good _____[9] what they do and this will mean them being given further opportunities at work. Personally I am optimistic _____[10] the future as I think it will lead to amazing opportunities for the graduates of today.

Progress Check 3 Units11–15

1 Complete each sentence with a correct word from the box. Four of the words cannot be used.

> down   out   ways   ring   tune   tack   so
> chop   means   less   off   near

1 You've changed your _____: yesterday you couldn't stand her and now you're best friends!
2 This is not, by any _____, the first time he has beaten me at tennis.
3 They've decided to wind _____ their catering business so they have more time for themselves.
4 I'm sorry but this report is nowhere _____ up to the expected standard.
5 Children are more likely to eat different foods if you _____ the changes and provide plenty of variety.
6 They just grew apart and in the end the relationship fizzled _____ completely.
7 We're going to have to decide which restaurant to book. We can't just _____ and change all the time.
8 The state that he kept those animals in was nothing _____ than appalling.

2 Punctuate the text using capital letters, fullstops, commas, apostrophes, semicolons and colons as appropriate.

Climbing to the Top

employers are using a wide variety of interviewing techniques these days to find the best people for their company questionnaires unusual questions personality tests skills tests and group interviews some of these can be pretty challenging

recently however one company in Japan has done something much more unusual the company imagenet left a message with potential interviewees asking them to climb the highest mountain in the country and be ready for an interview at the top the company has nothing to do with mountain climbing theyre one of that countrys top online fashion labels

fifteen out of the twenty candidates accepted the challenge to climb mount fuji japans highest mountain which is about 12,388 feet high of those twenty eleven reached the top some with the assistance of oxygen tanks of those eleven top candidates who were interviewed at the summit four were offered positions with imagenet

3 There are mistakes in seven of these sentences. Find the mistakes and correct them.

1 I told him he had better have his presentation finished immediately!
2 You aren't going to the post office now, aren't you?
3 He's had series of rows with his boss so he's thinking of leaving.
4 Who did explain what you had to do?
5 I always say that no news is the good news.
6 Nobody's seen him today, have they?
7 Did he tell you he had got his car stolen in London?
8 She got the huge audience for her talk.

4 Read the text and decide which answer A, B, C or D best fits each gap.

Tricks of the trade

Last year, I became more and more dissatisfied with my job and decided I needed to try to _____ ¹ my prospects of finding something more exciting. So I decided to find out what kind of training course there might be to help me. I happened to be _____ ² through a magazine one day, when I came across an interesting article. It was all about magic and it claimed that learning the skills the magicians use could really improve your chances of _____ ³ a promotion, a pay rise, or whatever.

Although I was a little sceptical, I was also curious _____ ⁴ what skills a magician really might be able to teach me. So, the following Thursday, I set off to attend the first of three evening classes. I was nervous, but also _____ ⁵ about what would happen. The course was run by a professional magician, Charlie Chester, who three years ago had _____ ⁶ up his own business teaching people how a magician's skills could be used in the corporate world.

Most of that first session focused on the art of public speaking. Like many people, I am anxious _____ ⁷ public speaking; I forget my words, start _____ ⁸ and it all goes from bad to worse. Charlie showed us that in a magic performance, the tricks are only a small part of the show; for example, getting people's attention and looking directly at people's eyes lets them know that you mean business. After three fascinating sessions, I feel incredibly _____ ⁹ of my progress. I haven't got a new job yet, but it has given me hugely increased confidence _____ ¹⁰ myself and I can also do a couple of card tricks!

1 A prove	B provide	C boost	D burst
2 A bruising	B breezing	C browsing	D brawling
3 A getting	B putting	C setting	D taking
4 A of	B about	C by	D to
5 A aware	B familiar	C optimistic	D satisfied
6 A set	B put	C took	D made
7 A in	B by	C with	D about
8 A screeching	B stuttering	C grumbling	D mouthing
9 A proud	B pleased	C amazed	D satisfied
10 A to	B for	C in	D with

Progress Check 3 Units 11–15

5 Use the word given in capitals at the end of some of the lines of this text to form a word that fits in the gap in the same line.

Change your life?

Have you ever wished you could dump your current life and (1) _____? You may have thought about going somewhere else, perhaps to the other side of the world, and living completely differently. Many of us dream about this, especially when we feel (2) _____ and overworked! Although those who've done it give the (3) _____ it's easy, it can be a great deal harder than it seems. Living in a new community means making new friends – and those friends have no (4) _____ with your past and so you will have no (5) _____ you can call on to bind you together. What may at first appear exciting or exotic can rapidly become strange and distancing. (6) _____ we often find it easier to fit into more similar cultures than dissimilar ones. We can feel more (7) _____ towards them, more ready to accept the differences and less (8) _____ by approaches from strangers.

APPEAR

PAY
IMPRESS

CONNECT
REFER

INTERESTING

SYMPATHY
THREAT

6 For each group of sentences 1–5, think of one word which can be used appropriately in all three sentences.

1 The children seem to want to _____ around the house all day, playing all sorts of chasing games.
   He won the _____ by a huge margin, leaving the other competitors miles behind.
   It was a _____ against time as the dogs set off in search of the missing walkers.

2 Just take the first one, please. There's no time to _____ and choose.
   I'd be very grateful if you could _____ me up from the airport when I arrive.
   Be careful that someone doesn't _____ your pocket or steal your bag when you're in that café.

3 I'm going to take _____ of my grandmother now as she is too old to live alone.
   I feel very nostalgic for my childhood when I didn't have a _____ in the world.
   Could you send the parcel _____ of Auntie Elsa as I'll be staying with her all summer?

4 We sat on the beach and watched the sun _____ behind the mountains.
   There was very little help given. We were just left to _____ or swim really.
   I couldn't believe how much washing up had been left in the _____.

5 The club has grown very quickly, with three _____ the number of members we had last year.
   I've just read a really good biography about the life and _____ of Charlie Chaplin.
   There are _____ when I wish I could go back to my school days.

7 Complete the second sentence so that it has a similar meaning to the first sentence, using the word given. Do not change the word given. You must use between three and six words, including the word given.

1 I regret not telling him about the problem.
   wish
   I _____ about the problem.

2 I had only just arrived when the man grabbed my bag.
   sooner
   _____ the man grabbed my bag.

3 I had a book from him for my birthday.
   gave
   He _____ for my birthday.

4 I didn't realise I had met him before until later.
   only
   _____ I had met him before.

5 She told me what the problem was.
   explained
   She _____ me.

6 Why did he take my car?
   if
   _____ my car!

7 We had left early to get good seats.
   was
   The _____ to get good seats.

8 We lost our bags, which really bothered me.
   was
   _____ our bags.

Selected audioscripts

UNIT 06

R.18

A: Did you see that hysterical video on YouTube of that couple dancing at their wedding?

B: Yeah, I did. I don't understand why people thought it was funny. I thought it was rubbish. It looked like a set-up.

A: Do you think so? I thought it was good because you expected them to do a normal wedding dance and they didn't. They did that rap singing instead. You've got to admit it was much more entertaining than most wedding videos!

B: Huh! I thought they'd filmed it like that deliberately just to get on YouTube. Some people'll do anything to be famous!

A: Well, it made me laugh.

B: Hm – well, you could tell it was fixed 'cos the rap music is supposed to be a surprise but you can see them smile just before they start dancing to the rap.

A: I don't see how you could tell! Anyway it's only a joke – they're not supposed to be serious videos …

R.19
Extract 1

A: So, Mark, a James Bond film! You must be excited. When does filming start?

B: Next month – I'm really looking forward to it, but really nervous at the same time.

A: And do you know anybody who'll be working with you or not?

B: I don't know the main actors at all, but the director and I have worked together before. The locations are all very carefully worked out beforehand, which means the difficult work is confined to things like lighting and the weather. Of course, it all looks a lot simpler than it actually is when you're filming!

A: And what does this job mean to you?

B: Well, I'm getting older now – though I'm not sure you ever outgrow the job – and I certainly can't imagine myself matching anything like this in the future. It means I really can't afford to mess up.

A: And are you doing the camerawork for the whole film?

B: Yes – that's what's so daunting! I can't tell you what it's about though – the plot is a closely guarded secret.

A: Well, I'll have to go and see it, then, won't I?

Extract 2

A: Censorship is under much discussion now because they were going to tighten the censorship on films but the film censors still seem to allow very violent films to go on general release.

B: But that's because the censorship board never come up with any resolutions. I mean, by March this particular committee will have been in office for six months and they've done nothing. If they think violence in films has an effect, then they should do something about it.

A: Apparently there was a huge row at their meeting yesterday so I think it's going to come to head now. It's disgraceful that they have allowed some films through the system with no cuts at all.

B: I do wonder why they've done that, though …

A: You have to remember that the committee will have been getting funding from the Film Academy for over thirty years this summer – they couldn't function without it – so they're very conscious of not antagonising the industry. Of course the film industry shouldn't police itself in this way and it doesn't help that they only seem to appoint their friends onto the committee. Personally I feel it needs some form of government intervention or I can foresee big problems …

Extract 3

A: Hi, Hi – Leon, over here. Are you excited to be here tonight?

B: Yeah, the crowds are great; it's fun. Even though I'm not up for an award, it's great to be here. I was going to stay home but – no, just joking – glad I came.

A: Why do you think the Oscars are so important to everyone?

B: Well, of course it's an honour. I know everyone says that, as an actor, it's great to be recognised by your peers – but you know it's a chance for the backroom boys, like the editors and make-up artists, to get some praise as the public rather take them for granted, I think. And everybody just has a really great evening. How fun is that?

A: And who are you with tonight?

B: Actually, you know, I don't have a date. I was hoping to meet someone at the party later!

A: Oh, I'll come with you, then! No, seriously, didn't you bring your mom?

B: Well, I know that's the fashion now but my mom's really shy. I did ask her, but she told me I was not to worry about her. I can understand why she didn't come – sometimes all this noise and flashing lights is too much. As actors we're used to it, but it's not for everyone.

A: OK, Leon. Thanks, have a good evening …

UNIT 08

R.25

A: OK, the next person in this competition to select a wonder of the world is Marlene from Manchester. Marlene, you have one minute to present your case for your chosen place. Go ahead.

B: I am going to propose that the Alhambra in Granada, Spain, should be considered a wonder of the world. This magnificent building was originally a fortress which stretched across 13 hectares and now it is a great, imposing castle rising from the oldest quarters of the city. I think there are basically three reasons why it should be chosen.

Firstly, the decorations are incredible: the palace, in the centre of the complex, is famous for its intricate frescoes and interior detail. Can you imagine how long this decoration took? Years and years of work by the most highly skilled craftsmen. I defy anyone not to be enchanted by all this – the exquisite detail on its marble pillars and arches; its ceilings with ornamental bands; the painted tiles on the walls. The colours on the walls, a little faded from time and exposure, have become almost transparent. As you walk round, the wind blows through the rooms and the sunshine streams in – and this brings me to the second reason: the effect the building makes; the whole effect is one of airy lightness and grace. If you visit it, you are sure to be entranced by the central court and the calming effect of the water decorations. The whole place is a unique mix of beautifully laid out buildings and stunning decoration. Finally, there is nowhere else quite like it – and the work would be impossible to replicate in the modern age. So in my view, for these three reasons, it should definitely be considered a wonder of the world.

Communication Activities

Unit 3, page 31 CAE close-up
Practice task

Work in pairs and decide which of you is Candidate A and which is Candidate B. Listen to the recording and follow the instructions.

Candidate A

- What different aspects of keeping fit do they show?
- How might the people be feeling?

Candidate B

- Why might these people be running?
- How might they be feeling?

Unit 3, page 35, Exercise 3

A

The Greatest Tennis Player ever. That's not a title you should use lightly. But what if it just happens to be true? What if it's describing someone who, for years, has been virtually unbeatable? Someone who almost every young sportsperson looks up to as a hero and a role model? Who is it? In my view, there's no competition – it's Roger Federer.

B

A role model can be defined as 'someone whose behaviour, attitudes, etc. people try to copy because they admire them'. That's a lot to live up to. So how do you choose a sporting role model for young people? Two things are important: the person's achievements and the characteristics that make this person special.

Unit 5, page 51, Exercise 4

Student A

- How is the situation of each animal different?
- How might the people watching the animals be feeling?

Unit 5, page 53, Exercise 3

Answers

All As: You don't have much sympathy for animals!

All Bs: You are very concerned to protect animals.

All Cs: You quite like animals, but not too close!

Mixed: How you think about animals depends on the situation you are in.

Unit 7, page 70, Exercise 2

You have 30 seconds. How many names can you remember?

Unit 14, page 147, Exercise 3

Answers

all As = You like change and embrace it.

all Bs = You resist change and want to stay as you are.

mixed = You are prepared to change some things but not always.

Unit 13, page 134, Exercise 5

1 He's a brilliant scientist, but he's not much of a teacher.
2 There is no reason why you shouldn't pass your physics exam.
3 Every so often you come across a new invention which sounds too good to be true.
4 I'd like to thank each and every one of you for helping us finish the project on time.
5 We have every reason to believe that he will go on to become a famous scientist.
6 We're expecting nothing less than the best from you all.
7 All too often people say they can't do something, when actually they're really capable.

Unit 11, page 115, Exercise 3

Add the verbs in your box to the correct columns in the table in Exercise 2. Look at the patterns that follow the verbs to help you.

Group A

> take   pull   start   describe   shut   miss   inform
> wait   give   want   play   offer   lend   sit

1 I pulled the door really hard until it opened.
2 She wanted me to buy a newspaper, but I forgot.
3 When my grandmother died, I missed her terribly.
4 I need to take the dog to the vet today.
5 She gave me three CDs for my birthday.
6 He played me a beautiful piece on the guitar.
7 I offered him some money, but he wouldn't take it.
8 You should never lend money to friends.
9 He described the book to us in great detail.
10 The teacher will inform you about the arrangements for the exam next week.
11 We had to wait for over half an hour at the bus stop.
12 When I walked in, she was sitting on the sofa, watching TV.
13 You're late – the lesson started ten minutes ago.
14 I couldn't start the car today so I had to walk to work.
15 When I was young, the shops used to shut early on Thursdays.
16 Can you shut that door when you go out?

Group B

> lose   explain   stop   make   eat   assure   sleep
> fall   happen   invite   tell   bring   warn   forget

1 I lost my watch today when I went to the swimming pool.
2 He was so hungry that he ate three platefuls of pasta for dinner.
3 Shall we invite the neighbours to the party?
4 My dog brings me his lead when he wants to go for a walk.
5 They made me a fantastic chocolate cake for my birthday.
6 My mother used to tell me a story every night before I went to bed.
7 He explained the idea to us very quickly before he left.
8 They assured us that all the equipment was safe.
9 You need to warn everyone about the cost of the trip.
10 I can't believe what happened yesterday.
11 I was so tired that I slept for over twelve hours.
12 Be careful that you don't fall – the pavements are very slippery.
13 She stopped, turned round and then carried on walking.
14 He heard a strange noise and stopped the car immediately.
15 I meant to phone her yesterday but I completely forgot.
16 I really think you should just forget her now and move on.

Unit 7, page 75 CAE close-up Practice task

Work in pairs and decide which of you is Candidate A and which is Candidate B. Listen to the recording and follow the instructions.

> How might each idea help to improve your brain power?
> Which picture shows the most effective way?

Communication Activities

Unit 7, page 74, Exercise 1

The second time should have been easier, despite the fact there were more numbers, because the digits were grouped together. Tasks involving remembering numbers still appear in tests of general mental ability. Our capacity for remembering numbers has been used to determine the maximum number sequence for telephone numbers in many countries.

Unit 5, page 51, Exercise 4

Student B

- What different attitudes to animals do the pictures show?
- How might the people be feeling?

Unit 4, page 42, Exercise 4

A

A particularly special event that the club has organised recently was an outing to see the musical of the *Phantom of the Opera* with everyone wearing fancy dress of the characters. It was a fantastic musical with masks, costumes and a meal after. Everyone thought it was a great evening.

B

One of the most successful events that the club has organised recently was a superb fancy dress outing. Club members spent a long time getting masks and costumes sorted out and we all went to the musical of the *Phantom of the Opera* dressed up as some of the characters. We went to a restaurant afterwards, where we carried on singing some of the songs from the musical, and everyone had a really enjoyable evening.

Unit 12, page 124, Exercise 3

A Words which can be singular or plural (depending on your point of view)	B Words which are always plural	C Words which look plural but are not

Index

Ability, possibility and obligation	171
Articles	170
Causative *have* and *get*	171
Cohesion in text	174
Complex sentences	187
Confusable structures	179
Countable and uncountable nouns	183
Degrees of certainty	178
Emphasis with inversion	186
Emphasis with *what*, *all* and *it*	174
Future forms	176
Future in the past	172
Hypothetical meaning	188
if structures	176
-ing forms and infinitives	169
Introductory *it*	180
Linking phrases	178
Linking words	175
Modifying comparison	171
Narrative tenses	173
Noun groups	183
Participle clauses	180
Passives	179
Past continuous	173
Past simple	173
Past perfect continuous	173
Past perfect simple	173
Present perfect continuous	174
Present perfect simple	172
Punctuation	189
Quantifiers – phrases	185
Question forms	184
Relative clauses and pronouns	175
Reported speech	181
Reporting verbs	182
Verb patterns	182

Unit 01

-ing forms and infinitives

Certain grammatical constructions and certain verbs are followed by:

1 The infinitive without *to* (e.g. *do*)
2 The infinitive with *to* (e.g. *to do*)
3 the *-ing* form (e.g. *doing*)

Grammatical constructions/patterns

1 Use the infinitive without *to* (e.g. *do*):
   after modal verbs
   *I **could give** you a lift if you want.*
   after *make* and *let*
   *My boss **let me finish** work early.*
   after *I'd better* and *I'd rather*
   *I'd **rather get** a taxi than walk.*

2 Use the infinitive with *to* (e.g. *to do*):
   after certain adjectives
   *She was very **happy to be** invited.*
   after the construction *too ... to ...*
   *It's **too late to go** shopping now.*
   to express purpose
   *I'm learning English **to improve** my work prospects.*

3 Use the *-ing* form (e.g. *doing*):
   after prepositions
   *She's interested **in working** with animals.*
   when an action (not a noun) is the subject or object of a sentence
   ***Reading** a lot is a good way of increasing your vocabulary.*

With certain verbs:

1 Verbs followed by the *-ing* form (gerund)
   Here are some common verbs which are followed by the *-ing* form:
   admit, deny, appreciate, can't help, can't stand, consider, delay, deny, detest, dislike, enjoy, escape, excuse, face, feel like, finish, forgive, give up, imagine, involve, mention, mind, miss, postpone, practise, put off, resent, risk, suggest, understand
   *I'd never even **consider travelling** on my own.*

2 Verbs followed by an infinitive with *to*
   Here are some common verbs which are followed by an infinitive with *to*:
   afford, agree, appear, arrange, ask, attempt, bear, begin, care, choose, consent, decide, determine, expect, fail, forget, happen, hate, help, hesitate, hope, intend, learn, like, love, manage, mean, offer, prefer, prepare, pretend, promise, propose, refuse, regret, remember, seem, start, swear, trouble, try, want, wish
   *She **managed to get** tickets in the front row.*

3 Verbs followed by object + infinitive with *to*
Here are some common verbs which are followed by an object and the infinitive with *to*:
advise, allow, ask, cause, command, encourage, expect, forbid, force, get, hate, help, instruct, intend, invite, leave, like, mean, need, oblige, order, permit, persuade, prefer, press, recommend, remind, request, teach, tell, tempt, trouble, want, warn, wish
They **persuaded me not to resign** from my job.

4 Verbs followed by an object + the infinitive without *to*
Here are some common verbs which are followed by an object and the infinitive without *to*:
feel, hear, help, know
I'd really like to **hear him play** the piano.

In passive sentences these verbs are followed by an infinitive with *to*.
The new curriculum **was felt to be** too limited.

5 Verbs followed by a gerund or an infinitive with a difference in meaning
remember, forget, stop, try
remember: the gerund is used when the action happens before the remembering; the infinitive refers to an action that happens after.
I **remember posting** the letter on the way to work.
Did you **remember to send** her a birthday card?
forget: when used with the gerund, this means 'forget what you have done'; when used with the infinitive with *to* this means 'forget what you have to do'.
She'd **forgotten having** a conversation with me last week.
I **forgot to buy** a newspaper when I went out.
stop: when used with the gerund, this means 'stop something you do'; when used with the infinitive with *to*, this means 'stop in order to do something'.
I **stopped paying** for my gym membership because I didn't go enough.
We **stopped to get** some more petrol on the way.
try: when used with the gerund, this means 'make an experiment' – doing the action may not be successful; when used with the infinitive this means 'make an effort' – the action may be difficult or impossible to do.
You should **try cutting** out all dairy products.
Try to get an early night before the exam.

6 Verbs followed by a gerund or an infinitive with almost no difference in meaning
can't bear/stand, hate, like, love, prefer
When these verbs are used with the infinitive, they refer to more specific situations. When they are used with the gerund, they refer to more general situations. The difference in meaning is very slight.
I **like to go** to the dentist regularly.
I **can't stand listening** to music when I'm studying.

Articles

The definite article: *the*
Use the definite article *the* to talk about the following:

inventions: *I'm not sure when* **the** *umbrella was invented.*
species of animal: *My favourite kind of animal is* **the** *panda.*
oceans and seas: *They rowed across* **the** *Atlantic Ocean.*
mountain ranges: *We're going skiing in* **the** *Rockies this year.*
island groups: *We spent three weeks in* **the** *Shetland Islands.*
areas: *The most heavily-populated part of England is* **the** *south-east.*
rivers: *She's just bought a house on the banks of* **the** *River Dee.*
deserts: **The** *Sahara desert is the biggest desert in the world.*
hotels: *They went for tea at* **the** *Savoy Hotel in London.*
cinemas: *That new film is coming to* **the** *Odeon next week.*
theatres: *We went to 'The Lion King' at* **the** *Lyceum Theatre in London.*
newspapers: **The** *Guardian Weekly is one of my favourite newspapers.*
national groups: *People sometimes think* **the** *British are a bit eccentric.*
Also:
with superlatives.
That's **the** *most ridiculous excuse I've ever heard.*
when there is only one thing.
We could see where we were going because **the** *moon was so bright that night.*
to talk about particular nouns when it is clear what we are referring to.
Can you pass me **the** *milk, please?*
to talk about previously mentioned things.
I've lost an umbrella and a small purse. **The** *umbrella is red and black and* **the** *purse is brown leather.*

The indefinite article: *a/an*
Use the indefinite article *a/an*:

with (singular) jobs, etc.
He's **an** *engineer in the construction business.*
with singular countable nouns (mentioned for the first time or when it doesn't matter which one).
She sat under **a** *tree and read her book all afternoon.*
with these numbers: 100, 1,000, 1,000,000.
Over **a** *thousand people responded to the survey.*
in exclamations about singular countable nouns.
What **an** *awful mess!*

The zero article
Use no article (the zero article) to talk about:

continents: *I've never been outside Europe.*
countries: *We went to Spain last summer.*
mountains: *He's taken some amazing photos of Mount Fuji.*
lakes: *Lake Garda is the largest lake in Italy.*

villages, towns, cities: *Is this the right train to Krakow?*

streets, roads, etc.: *I live in Oak Gardens. It's not far from here.*

magazines: *He often reads 'GQ' magazine on the train to work.*

illnesses: *I've had flu for the last four days. (But: I've got **a** headache.)*

uncountable, plural and abstract nouns used in their general sense:

Laziness is something that we won't put up with here.

I'm not keen on keeping dogs as pets.

Also use no article in the following expressions:

to/at/from school/university/college
in/to class
to/in/into/from church
to/in/into/out of prison/hospital/bed
to/at/from work
for/at/to breakfast/lunch/dinner
by car/bus/bicycle/plane/train/tube/boat
on foot

Unit 02

Modifying comparison

The standard forms of comparison can be modified in several ways:

1 Intensifying comparison
   *The restaurant is **much more comfortable than** it used to be.*
   *This holiday is **far better than** I expected it to be.*
   *We arrived **three times faster than** our nearest rivals.*
   *She's **twice as** pretty **as** her sister.*
   *He's **not half as** clever **as** he thinks he is!*
   *I'm **not nearly as** good at cooking **as** my boyfriend.*
   *It's **by far the largest** house in the road.*

2 Comparative meaning 'relatively' (*one of …; one for …*)
   *He is **one of the more colourful** artists from that period.*
   *This exercise is **one for the cleverer** students in the class.*

3 Comparative for abstract ideas (*all; any; none*)
   *He was **none the wiser** despite her careful explanation.*
   *I feel **all the better for** having gone on that yoga holiday.*

4 Progressive comparison
   *He's getting **richer and richer** by the minute.*
   *We've finding it **harder and harder** to keep up.*

Other forms of comparison

1 Comparison to describe things changing or varying together (*the …, the …*)
   ***The more** you study, **the easier** it is.*

2 Ellipsis
   than can replace a subject or object pronoun or an adverbial expression:
   *They were earlier **than we expected**. (Not … than we expected them.)*
   *I ate more food **than was comfortable**. (Not … than it was comfortable.)*

Ability, possibility and obligation

Ability – can, could

1 *can* and *could*
   We use *can* and *could* to talk about present and future ability.
   After months of lessons, she can finally drive!
   I've cancelled my appointment so I can come shopping with you on Saturday.
   I could see you next week if that's easier.

2 *could* in the past
   We use *could* to talk about general past ability.
   I could swim quite well when I was at school.
   We do not normally use *could* to say that somebody did something on one occasion. Instead we use other expressions.
   *He **succeeded in** his ambition of becoming a pilot.*
   *Did you **manage to** climb the mountain in three days?*
   *We **were able to** see him before he left for Zurich.*

3 We use *could have* for unrealised past ability.
   *I **could have gone** to college, but I chose to get a job instead.*

4 We use *can/could always* meaning 'if there is nothing better'.
   If you're stuck, you could always ask Peter for a lift.
   If I don't get my degree, I can always work for my uncle.

Possibility – can, could, may, might (not)

1 We use *can* and *could* for a general possibility in the present and future (without saying what chance there is that it will happen).
   Everyone could come if they wanted.
   You can shop online to save time.

2 We use *could*, *may* and *might* for a chance that something will happen or is happening.
   We may see him when we are in Rome.
   The weather could be good by March.
   I might pop in later if I've got a minute.
   I might not be able to come on Friday.

   may and *might*: the difference
   might is mostly used as a less definite form of *may*, suggesting a smaller chance.
   I may take an extra course next year as I want to qualify sooner.
   I might go to the Maldives, but I'm not sure I'll have enough money!

Grammar Reference

Obligation

should and **ought to**

We use *should* and *ought to* to talk about obligations in the past present and future.

You should go to see your grandmother.

Shouldn't you have started revising by now?

You ought to start saving for your holidays.

should have and *shouldn't have* are used to criticise people's behaviour.

She shouldn't have told him about losing the money.

strong obligation – must, have to, have got to

A *must*

We use *must* to:

1 Talk about present and future strong obligations and necessities that come from the speaker.

*You **must** have proper lessons if you want to kite-surf.*

*I'm really tired so I **must** go now.*

2 Ask about what the listener wants you to do.

***Must** I make an appointment if I want to see you?*

3 Tell people not to do things.

*You **mustn't** leave anything valuable in the hotel room.*

B *have to/have got to*

We use *have to/have got to* to:

1 Talk about present and future strong obligations that do not come from the speaker. *Have got to* is used more in British English than it is in American English.

*We **have to** vacate our university accommodation at the end of the academic year.*

*Where do we **have to** leave our luggage? (more common in American English)*

*I **haven't got to** hand in my project until next week. (more common in British English)*

2 Talk about past and reported obligations of all kinds.

*He said I **had to** wait for him at the station if I wanted a lift.*

*I **had to** get a visa for Australia before I could book the flight.*

*She **didn't have to** do any exams – she only had coursework.*

lack of obligation – don't need to, needn't, don't have to

1 *needn't, don't need to* and *don't have to*

We use *needn't, don't need to* and *don't have to* to talk about a lack of obligation in the present or future.

*You **needn't/don't need to** call, just come straight over.*

*You **don't have to** come with us if you'd rather stay at home.*

2 *needn't + have + past participle*

We use *needn't + have + past participle* to say that somebody did something but it was unnecessary.

*You **needn't have** paid for the meal. We could have shared the cost.*

3 *didn't need to + infinitive*

We use *didn't need to + infinitive* to say that something wasn't necessary without saying if the person did it or not.

*They **didn't need to** bring money as it was all paid for.*

The future in the past

Sometimes when we are talking about the past, we want to talk about something that was in the future at that time; something which had not yet happened. To do this we use future structures but we make the verb forms past.

*I **was going to** call him but I ran out of time.*

*She had no way of contacting him as she **was about to** get on the plane.*

*Later that year I met the woman who **would** later become my wife.*

Unit 03

Present perfect simple

FORM

have/has + past participle

USE

We use the present perfect simple:

1 To talk about an experience or an action in the past when the time is not important or not known. (It is often used with *ever* and *never*.)

I've never eaten meat in my life.

Have you ever played basketball?

2 To talk about an action that started in the past and continues to the present. (It is often used with *for* and *since*.)

When you're focusing on the finished action.

I've cleaned the whole house from top to bottom.

When you're focusing on the number of times the action has been completed up to the time of speaking.

I've left a message three times now.

With 'state' verbs, e.g. *be, have, like, believe, know*.

She's always known she was adopted.

3 To talk about an action that happened in the past but has the result in the present. (It is often used with *just, yet, already* and *still*.)

She's just cancelled her appointment.

Have you seen that new film yet?

I've already told him we can't come to the meeting.

He still hasn't replied to that email I sent on Monday.

4 To talk about our first/second experience of something with the phrase *This is the first/second time …*

This is the first time I've tried anything like skiing.

5 When used with the superlative. (It is often used with *ever*.)

I think that's probably the funniest joke I've ever heard.

Present perfect continuous

FORM
have/has + been + -ing

USE
We use the present perfect continuous:

1 To suggest that an action is not complete.
   I've been writing my essay all day and it's nowhere near finished.

2 To emphasise how long the action has been going on for.
   I've been learning Spanish for over a year and I still feel like a beginner.

3 To describe a recent activity when you can still see the results of that activity.
   A: *This looks good!*
   B: *Yes, I've been clearing the garden.*

ever
Ever indicates that the speaker is talking about 'at any time in your life'. It generally comes before the past participle in questions.
Have you ever joined a gym?

for/since
For is used to talk about a period of time.
I've worked at this school for nearly ten years.
Since is used to talk about the starting point.
He's lived in that village since he was born.

just/yet/already/still
Just means a short time ago. It usually comes between *has/have* and the past participle.
I've just noticed something.

Yet shows that the speaker expected something to happen before now. It is used at the end of negative sentences and questions.
I haven't sent out the invitations **yet**.
Have you decided what to do **yet**?

Already shows that something happened sooner than expected. It usually comes between *has/have* and the past participle or at the end of the sentence.
Don't worry about the washing up, I've already done it.

Still shows that something is continuing to happen.
She still hasn't phoned me.

Unit 04

Narrative tenses

Past simple

FORM
verb + -ed (remember there are many irregular verb forms)

USE
We use the past simple:

1 To talk about events in the past that are now finished.
   We went to a really fantastic show last Saturday.
   He looked at her and smiled, but he didn't say anything.

2 To talk about habits in the past.
   When I was a child, I walked a mile to school every day.

3 To talk about situations in the past.
   I lived in Madrid in my early twenties.

4 In reported speech.
   He told me you wanted to see me.

Past continuous

FORM
was/were + -ing

USE
We use the past continuous:

1 To talk about actions in progress in the past.
   He was sitting at his computer, staring hard at the screen.

2 To talk about temporary situations in the past.
   I was staying at my aunt's while the builders were at my house.

3 To talk about anticipated events that did not happen.
   They were having a meeting on Monday, but it didn't happen till Thursday in the end due to staff sickness.

4 To talk about an event that was in progress when another event happened.
   I was standing on the station platform when I noticed a £20 note on the ground.

5 To talk about actions in progress at the same time in the past.
   The doctor was looking after the injured man while the policeman was making sure the damaged car was removed from the road.

Past perfect simple

FORM
had + past participle

USE
We use the past perfect simple:

1 To refer to a time earlier than another past time.
   When I last saw Sarah, she had just started her new job.

2 In reported speech.
   He asked me if I had seen that new Brad Pitt film.

Past perfect continuous

FORM
had been + -ing

USE
We use the past perfect continuous to talk about actions or situations which had continued up to the past moment that we are thinking about.

*I **had been feeling** more and more dissatisfied with my job so I decided to resign and go travelling.*

Emphasis with *what*, *all* and *it*

We can use sentence structures starting with *what*, *all* and *it* to emphasise an action and make what we are saying sound more dramatic and interesting. When speaking, we often stress the main words more and use emphatic intonation to add to the dramatic effect.

For sentences starting with *what* or *all*, the two parts of the sentence are joined by *is* or *was* and we think of the first clause as singular.

What
Using *what* at the beginning of the sentence, emphasises an action or a series of actions.

***What I really love is** all my family having lunch at my place on a Sunday.*

***What he said was** that he was going to pack everything up and leave at dawn.*

***What they do is** go out every night and wait for the badgers to appear.*

All
Using *all* at the beginning of the sentence, suggests that this is the only thing that is important.

***All I know is** that I need to see her before tomorrow.*

***All people want is** reasonably priced food and a pleasant atmosphere.*

***All she said was** that she didn't want anyone to be late.*

It
We can use emphatic *it* sentences to emphasise a noun (including an *-ing* form).

***It was the tone** of his voice which gave it away in the end.*

***It is cycling** to work every day that really keeps me fit.*

***It's the way** he whistles all the time that annoys me.*

We can also use emphatic *it* sentences to emphasise the reason (with *because*) and the time (with *when* or *until*).

***It was because** he booked early that he got such good seats.*

***It is when** she doesn't talk to me about things that we start drifting apart.*

***It wasn't until** I woke up the next day that I realised what I'd done.*

Unit 05

Cohesion in text

We can avoid repeating words or phrases we have already used or specified by means of substitution (referring back, using pronouns or nouns) and ellipsis (leaving words out).

Substitution (referring back, using pronouns or nouns)
Substitution involves using other words. Nouns can be substituted by pronouns or text-referring nouns.

1 pronouns
 *This is my car and that **one** is hers.*

 *We decided not to leave our bags **there** as it was too risky.*

 *Marcus tried to carry the luggage but it was too heavy for **him**.*

 *I looked for the number but I couldn't find **it** in the book.*

2 text-referring nouns
 *She had <u>a continual itch on her leg</u>. She went to see her doctor because **the problem** wouldn't go away.*

 *They were <u>very short of money</u> and extremely worried about **the situation**.*

 *<u>He doesn't think we should pay the company</u> but I don't agree with **his view**.*

 *<u>Should we build more houses or not</u>? Most people think the government should decide on **this issue**.*

Verb phrases can be substituted with auxiliaries and *so, too, as well*, etc.

*If he could have left the house early in the morning, he would have **done so**.*

*She went to the post office and I **did, too**.*

Ellipsis (leaving words out)
Nouns, verbs and verb phrases can be left out of sentences to avoid repetition.

A nouns
1 *They came late and then (they) left early.*
 This is my car and that (car) is hers.
 The men ran up the hill. A few (men) fell as they ran.
2 with *and, but, or*
 Martin speaks French and Anna (speaks) Italian.
 They've got a dog and (a) cat.
 She was penniless but (she was) happy.
 Would you like orange (juice) or apple juice?

B verb phrases
1 at the end of a verb phrase
 If he could have left the house early, he would have (left the house early/done so).
2 with infinitives
 I never go swimming now but I used to (go swimming).
 I'm not sure I can see you then but I'll try to (see you then).

3 Clauses can be dropped after question words.

*If you want to be a writer, this article tells you **how**.*

*I asked for an appointment, and they said they would phone to tell me **when**.*

C after superlatives

I wanted to buy a new TV. He told me to buy the largest (TV) I could afford.

D before a complete form, usually in sentences beginning with *if*

If he could, he would have left the house early in the morning.

If I can, I'll call you tomorrow.

If you prefer, I can pick you up first.

Relative clauses and pronouns

Relative pronouns have a double use: they act as subjects or objects inside relative clauses, and at the same time they connect relative clause to nouns or pronouns in other clauses and so they act as conjunctions.

Defining relative clauses

1 The relative clause defines or identifies the person, thing, place, time or reason.

My boss is the person who told me about the training course.

This hotel is where Marco asked me to marry him.

2 *that* can be used instead of *which* and *who*.

*The girl **that** (who) was at reception has left now.*

*The course **that** (which) you want to attend is fully booked.*

3 The relative pronoun can be omitted when the clause defines the object of the clause.

The lecturer (who/that) the university just appointed is very well known.

The reason (why/that) he wants you to be there is to support him.

4 No commas are used before and after the relative clause.

Non-defining relative clauses

In non-defining relative clauses the relative clause gives extra information which can be left out. Commas are used before and after the relative clause.

The holiday, which we had booked months in advance, was a disaster.

The dog, whose owner clearly doted on him, chased the boys away.

Prepositions in relative clauses

Prepositions can come before the relative pronoun or at the end of the relative clause depending on whether the sentence is formal or informal.

The woman to whom you need to speak is away from the office for three days. (formal)

His routine, which you can usually set your clock by, has changed lately. (informal)

Reduced relative clauses

1 We can sometimes leave out a relative pronoun and the verb *be* before participles or adjectives such as *available* and *possible*.

The person (who is) taking us has been a guide for several years.

Who are the boys (who are) talking at the back?

Please tell me all the dates (which are) available.

I'm sorry but this Friday is the only date (which is) possible.

2 In informal style, *when, where*, etc. can be replaced by *that* or dropped after common nouns referring to time.

*Call me any **time** (that) you're free.*

*1998 was the **year** (that) I first fell in love!*

*It was the first **day** (that) we had free.*

Unit 06

Linking words

Linking words connect ideas, either between what a speaker is saying, or with what has been, or what is going to be, said or written. Some are used mostly in informal speech and writing; others are more common in formal styles of communication.

A Types

1 meaning 'and', these words introduce additional information or arguments:

also, plus, too, additionally, furthermore

2 meaning 'if', these words introduce a condition:

if, unless, provided (that)

3 meaning 'but', these words balance or emphasise contrasting points:

however, although, but, while, whereas, though, nevertheless, yet, despite, nonetheless

4 meaning 'because', these words introduce a reason for what has gone before or what is about to be said:

because, as, since, through

5 meaning 'therefore', these words show that what is said follows logically from what went before:

so, therefore, thus, hence, accordingly, consequently

6 meaning 'in order to', these words introduce a reason for something previously said:

for, so (that)

7 used for comparing, these words show a similarity or difference:

(just) as, unlike, similarly

8 meaning 'or', these words introduce an alternative idea:

instead, alternatively

B Examples of position and punctuation

Most linking words come at the beginning of their clauses and can appear at the beginning or in the middle of a sentence, e.g.:

We spent hours in the art gallery. **Therefore**, *we had very little time left for shopping.*

We spent hours in the art gallery and, **therefore**, *had very little time left for shopping.*

Some can be used at the end of clauses, e.g.

He agreed to take her to the interview. **However**, *he felt nervous about driving.*

He agreed to take her to the interview. He felt nervous about driving, **however**.

Most linking words need a comma. This is usually after the word if it is at the beginning of a sentence, or before and after the word if it appears in the middle of a sentence.

C Using two linking words

1 *and, but* and *or* can go before linking words which introduce a subordinating clause or before *yet* and *so*, e.g.

They could not find him **and so** *they didn't know whether to wait or not.*

We liked him **but, although** *he was the best on the list, he didn't get chosen.*

You can pick me up now **or, if** *you're busy, I'll wait.*

2 Some linking words can be used in the same sentence for emphasis. They must each be attached to their own clause.

While *I like him I do,* **however**, *think he's hard to get on with.*

Although *he was right, I think,* **nevertheless**, *he should apologise.*

Future forms

FORMS

will (shall) going to + infinitive
Present continuous
Present simple
Future continuous (*will + be + -ing* form)
Future perfect (*will + have +* past participle)
Future perfect continuous (*will + have been + -ing* form)
Future in the past

USES

1 We use *will* + infinitive for predicting something based on what we know or believe.

I think he'll be here in time for dinner. He's not usually late.

I'm sure you'll be fine in the interview because you're just what they need.

Note: *going to* + infinitive is also possible in this case.

2 We use *going to* + infinitive for predicting something based on what we can see or hear.

Mind that car –you're **going to crash**!

He's **going to slip** *if he doesn't put some proper shoes on.*

Note: we cannot use *will* + infinitive or the present continuous in this case.

3 We use *will* + infinitive for promises, threats, offers and requests.

If you shout at me one more time, I'll leave.

I promise I'll email you every day.

I'll help you with that presentation if you're stuck.

Will you show me how to play tennis properly?

Note: We cannot use *going to* in this case.

4 We use *going to* + infinitive and the present continuous to talk about things that have already been decided. We usually use the present continuous if the plans are more certain and more details have been decided.

I'm arriving early on Saturday so I can help them prepare.

He said he's meeting her in Bristol on Friday.

Note: We cannot use *will* + infinitive in this case.

5 We use *will* + infinitive to talk about future actions decided at the time of speaking.

I think I'll give her a call now.

I'll make a cup of tea.

Note: We cannot use the present continuous in this case.

6 We use the future continuous (*will + be + -ing* form) to say that an action will be in progress at a definite time in the future.

She'll be travelling to Sydney this afternoon.

7 We use the future perfect (*will + have +* past participle) to describe something that will be completed before a definite time in the future. This focuses on the event.

I'll have completed my degree by this time next year.

8 We use future perfect continuous (*will + have been + -ing* form) to describe something that will be completed before a definite time in the future. This focuses on the length of time taken.

I'll have been studying for three years by this time next year.

Unit 07

if structures

Linking words in *if* structures

Some common conditional linking words are:

if, when, until, unless , even if, no matter how/who/what/where/when, provided (that) imagine (that), supposing (that), providing (that), as/so long as, on condition (that)

Punctuation in *if* structures

When the clause with the conditional linking word (*if, unless*, etc.) is at the beginning of the sentence, there is a comma. When the main clause begins the sentence, there is no comma.

If I see her, I'll give her the money back.

As long as you pay me back by Friday, I'll lend you some money.

I'll give her the money back when I see her.

*I won't lend her any money **unless** she promises to pay me back.*

Different types of *if* structures

A

FORM
if + present simple + present simple in the main clause

USE
To talk about something which is always true or describe what always happens. (Sometimes called the **zero conditional**.)

*If you **heat** water, **it boils**.*

*The dog **barks** if you **disturb** her.*

B

FORM
if + present simple/present continuous/present perfect + future/present continuous or imperative in the main clause

USE
To talk about something that is a real possibility in the future. (Sometimes called the **first conditional**.)

*If she **gets** the job, she'**ll earn** more money.*

*Unless you **tell** me, I won'**t be able to** help you.*

***Tell** Alan to give me a call if he'**s** in this afternoon.*

*As long as you'**ve prepared** for the interview, you'**ll be** OK.*

*No matter what you **do**, she'**ll never apologise**.*

C

FORM
if + past simple/continuous + conditional in the main clause

USE
To talk about something:
1 that is impossible and just imagined.
2 which is very unlikely to happen in the future.
(Sometimes called the **second conditional**.) Also, this form is often used to give advice.

*If she **was** richer, she'**d buy** that new car.*

*I **wouldn't go camping** even if the weather **was** warm!*

*If I **were** you, I'**d tell** him what you've done.*

*He only **agreed** to pay on condition that we **would pay** him back next month.*

*Supposing she **went** to university, what do you think she **would study**?*

D

FORM
if + past perfect + *would have* + past participle in the main clause

USE
To talk about something in the past that could have happened, but didn't, or something that shouldn't have happened, but did. (Sometimes called the **third conditional**.)

*I **wouldn't have taken** the bus if I'**d known** the journey was so long.*

*If you'**d told** me, I **would've been able** to help you.*

*Provided that you **had paid** before the sixteenth, you **should have had** the tickets by twentieth.*

E

FORM
an *if*-clause referring to the past with a main clause referring to the present or the future

USE
To talk about if something had been different in the past, the present (or future) would be different. (Sometimes called a **mixed conditional**.)

*If she'**d worked** harder, she **would have got** that promotion.*

*I'**d be** still living in Newcastle if **I hadn't taken** that job.*

*Imagine he **had gone** to India, he **would** still **be** living there now.*

F

FORM
an *if*-clause referring to the present or future with a main clause referring to the past

USE
To talk about if something in the present (or in general time) were different, the past would have been different. (Also sometimes called a **mixed conditional**.)

*If I **knew** her address, I **would have sent** her an invitation.*

*She **wouldn't have gone out with** him if she **didn't like** him.*

Leaving words out after *if*
We sometime leave out the subject + *be* after *if*. This is especially true with certain fixed expressions, e.g. *if necessary, if any, if anything, if ever, if in doubt.*

*I'll do the shopping for you **if necessary**.*

*I'm not sorry I did it. **If anything**, I wish I'd done more.*

Polite expressions using *if*, *would* and *should*
Would can be used after *if* in polite expressions.

*If you **wouldn't mind** waiting for a moment, the manager **will see** you shortly.*

Should is used in the *if* clause to make it even less likely. This is common in formal letters.

*If you **should require** any further information, please **do not hesitate** to contact us.*

Should can replace *if* in formal letters.

***Should you wish** to contact me, I **can be reached** at the above address.*

Grammar Reference

Linking phrases

Linking phrases connect ideas, either between what a speaker is saying, or with what has been, or what is going to be, said or written. Some are used mostly in informal speech and writing; others are more common in formal styles of communication.

A Types

1 meaning 'and', these phrases introduce additional information or arguments:
   in addition to, not to mention, on top of which

2 meaning 'because', these phrases introduce a reason for what has gone before or what is about to be said:
   in view of, out of, owing to

3 meaning 'but', these phrases balance or emphasise contrasting points:
   by contrast, in spite of, in any case, even so

4 meaning 'if', these phrases introduce a condition:
   whether or not, as long as, on condition that, in the event of, in case, assuming that

5 meaning 'therefore', these phrases show that what is said follows logically from what went before:
   as a result, for this reason, with the result that, this means that, as a consequence

6 meaning 'in order to', these phrases introduce a reason for something previously said:
   in order to, with the aim of -ing, with a view to -ing, so as to

B How the phrases connect clauses

Some of the phrases can be used to introduce coordinating clauses (i.e. clauses which can each form complete sentences on their own) and some can be used to introduce a subordinating clause (i.e. a clause which cannot be a complete sentence on its own but which is dependent on another clause). Some can be used for both.

1 coordinating clauses
   *He didn't have any money. **As a result**, he could not afford to go to Australia.*
   *I'm busy this evening. **In any case**, I don't want to go to the party.*
   *We will supply you with books **on condition that** they are returned.*

2 subordinating clauses
   *I can't stand his wife, **not to mention** his ghastly daughters!*
   ***In view of** his lateness, I have no option but to sack him.*
   ***In spite of** his illness, he still came to the party.*
   ***In the event of** fire, please gather in the car park.*
   *We spoke to him this morning **with a view to** getting his agreement.*

3 coordinating pairs
   There are several coordinating conjunctions which consist of pairs of words. The first word adds emphasis to the meaning of the second.

*****Not only** did he lose the match, **but** he also **broke** his ankle.*
*****Not only** is she beautiful, she is clever **as well**.*
*****On the one hand**, I think Venice is beautiful. **On the other, hand** I find it very expensive.*

Unit 08

Degrees of certainty

We can use *can, could, must, may* and *might* to make a logical deduction about what has happened or is happening based on information we have and the possibilities available. *Must* and *can't* express what we think is either inevitable or impossible; *can, could, might* and *may* express less certainty.

Suggesting a likely possibility
A *could, may* and *might* (not)
We use *could, may* and *might (not)* to:
1 say that something is possibly true at the moment of speaking

FORM
might/may/could + infinitive
*She **might** be late if the traffic is bad.*
*He **may** be in a meeting still.*
*That train **could** be very busy so I'd take an earlier one.*

Note: We don't use *can* in this case (to talk about possibility in the present): ~~He can be coming to dinner but I'm not sure.~~

2 talk about the possibility that past events happened

FORM
could/may/might + *have* + past participle
*They **may have** left the keys in the car.*
*She **might not have** spoken to him about the problem yet.*
*She **could have** taken the bag with her when she left.*

B *can*
We use *can* to:
1 ask, speculate or guess about past events
Note: This is only in questions.

FORM
(*Wh*-word +) *can* + subject + *have* + past participle
*****Can** he really have thought she didn't like him?*
*Where **can** they have gone?*

Certainty based on logical conclusion
A *must*
We use *must* to:
1 talk about something which is certain or highly probable to be true, or for which we have excellent evidence for believing to be true in the present or future

FORM
must + infinitive
*They **must** be tired after walking round Rome all afternoon.*

2 express conclusions about things that happened in the past when we are certain, or it is highly probable, something was true, or for which we have excellent evidence for believing to have been true

FORM
must + have + past participle

He **must have** picked it up because it's not on the table.

B *can't*

We use *can't* to:

1 talk about something which is certain or highly probable not to be true, or for which we have excellent evidence for believing *not* to be true in the present or future

FORM
can't + infinitive

That **can't** be the postman – it's too late.

2 to express conclusions about things that happened in the past when we are certain, or it is highly probable, something was *not* true, or for which we have excellent evidence for believing *not* to have been true

FORM
can't + have + past participle

She **can't have** taken the bus or she'd be here by now.

Note: We can also use *couldn't* in this case (to talk about certainty):

That **couldn't** be the postman – it's too late.

She **couldn't have** taken the bus or she'd be here by now.

We don't use *mustn't* in this case (to talk about certainty): ~~He mustn't have liked the film because he left halfway through it.~~

C *should*

We use *should* to:

1 talk about something which is certain or highly probable to be true, or for which we have excellent evidence for believing to be true in the present or future

FORM
should + be

It's 6 o'clock – he **should** be in Warsaw by now.

We don't use *should + infinitive* (except *be*) in this case. *Should + infinitive* is only used for obligation or advice:

He **should** apply for that job.

He **should** do some revision.

2 to express conclusions about things that happened in the past when we are certain, or it is highly probable, something was true, or for which we have excellent evidence for believing to have been true

FORM
should + have + past participle

He s**hould have** arrived at 8.00 p.m. if the roads were OK.

We don't use *should + have + not* in this case. Instead, we use *can't + have*: ~~He shouldn't have got there by 8.00 p.m. as the traffic was awful.~~ He **can't have** got there by 8.00 p.m. as the traffic was awful.

Confusable structures

1 *like, as if*

We use these expressions to say we think something is going to happen based on present evidence. Usually this is evidence based on our senses. There is no difference in meaning.

A *looks/feels/seems/sounds like* + noun phrase or + clause

It **feels like** silk.

It **looks like** he's forgotten.

It **sounds like** complete rubbish to me.

B *looks/feels/seems/sounds as if* + clause

It **feels as if** it is made of silk.

It **looks as if** he's forgotten.

It **sounds as if** it's complete rubbish to me.

2 *suppose, to be supposed to, to suppose*

A *suppose* (conjunction) = 'if'

Suppose he doesn't call me, what will I do?

Suppose you had a million pounds, would you give some to me?

B *to be supposed to* (verb) = 'meant to'

This usually refers to the present or future.

It **is supposed to** be sunny this afternoon.

to be supposed to (verb) = 'have to'

This can be used to refer to an obligation in the present, future or past.

You **are supposed to** be writing that report now.

He **was supposed to** call me when he had finished.

We **were supposed to** give him the money yesterday.

C *suppose* (verb) = 'think' or 'guess'

I **suppose** it will be too late to go to the party now.

We **suppose** the roads will be busy.

3 *used to, to be used to*

A *used to* + infinitive for a past habit

I **used to be** in the sun a lot as a child.

B *to be used to* + *-ing* for 'accustomed to'

People who live in hot climates **are used to being** in the sun.

Unit 09

Passives

FORM
appropriate tense of *be* + past participle

Present simple: All the figures **are checked** by at least two people.

Present continuous: I came by bus because my car **is being repaired** at the moment.

Past simple: We **were told** to arrive at least half an hour early.

Past continuous: We couldn't go into the building because the floors **were being cleaned**.

Present perfect: You **have been warned** about the consequences of being late.

Past perfect: He **had been arrested** on two previous occasions.

Future will: She**'ll be trained** up in the first week and then left to get on with it.

Future perfect: Your seat **will have been taken** by someone else by now.

going to: The new library **is going to be paid** for by an anonymous donor.

Modals: She **must have been persuaded** to go by her brother.

Passive gerund: My dog loves **being taken** for walks by the sea.

Note:

1 Verbs that do not take an object (e.g. *ache, arrive, sit down*) do not have passive forms. It is not possible to say: ~~My legs were ached~~.

2 Stative verbs like *have, fit* and *suit* are not used in the passive with the same meanings.

Do you have any pets? (*have* = own)

The builders charged us double what we expected. We**'ve been had**. (*have* = deceived)

That dress **fits** you perfectly. (*fit* = be the right size)

My new kitchen **is being fitted** this week. (*fit* = installed)

Her new haircut really **suits** her. (*suit* = look nice)

Helen and her new boyfriend **are** really **suited** to each other. (*suit* = are compatible)

USE

The passive is used for the following reasons:

1 To talk about actions, events and processes when the action is more important than the agent (or when we don't know the agent, or when the agent would be a vague subject word like *someone* or *people*). This is often the case in scientific writing.

The pyramids at Giza **were built** around 4,500 years ago.

The animals **were given** varying doses of the new drug.

2 To put new information later in the sentence.

This watch **was given** to me by my best friend.

3 To put longer expressions at the end of the sentence.

The decision **was made** by the head teacher, the teachers and the governors as well as the students themselves.

4 To give a general opinion with the verbs *think, believe, feel, know* and *say*.

It **is believed** that the world is getting warmer.

It **is thought** that most people are unhealthier than they think they are.

5 To make a statement sound more impersonal and less connected to the speaker.

Learning about nutrition is something which **should be compulsory** in all schools.

Introductory *it*

1 *It* as a subject may refer forward to a noun clause (starting with *to* infinitive, *-ing*, a *that* clause or a *wh-* clause). This structure is used to emphasise the adjective.

It's difficult to hear him.

It's great working with you.

It turned out that he was lying all the time.

It was too late when we found out about it.

2 *It* is often used to talk about the weather and the time.

It's raining again.

It's half past six.

3 *It* as a subject can be used to avoid using noun clauses in a subject position, which sounds too formal.

It frightens me that there is so much crime in big cities today.

That there is so much crime in big cities today frightens me.

4 *It* is common with reporting verbs used in the passive.

It is thought that crime rates are now falling.

5 *It* + *(would) seem/appear* + *that* is also common when reporting events.

It seems that someone broke into the school last night.

It would appear that a number of computers were taken.

6 Some common phrases used with *it* are:

It's no use -ing

It's no good -ing

It's pointless -ing

It occurs to me that …

It strikes me that …

It doesn't matter what/when, etc. …

It's a waste of time …

Unit 10

Participle clauses

Participles can combine with other words into participle clauses. These are used to add information to sentences, or to combine two sentences into one more concise sentence. They are often quite formal.

1 They can be used after nouns.

They function in a similar way to relative clauses (adding information about the noun), except they have participles instead of complete verbs.

Present and past participles are used in this way, but not usually perfect participles.

There were over fifty people **applying** for the job I wanted. (*… who were applying …*)

The total amount of money **collected** for the new building appeal came to over £500,000. (*… which was collected …*)

2 They can be used in similar ways to adverbial clauses.

They can express condition, reason, time relations, result, etc. Present, past and perfect participles can be used in this way.

*I felt safer **travelling** with a group of people than on my own. (... because I was travelling with ...)*

***Determined** to be a professional musician, she spent hours practising her violin every day. (She was determined to be ..., so she practised ...)*

***Having seen** their terrible living conditions, he decided to try to do something to help. (As a result of seeing ...,/When he saw ...,)*

Reported speech

Direct speech

This is when we report the exact words that someone says or writes.

'Come here immediately!' he shouted.

Reported speech

This is when we report something that has been said or written. If the report is after the time the thing was said or written, the verb form generally changes as follows. The changes are almost always used in written, more formal English. (However, in spoken English, the reported speech is often the same as the direct speech – see below.)

Direct speech	Reported speech
1 Present simple/continuous	Past simple/continuous
*'I **want** to go to Florida,' he said.*	*He said he **wanted** to go to Florida.*
2 Past simple/continuous	Past simple/continuous or past perfect simple/continuous
*'I **saw** him enter the building,' the witness said.*	*The witness said (that) he **had seen** him enter the building.*
3 Present perfect simple/ continuous	Past perfect simple/continuous
'I've always wanted to go to New Zealand,' she said.	*She said that she **had** always **wanted** to go to New Zealand.*
4 *will*	*would*
*'I**'ll give** you a lift to the station,' he said.*	*He said he **would give** me a lift to the station.*
5 *must* (obligation)	*had to*
*'You **must get** your assignment done by Friday,' she told me.*	*She told me that I **had to get** my assignment done by Friday.*
6 *can*	*could*
*'I **can't reach** the shelf,' she said.*	*She said (that) she **couldn't reach** the shelf.*

The verb form does not need to change when:

1 The thing being reported is still true – especially in spoken English.

*'Spaghetti **is** my favourite type of pasta,' he said.*

*He said (that) spaghetti **is** his favourite type of pasta.*

2 The thing reported contains the modals *would, could, might, ought to* and *should* as well as *must* for logical deduction.

*'I **might have** a party next weekend,' she said.*

*She said (that) she **might have** a party the following weekend.*

3 The thing being reported contains the past perfect.

*'The bus only came after I**'d been waiting** for ages,' he said.*

*He said (that) the bus only came (had come) after he**'d been waiting** for ages.*

Other changes that occur in reported speech are:

Direct speech	Reported speech
today	*that day*
this morning	*that morning*
tomorrow	*the next day, the day after, the following day*
next Friday	*the following Friday*
yesterday	*the day before, the previous day*
last week	*the week before, the previous week*
ago	*before*
here	*there*
this/that/these/those	*the*

Reported questions

1 Reported *Yes/No* questions

FORM

When there is no question word (a *Yes/No* question) in the direct speech question, we use *if/whether*. Word order is the same as in the statement. The verb tense and other changes are the same as for other types of reported speech.

'Have you got a driving licence,' he asked.

*He asked me **if/whether I had** a driving licence.*

2 Reported *wh-* questions

FORM

When *wh-* question words are used, the *wh-* word is followed by statement word order, that is the subject followed by the verb. All the tense and other changes are the same as for other types of reported speech.

'What do you want to do today?' she asked.

*She asked me **what I wanted** to do that day.*

Reported orders

FORM

verb + (*that*) + clause or verb + object + infinitive with *to*

'Go and do your homework,' she said.

*She **told me to go** and do my homework.*

Reported suggestions

FORM

suggest + -ing

suggest + that + should + infinitive without *to*

suggest + past simple

'I think we should go to the Italian restaurant,' she said.

She **suggested going** to the Italian restaurant.

She **suggested that we should go** to the Italian restaurant.

She **suggested we went** to the Italian restaurant.

Note: We cannot say: ~~She suggested to go to the Italian restaurant.~~

Reporting verbs

Note: Some verbs can be used with more than one pattern.

1 Verb + object + infinitive

   She **invited me to take** part in the competition.

   Other verbs with the same pattern are:

   beg, encourage, invite, order, advise, persuade, remind, tell, warn

2 Verb + object (+ *that*) + clause

   They **told us (that) they were** new to the area.

   Other verbs with the same pattern are: *advise, persuade, remind, tell, warn*

3 Verb (+ *that*) + clause

   She **says (that) she'll explain** everything later.

   Other verbs with the same pattern are:

   say, claim, explain, admit, deny, recommend, agree, decide, promise, suggest

4 Verb + *-ing* form

   He **recommended booking** tickets online.

   Other verbs with the same pattern are:

   admit, deny, recommend, suggest

   He **admitted that he hadn't paid** his bus fare.

   She **suggested that** we should go for a walk.

5 Verb + infinitive

   We **agreed to talk** to the head teacher.

   Other verbs with the same pattern are:

   agree, decide, promise, offer, refuse, threaten

6 Verb + (object) + preposition + *-ing* form

   She **apologised for arriving** late.

   He **accused me of lying** to him.

   Other verbs with the same pattern are:

   accuse (of), apologise (for), blame (for), congratulate (on), discourage (from), insist (on)

Unit 11

Verb patterns

There are different patterns that different verbs take depending on whether they are **transitive** (= followed by one or two object(s)) or **intransitive** (= not followed by an object). Some verbs can be both transitive and intransitive (see below).

This information can be found in dictionaries, with the following symbols:

[T] = transitive   [I] = intransitive.

Looking at the examples given in dictionaries can also help with working out what the pattern is.

Some common verbs:

1 Transitive verbs with one object:

   believe, pull, lose, want, eat, miss

   I **believed him** when he said he urgently needed money.

   He sat down and **ate his dinner** in silence.

2 Transitive verbs with two objects:

   send, take, invite, give, bring, play, make, offer, tell, lend, explain, describe, assure, inform, warn

   She's **sent me three emails** already this morning.

   I'm sure he's **telling us the truth**.

   When there are two objects, usually the first object is a person and the second object is a thing. With many of these verbs, we can reverse the order of the objects by using *to* or *for*.

   He **gave me the tickets** yesterday and now I can't find them.

   He **gave the tickets to me** yesterday and now I can't find them.

   She's going to **make me a scarf** for my birthday.

   She's going to **make a scarf for me** for my birthday.

   Certain transitive verbs, however, always need a preposition before the person.

   She **explained the instructions** to me carefully.

   ~~She explained me the instructions carefully.~~

3 Intransitive verbs:

   happen, wait, sleep, sit, fall, laugh

   We **waited** until 9 o'clock but nobody came.

   He **fell** and broke his leg while playing football last weekend.

4 Verbs which can be both transitive and intransitive:

   wake up, start, stop, shut, forget

   I need to **wake up** early tomorrow morning.

   Please **wake me up** early tomorrow morning.

   The minute the door **shut**, I realised I'd left my keys inside.

   Can you **shut the door**, please?

   Transitive verbs can have passive forms.

   The parcel **was sent** by registered post.

With some transitive verbs you can miss out the object if it is obvious what it is:

park the car, cook the food, smoke a cigarette, ride a horse

*I like driving but I find it very difficult to **park**.*

*Who's going to **cook** tonight?*

Noun groups

It is sometimes possible and desirable to use a noun group instead of a verb and adjective group. This is sometimes called *nominalisation*.

Noun group: ***His poor health** meant that he had to cancel his holiday.*

Verb and adjective group: ***He wasn't very well** so he had to cancel his holiday.*

The main reasons for using a noun group are:

1 To change the emphasis of the sentence (usually making one clause instead of two).

   ***Her bravery** was noticed by everyone.*

   Everyone noticed how brave she was.

2 To make sentences shorter and more concise, (leaving room for new information at the end of the sentence) .

   ***The main reason for the trip** was to go on a boat trip round the islands.*

   The main thing that we wanted to do on the trip was to go on a boat trip round the islands.

3 To refer back to phrases already mentioned.

   *He managed to win every race in his first season of competition. **This amazing achievement** brought him many fans.*

4 To make sentences more impersonal.

   ***Your promotion prospects** are increased if you're a good team player.*

   You're more likely to be promoted if you're a good team player.

5 Noun groups are often used in formal, academic or scientific English.

   ***The conclusion** was that most people are basically honest.*

   We concluded that most people are basically honest.

Unit 12

Countable and uncountable nouns

Uncountable nouns

These have no plural. The following are common nouns that are usually uncountable:

accommodation, advice, behaviour, bread, copper (and all other metals), *English* (and all other languages), *furniture, health, information, knowledge, luggage, news, progress, research, rice*

(and all other grains and cereals), *rubbish, salt* (and all other condiments, e.g. pepper), *scenery, spaghetti, traffic, travel, trouble, water* (and all other liquids), *weather, work*

Nouns which can be countable or uncountable

The following nouns can be both countable and uncountable:

1 Nouns we think of as single things or substances.

   ***Egg**: I'll have **an egg**, please. You've got **egg** on your tie.*

   ***Chicken**: Can you get **a chicken** from the supermarket? We had **chicken** and chips for dinner.*

   ***Iron**: Have you got **an iron** I could borrow? She's got an old bed made of **iron**.*

   ***Glass**: Would you like **a glass** of water? Vinegar is very good for cleaning **glass**.*

   ***Hair**: I found **a hair** in my soup. She's got very long, straight **hair**.*

2 Normally uncountable nouns which are used to refer to particular varieties.

   *Would you like some more **wine**?*

   *They produce **a very good wine** in that region.*

3 Words for drinks, e.g. *coffee, tea, beer*. The countable noun means *a glass of, a cup of, a bottle of*, etc.

   ***Coffee** is fine as long as you don't drink too much.*

   *Shall we meet for **a coffee** on Tuesday morning?*

   *I like drinking **beer** when the weather's really hot.*

   *There's **a beer** in the fridge if you want one.*

4 *time, space, room*

   *I won't have **time** to go shopping until tomorrow.*

   *We had **a really good time** at her party last night.*

   *We haven't got **space** for a bigger table in here.*

   *I'll try to find **a space** for you.*

   *There's **room** for at least five more people to come in.*

   *I'd like **a room** with a view of the sea, please.*

5 Words which can be singular or plural, depending on your point of view.

   team, public, staff, cast, crew, company, police, media, army, community, committee, audience

   *The **team has** worked very hard this year. (Singular verb = the team as a whole)*

   *The **team have** worked very hard this year. (Plural verb = the team as made up of many individuals)*

Singular and plural nouns – confusing cases

1 Words which are always plural.

   goods, stairs, proceeds, lodgings, contents, acoustics, outskirts
   Some tools, instruments, pieces of equipment, *e.g. scissors, pliers, glasses, headphones, goggles*, etc.
   Some clothes, e.g. *trousers, shorts, tights, leggings, pyjamas*, etc.

   *The safety **goggles are** made of heat-resistant plastic.*

   *The **acoustics** in the concert hall **were** fantastic.*

2 Words which look plural but are not.

news, series, means

Some games, e.g. *billiards, darts, dominoes, cards*, etc.

Some activities and subjects, e.g. *economics, maths, physics, aerobics, gymnastics*, etc.

*The new **series** of 'Doctor Who' **is** absolutely brilliant.*

*When I was at school, **maths was** one of my favourite subjects.*

Determiners used with countable and uncountable nouns

Before countable nouns, we can use:

a/an, few(er), a few, many, a great many, not many, several

Before uncountable nouns, we can use:

(very) little, a little, much, not much, a great deal of, a small/large amount of

Before both countable and uncountable nouns, we can use:

some, any, (quite) a lot of, lots of, plenty of, a lack of

1 *few/a few* and *little/a little*

Use *few/a few* with plural countable nouns and *little/a little* with uncountable nouns.

A

a few (for countables) and *a little* (for uncountables) are used to talk about positive ideas. *A few* means 'some but not many' and *a little* means 'some but not much'.

*I invited **a few** friends round for dinner on my birthday.*

*There's **a little** cake left – do have some!*

B

few (for countables) and *little* (for uncountables) are used to talk about negative ideas. *Few/little* are generally used to mean 'not enough'/'almost none'.

***Few** people do enough recycling to really make a difference.*

***Little** time was left to discuss the most important issues.*

2 *many/much*

Use *many* with plural countable nouns and *much* with uncountable nouns.

*How **many** people are coming to the meeting?*

*She hasn't got **much** support for her plans yet.*

3 Some determiners can be used with both plural countable nouns and uncountable nouns.

*I've got **some** time spare if you need help.*

***Some** computers have been stolen from the school.*

***A lot of** people must have seen what happened.*

*There's **a lot of** cheese in this particular recipe.*

4 *a piece, a bit, a slice, a lump*, etc.

Use specific words to make uncountable nouns countable.

a piece is a general word and can be used with many different uncountable nouns, e.g.

a piece of bread, advice, furniture, music, equipment

a bit is also a general word and can be used with many different nouns (both countable and uncountable). It is slightly more informal than *piece* and it usually suggests a smaller amount than *piece*, e.g.

a bit of bread, cheese, information, advice, chocolate

There are a number of other words with go with specific uncountable nouns. The most common ones are:

a tube of toothpaste

a slice of bread, toast, cheese, ham, meat

a loaf of bread

a bar of chocolate, soap

a carton of milk, juice

a lump of sugar, cheese, coal

a joint of meat

a fit of temper

a breath of fresh air

a spot of bother, rain

a rumble of thunder

a gust of wind

a stroke of luck

an item of news, clothing

a state of emergency, confusion, chaos

There are also a number of other words which go with specific 'collective' nouns to describe groups. The most common ones are:

a crowd of people

a gang of thieves, hooligans, young people (mostly used negatively)

a flock of sheep, birds

a herd of cows, deer, elephants

a swarm of bees (and other flying insects)

a shoal of fish

a pack of (playing) cards, dogs, wolves

a bunch of flowers, grapes, bananas

a set of tools, saucepans, paintbrushes

a pile of papers, clothes, dishes

a stack of chairs, boxes (usually large things piled up)

a couple of people, books (vague way of saying two, not necessarily exactly two)

Question forms

Direct questions

There are three main types of direct questions:

A *Yes/No questions* (which expect the answer 'yes' or 'no')

1 Most verbs need to use the auxiliary *do/does/did* to make questions.

***Does he speak** German?*

2 Verbs with *be, can* and *have (got)* don't need the auxiliary *do/does/did*.

***Is she cooking** dinner tonight?*

***Can you play** tennis?*

***Have you got** any money?*

3 Negative *Yes/No* questions expect a particular answer.

Didn't he go to Australia last summer? (expected answer 'yes')

Haven't you finished your essay yet? (expected answer 'no')

B *Wh-* questions

1 Question words (*who, what, where, when, whose, why, which* and *how*) come at the beginning of the question.

Where did you live when you were a child?

What are you doing at the weekend?

2 If *who, what* or *which* is the subject of the sentence, we don't use the auxiliary *do/does/did*, and we use normal sentence word order (not the inversion of subject and verb as for other questions).

Who gave you those flowers?

What happened yesterday?

Compare:

Who gave you those flowers? (asking about the subject)

Who did you give those flowers to? (asking about the object)

3 If there is a preposition, it comes at the end of the question (unless it is very formal speaking or writing).

Who are you going to give that **to**?

(Very formal: **To whom** are you going to give that?)

What were you talking **about**?

(Very formal: **About what** were you talking?)

C Alternative questions (which expect the answer to be one of two options)

There are two types of alternative questions; (a) a *Yes/No* type and (b) a *Wh-* type.

Do you want to go to a restaurant or stay in tonight?

Which would you rather do, have a skiing holiday or a beach holiday?

Other types of questions
A Indirect questions

Indirect questions use statement word order (you don't invert the subject and verb). They are often used to be more polite or tentative when you're asking a question (e.g. if you don't know someone very well/at all, if you're asking for something quite big or difficult). We use *if/whether* for *Yes/No* type indirect questions.

Common ways of starting indirect questions are in **bold**:

I'd like to know if your report is finished yet.

Could you tell me what the time is, please?

Would you mind telling me where the manager is?

Do you know whether there have been any cancellations?

B Question tags

Question tags are short questions at the end of a statement. The speaker often expects a particular answer and is using a question tag to confirm what he or she already knows.

The most common question tags are formed as follows:

1 positive statement + negative question tag

*She does a lot of yoga, **doesn't she**?*

*You've played tennis before, **haven't you**?*

2 negative statement + positive question tag

*You didn't cook me any dinner, **did you**?*

*He isn't going to be late, **is he**?*

If the main sentence has an auxiliary verb, this is repeated in the question tag.

*He can't hear us, **can he**?*

If the main sentence has no auxiliary verb, the question tag uses do, does or did.

*You speak French, **don't you**?*

If the main sentence contains negative words like *never, no, nobody, hardly, scarcely* and *little*, non-negative question tags ar used.

***Hardly** anyone turned up to the meeting, **did they**?*

*It's **no** good saying that now, **is it**?*

There are other exceptions as follows:

1 *aren't I?*

The question tag for *I am* is *aren't I?*

*Oh dear! **I'm** late, **aren't I**?*

2 *let's*

The question tag for *let's* is *shall we?*

*Let's see what Jane thinks, **shall we**?*

3 imperatives

will, would, can and *could you?* can all be used to tell or ask people to do things. After a negative imperative, we use *will you?*

*Close the window, **could you**?*

*Carry those suitcases, **would you**?*

***Don't** forget to call me, **will you**?*

Unit 13

Quantifiers – phrases

1 *Both* and *all*

We can use *both* and *all* as determiners and pronouns. They take a plural verb.

***Both brands** of jeans look the same to me.*

***Both of those shops** are owned by the same person.*

***All dogs** need to go for walks.*

*I'll have **all of them**, please.*

2 *Neither* and *either*

We can use *neither* and *either* as determiners and pronouns. They usually take a singular verb, although sometimes in spoken English, we can use a plural verb.

***Neither room** is very suitable for the meeting.*

***Neither of the books** was very interesting.*

Grammar Reference

*I don't like **either photograph**.*

***Either of the restaurants** you've mentioned would be fine.*

3 No and none

No is a pronoun and takes a plural verb. *None* is a determiner and can be used before singular, plural and uncountable nouns. *None* takes a singular verb (but in less formal English a plural verb can be used).

***No two snowflakes** are exactly alike.*

***None of us** could agree about where to go.*

4 Each and every

Each can be a determiner and a pronoun. *Every* is only a determiner. They usually take a singular verb.

Each and *every* are similar in meaning and in some contexts both can be used.

***Every/Each** person brought something to the picnic.*

Each is mostly used when we are thinking of separate individuals/items in a group. It is used to talk about two or more things.

***Each computer** in the new library cost over £500.*

***Each of the pieces** of homework took me ages.*

Each can also be used for emphasis:

*They **each** carried their own bag.*

Every is mostly used to refer to the group as a whole (rather than separate individuals). It is closer in meaning to *all*. It is used to talk about three or more things.

*We went to the same restaurant **every night**.*

Every can also be used with plural nouns in phrases of frequency:

*She went to see her grandmother **every six weeks**.*

Every can also be used with some abstract nouns to emphasise that something is correct or necessary.

*You have **every right** to say if you don't like it.*

5 One, another and ones

One and *another* can be used as determiners and pronouns. As pronouns, they are used to replace a countable noun. *Ones* is only used as a pronoun.

*I liked all the books but my favourite was this **one**.*

***One of the other departments** will deal with that.*

*Would you like **another**?*

***Another of the victims** has decided to report the crime.*

*Why don't you try on the bigger **ones**?*

6 Other and others

Other is usually used as a determiner. We can also use *other* as a pronoun with *the*. *Others* is only used as a pronoun.

***Other places** are far more interesting than here.*

*Here's one CD I lent you. What have you done with **the other**?*

*We couldn't find anything in this shop but there are plenty of **others**.*

7 One another and each other

We use *one another* and *each other* as objects of the verb. They mean the same.

*They looked at **each other/one another** for a long time before she spoke.*

8 Some and any

Some and *any* are used to talk about indefinite amounts. *Some* is generally used in positive statements and *any* in negatives and questions. They can be used as determiners and pronouns.

*I've got **some chocolate** left.*

*Have you seen **any birds** in the nest yet?*

*You don't need to bring any money because I've got **some**.*

***Some of the things** he's written are incorrect.*

*I hadn't seen **any of those people** before.*

9 Something, anything, everything, nothing, somewhere, anywhere, someone, anyone, etc.

These are all generally used as pronouns. They take singular verbs.

*I asked him but he didn't say **anything**.*

***Everyone** seems happy with the idea.*

For determiners *much, many, a lot of, (a) few, (a) little, most*, etc. see *Countable and uncountable nouns* on page 183.

Other common phrases:

*There were a lot of people at the party but he greeted **each and every one** personally.*

***Every single time** he sees me, he asks about my accident.*

*They picked up **every last** piece of litter from the campsite before they left.*

*I go to the cinema **every so often**, depending on how busy I am.*

*You have **every reason** to be annoyed with him.*

*I'm going to give out the marks **one by one**.*

***All too often** their discussions end up as huge arguments.*

***There is no reason** why you can't just turn up on the night.*

*His behaviour is **nothing less than** outrageous.*

*I'm sorry but you came **nowhere near** to passing this exam.*

*I'll do my best but I'm afraid I'm **not much of a** public speaker.*

*He's not **by any means** an expert in computers.*

Emphasis with inversion

We can change the emphasis of a sentence by putting a negative adverb, adverbial expression or restrictive word at the beginning, such as *In no circumstances, At no time, Hardly, Seldom, Only*, etc. In this case we put an auxiliary verb directly before the subject of the verb.

FORM

adverb/adverbial expression/ restrictive word + auxiliary + subject + verb

***In no circumstances** must you smoke in here.*

*At **no time** was he in danger.*

***Not until** much later **did she** realise the extent of his betrayal.*

***Hardly had I** arrived **when** she started shouting at me.*

***Seldom have I** seen such a stunning painting.*

***Little did I** realise that I would live to regret my decision.*

***Only then did I** see his letter on the table.*

***Only** after her accident **was she** able to appreciate what he did for her.*

***No sooner** had they withdrawn the money **than** he grabbed it from them.*

***Not only did we** arrive late **but** with no money as well.*

We can also use *Not until …* with a complete clause:

***Not until he had finished the journey was he** aware how much it had cost him.*

USE

These inverted sentences are used to alter the information structure of a sentence and emphasise the aspect at the beginning.

Not until later did I realise that I had been lucky.

This emphasises the time (or delay) in realising how lucky he had been.

I realised later that I had been very lucky.

This emphasises the fact that he was lucky.

Inversions are generally used in formal or literary English. They have the effect of drawing the reader deeper into the subject.

Unit 14

Complex sentences (writing)

We can use complex sentences to make our writing more effective and more sophisticated and/or interesting.

Presenting ideas or events more concisely

1 a shortened relative clause

   Katy was happy with what she had achieved. Therefore, she decided to leave the office.

   *Katy, **happy with what she had achieved**, decided to leave the office.*

2 a clause inside a clause

   The pilot had finally checked the plane. Then he decided to look in the luggage hold.

   *The pilot, **when he had finally checked the plane**, decided to look in the luggage hold.*

3 a very long object

   She had met the boy the previous week while travelling on a train. She asked him if he wanted to go out with her.

   *She asked **the boy who/whom she had met the previous week while travelling on a train** if he wanted to go out with her.*

Avoiding unnecessary repetition

1 a participle clause

   He was arrested as he was committing the crime. He was kept in the police station for three days.

   ***Arrested** as he was committing the crime, he was kept in the police station for three days.*

2 a very long object

   The books had been lying on his sitting room floor. He took the books to the library.

   *He took **the books which had been lying on his sitting room floor** back to the library.*

Emphasising an idea or event

1 the use of *It* at the beginning

   Maria couldn't get hold of Kim. It worried her.

   ***It** worried Maria that she couldn't get hold of Kim.*

2 emphasis with inversion

   I realised that I wanted to stay at home after I had travelled so far.

   ***Only** after travelling so far **did I realise** I wanted to stay at home.*

Causative *have* and *get*

1 *have/get* + object + past participle is used to talk about when somebody else does something for you (often when you arrange and pay them to do so). (*Get* in this case is sometimes considered slightly more informal.)

   *We're **having the house painted**.*

   *I must **get my watch repaired**.*

   *I'm going to **get my hair cut** this afternoon.*

2 *have/get* + object + past participle is used to talk about an experience or something that happens to you (often something which you have no control over). (*Get* in this case is sometimes considered slightly more informal.)

   *We **got our roof blown off** in the storm last week.*

   *I've just **had my first article published**.*

3 *get* + object + past participle is used to talk about completing work on something. (We cannot use *have* in this case.)

   *I'll **get the washing up done** and then I'll help you in the garden.*

4 *get* + object + *to* infinitive is used to talk about when you make (or persuade) somebody/something do something (often with the idea of difficulty). (We cannot use *have* in this case.)

   *You could **get Jim to help** us.*

   *I tried to **get someone to listen** to our complaint.*

Grammar Reference

Unit 15

Hypothetical meaning

Wish

wish + that clause expresses regret that things are not different. In informal style *that* can be dropped.

We use *wish + past simple* to express a wish that has not come true in the present or is impossible. We also use *wish + past simple* to talk about wishes that might come true in the future.

I wish (that) **I was** taller, then I could be a model.

I wish (that) **I had** a better job.

Don't you **wish** (that) **you lived** in a city?

If the verb is *to be*, we can use the past simple (*I/she/it was; you/we/they were*) or *were* with all persons (*I/you/she/it/we/they were*).

We all **wish** (that) the shopping centre **wasn't/weren't** so far from the town.

I wish (that) he **wasn't/weren't** so unhappy.

We use *wish + would/could* to refer to general wishes for the future.

I wish I could come to your wedding but I have to go away.

I wish they would spend more on training.

wish + would is often used to talk about other people's irritating habits. This form is not often used with *I* or *we*. To talk about our own irritating habits we use *could*.

I wish you would stop fidgeting. It's very irritating.

Don't you **wish she wouldn't** be so critical all the time?

I wish I could stop biting my nails.

We use *wish + past perfect* to refer to things we are sorry about in the past.

I wish (that) **I hadn't lost** my temper.

She **wishes** (that) **she hadn't resigned** from her job.

wish versus hope

wish + that clause is not generally used for wishes about things that seem possible in the future. We often use hope in this sense.

I hope (that) I get offered that job (not ~~I wish I get offered that job.~~)

If only

If only is used with the same verb forms as *wish*, and is used when your feelings are stronger. It is often used with an exclamation mark (!). It is used very commonly with *would/wouldn't* to criticise someone else's behaviour.

If only I could travel as much as you do!

If only I had the right qualifications for that job.

If only she hadn't lost my keys!

If only you wouldn't interrupt all the time!

regret

regret + -ing and *regret + the fact that + clause* looks back at the past and is used to express how sorry one is about what one did.

I regret sending him that letter now.

I regret not visiting the Vatican when I was in Rome.

I regret having spent so much money.

I regret the fact that I didn't apply for that job.

It's time

It's time is used with the past simple to talk about the present or future. We mean that the action should have been done before. We can also say *It's about time* and *It's high time*.

It's time you stopped complaining and got on with your work.

It's about time we thought about our holidays or they will all be booked up.

It's high time they got married. They've been going out for years.

I'd rather (would rather)

We use *I'd rather + past simple* when we want to say what we want someone or something else to do in the present or future.

I'd rather you didn't tell him just yet.

Would you rather go to the Italian restaurant or the Thai one?

We use *I'd rather + past perfect* when we want to say what we wanted to happen in the past.

I'd rather you hadn't borrowed my computer without asking.

I'd rather she had asked me about hotel before booking me in.

I'd rather + infinitive without to is used to talk about our preferences or other people's preferences in the present or future.

I'd rather get some training before I start the job.

We'd rather go by train. The plane is too expensive.

Suppose/supposing

Suppose or *supposing* mean 'What if …?'. They are used with:

The present simple to describe something that may possibly happen or may have happened.

Suppose there are jellyfish in the water, what will we do?

Supposing he has already left, how will we contact him?

The past simple to talk about something that is just imagination or which is unlikely to happen in the future.

Suppose you won the lottery. What would you do?

Supposing you could afford an expensive car, which one would you buy?

The past perfect to talk about something that could have happened but didn't in the past.

Suppose we had taken that train! Imagine how lost we would have been!

Supposing you had had the chance to travel, where would you have gone?

Punctuation (writing)

Ending sentences

Full stops (.), question marks (?) and exclamation marks (!) are used to close sentences.

We hadn't been there long when we heard a strange sound.

Would you like to come over for dinner tomorrow?

Then she asked me if she could borrow some money!

Separating clauses

A comma (,)

Commas are generally used to reflect pauses in speech.

To separate long coordinate clauses with *and, but* or *or*:

She was worried about money, but could not think of how she could earn more.

After subordinate clauses that begin sentences:

If you want to go tonight, give me a ring.

We do not use commas before *that* clauses:

It's understandable that you would want to see him.

To indicate unusual word order:

Jane, however, thought they should leave early.

Between adjectives:

She was wearing a long, green, silk dress.

In lists:

He spent his time at university going to lectures, playing rugby and socialising.

In direct speech:

Between a reporting expression and direct speech

She said, 'You will have to wait.'

Before a reporting expression which follows direct speech, before the closing quotation mark

'He's going to collect us at 3 o'clock,' said Anna.

To divide large numbers into groups of three

6,476,300

We do not use commas in some instances.

Grammatically separate sentences:

She wanted to go to the theatre. On the other hand, she didn't want to miss his call.

Identifying expressions:

The family in the last house would like to move.

Long subjects:

The man wearing a yellow coat is behaving suspiciously.

Indirect speech:

He explained that he would be late for dinner.

B semicolon (;)

We use semicolons instead of full stops where sentences are grammatically independent but the meaning is closely connected:

Some companies offer in-house training; others prefer to outsource their training.

He felt ill when his woke up; his head was aching from the previous night.

In lists when ideas or items are grammatically complex:

He was concerned that she wouldn't like him; that she would think he was naïve; that he was not as sophisticated as her previous boyfriends.

C colon (:)

The colon is usually used after a noun, especially *the following*.

To introduce an explanation or further details:

He told a funny story: it was about his dog.

To introduce lists:

Make sure you have the following: warm clothes, a map, a compass ...

You need to use all the equipment in the gym: running machines, weights and mats.

To show subdivisions in titles or headings:

Indian food: dishes from the south

D dash (–)

In informal writing, dashes are used in the same way as colons, semicolons or brackets.

We had a terrible time in London – we kept getting lost.

My brother – who is studying in Greece – hopes to get a job with the UN.

E apostrophe (')

To replace missing letters in contracted forms:

don't (do not)   haven't (have not)   who's (who is)

Before or after a possessive:

the boy's computer

Alice's brother

her parents' house

Note: An apostrophe is not used with s to make a plural noun from a singular, e.g. ~~apple's~~.

F quoting (" " or ' ')

Quotation marks are used to quote direct speech:

"She isn't coming," said Gemma. "She's stuck in traffic."

'Wait for me,' said Norman.

Quotation marks are often used when we want to convey the special use of a word:

Apparently he's not in work because he's 'ill', if you believe that!

In handwriting, quotation marks are used for book and film titles, though in printed texts these would usually be put in italics.

The book is called 'Travels with My Aunt'.

G parentheses/brackets ( )

We use parentheses to clarify or to add an afterthought or personal comment. If the parentheses are at the end of a sentence, the full stop must be outside the parentheses. If the parentheses contain a complete sentence, the full stop must be inside the parentheses.

*There are many ways of cooking the dish **(see page 00)** but what is essential is getting the best ingredients.*

*As he got out of the car, he tripped **(Oh, how I laughed!)** and looked around him.*

Report

(For work on reports, see pages 73, 107 and 119.)

1 Task

> A website you use regularly has asked users to send in a report about their experiences of using the website. You decide to send in a report.
>
> In your report:
>
> • explain what you find useful on the website and why
>
> • compare the website to other websites you use
>
> • suggest how the website could be improved.
>
> Write your **report**. (You should write between **220** and **260** words.)

2 Model answer

Website report: *'Vocabulary You Like'*

Explain the purpose of the report in the first paragraph.

Introduction

The purpose of this report is to provide feedback on the website 'Vocabulary You Like' and to recommend how the website could be improved.

Remember to give a title and use appropriate headings throughout the report.

Good points about the website

Include two or three points in each section.

The website has an excellent range of vocabulary for each level and a good range of exercises. This is particularly helpful for students studying for exams and the number of examples given means that the user can really see how the language is used in context. The site also has a very easy link for checking collocations so it is much easier to use than a dictionary, for example. As many students work online, this site is both useful and user-friendly.

Use formal register and be consistent.

Use a range of vocabulary.

Comparison with other websites

Give factual information and objective reasons for your views.

Compared with other websites for vocabulary, the site is actually slightly harder to use and some of the links are confusing. However, it does have a much broader range of vocabulary than most other sites. Compared to other general language learning sites, it is on the whole much better as there is a link to get help and advice and it also has links to other sites that can be used for grammar, etc.

Recommendations for improvements

Make your recommendations or suggestions in the last section.

The website could be improved by tidying up the layout of the individual pages and making the links clearer, even if this means adding more words. It would also be useful if there was a link to an online dictionary which students could access as they are working. In conclusion, it is an effective website but would benefit from some improvements.

Use a range of vocabulary.

USEFUL LANGUAGE

Openings

Stating the purpose:

The purpose/aim of this report is to describe/present ...

In this report I will ...

This report gives a description/presentation ...

This report is intended to ...

Closings

Final suggestions/recommendations:

I would strongly recommend ...

My suggestion is ...

If these changes are introduced, ...

I can recommend ...

In conclusion, ...

In my opinion, ...

Points to Remember

- Think carefully about how many sections you need.
- Check that you have not repeated any points.

3 Sample task, answers and comments

Task

While studying in UK, you recently attended a conference on creative thinking. The Course Director has written to you asking for a report.

Read the extract from the Director's letter below and the Course Programme, on which you have made some notes. Then, using the information appropriately, write a report for the Director saying how you benefited from the course, explaining what you were disappointed with and suggesting how aspects of the course could be improved.

> We are asking some participants for a short report. Did you enjoy the course? Did you learn anything? Also please let me know if you have any recommendations.
>
> Many thanks
>
> *(signature)*
>
> Course Director

Course Programme		
Day 1	Lecture: 'Training your brain'	— *Great! say why*
	Seminar: discussions	
Day 2	'Making creative ideas work'	— *too long*
	Practice sessions: free thinking	
Day 3	Film: 'Great ideas'	— *Met loads of people!*
	Practical test	
Day 1:	Evening reception. Discount on books.	— *Only 5%!*

Write your **report**. (You should write between **180** and **220** words.)

Answer

Introduction
This report does feedback on the creative thinking course run on May this year.

Success of the course
There were several good bits of the course. The lekture on Day I was good and give me lots of ideas. Then we have had discussions. These were nice and all about what we can do being more creative.
In the evening we had a reception which as very nice and I met lost of people. We talked a lot and this was good for me. The film was very nice too.

Bits of the course they were less successful
Some parts of the course were less enjoyable. The practic sessions were too long. They were two hours about and I couldn't concentrate. Another thing that made me crossed was it said a discount on books but this was only 5% – hardly nothing!

Recommendations
In my view, you should ask us all what we want and maybe we can chose when we get there. Also you need to sort out the problems above. If you will give bigger discount you can get more people.

Comments

- All content points have been addressed.
- The writer has used appropriate organisation and layout, but there is a lack of cohesive devices and complex sentences.
- There is a limited range of language (overuse of *good, nice*).
- The report contains several basic errors (*does feedback, two hours about, if you will give*) and the errors sometimes impede communication (*made me crossed, we can chose*).
- The tone is too personal in places (*I couldn't concentrate, made me crossed*) and the register is sometimes inappropriate (*bits, sort out*).
- The target reader would be confused.

Band 2

Writing Reference

Proposal

(For work on proposals, see pages 87, 135 and 156.)

 1 Task

> An international committee is giving money in the form of grants to protect historical buildings and sites. You decide to write a proposal saying which historical place you think should be preserved, explaining what damage has been caused to the place and why, and giving reasons why it is important for your chosen place to be preserved.
>
> Write your **proposal**. (You should write between **220** and **260** words.)

2 Model answer

Explain the purpose of the proposal in the first paragraph.

Proposal for Venice to receive a grant

The purpose of this proposal is to persuade the committee that the city of Venice should have a grant to help preserve some of its buildings.

Remember to give a title and use appropriate headings throughout the report.

The problems with the city

Give factual information and objective reasons for your views.

Although Venice has had a lot of money invested in it, it still has a lot of problems and there are still many buildings that need money to restore or save them. One of the most obvious reasons for damage is the sea that is so much part of the city. The movement of the tides plus chemicals released into the sea by nearby factories are destroying the foundations of the city. In addition, global warming has caused high water levels to rise, meaning that water now seeps into many buildings. Furthermore, air pollution and pigeons are causing damage to the exterior of the beautiful palaces that line the Venetian canals.

Use a range of advanced level vocabulary.

Why Venice should be saved

The reason why it is important for Venice to be preserved for future generations is that it is a completely unique city. Its buildings represent a past golden age and there are no other similar buildings anywhere else in the world. It was also a fantastic feat of engineering to build a city in the sea like this. Although some money is available to help the city, it needs an enormous amount to save it as almost every building on the Grand Canal needs some preservation work done.

Use formal register and be consistent.

Use a range of advanced level vocabulary.

Appeal to the reader and summarise why they should accept your proposal.

I urge the committee to consider the unique nature of the city and its historical importance and recognise that Venice deserves a grant.

USEFUL LANGUAGE

Formal language
The reason why …
It is essential to consider …

Objective language
It needs work done …
Work needs to be done …

Persuasive language
I urge you …
It is essential/critical that …
There is an urgent need …

Points to Remember

- Explain the benefits of adopting your idea or suggestions.
- Use persuasive language and strategies.
- Don't write a proposal as a letter.

3 Sample task, answers and comments

Task

You are studying in the UK and you and some other students at your college would like to start a music club in the evenings. You decide to write a proposal to the college principal.

Read the notice from the principal below, together with the ideas from other students. Then, using the information appropriately, write a proposal to the principal outlining what you would like to include in the club, explaining how it would benefit students and suggesting how the club could be funded.

Write your **proposal**. (You should write between **220** and **260** words).

CLUBS

Students can have clubs in the evening, but you must have a clear idea of how your club will operate and why it is necessary. The college cannot give you money so you will need to explain how the club will be funded.

Principal

Bring own instruments.

Get to know each other.

Give concerts and charge?

Make CDS to sell?

Write music and songs?

Practise more English

Answer

Proposal for music club

This proposal is for a music club to have in the evenings after classes.

What the music club will include

Our idea is to have the club one evening every week at about 6.00 p.m. after classes have finished. Everyone will be welcome just if they like music not only if they play an instrument. From the people who play instruments we will try make a band and compose music together. Once every term we could have concert. We can also make CDS of our good music.

How it will benefit students

The club will be a good benefit to students because first of all it is a good opportunity for us to get to know people all over the college and also we will all have to speak in English so it will be good practice for our English. It also means people which miss their practice of their instruments at home can get the chance to play them with other people here and it will develop students' creativity.

How we will get money for the club

To get money for the club we can ask everyone to pay a cost for the year, just a small sum. But most of our money could be from making CDs and selling them in college and also if we have a concert we can charge students and families something to come to the concert. I think so we could make quite a lot of money like this. Altogether we think the club would be no trouble for the school so we would really appreciate if you could consider this proposal.

Comments

All content points have been addressed.

The writer has used reasonable organisation with good paragraphing.

There is a reasonable range of structures and vocabulary.

There are errors when more complex language is attempted (*try make, people which miss, to pay a cost, appreciate if*).

The language and tone at times is rather informal and there are some clumsy structures and expressions, (*just if they like music not only if they play, a good benefit to students*).

Overall, the target reader would be informed.

Band 3

Writing Reference

Essay

(For work on essays, see pages 67, 103 and 125.)

 Task

> Your teacher has asked you to write an essay saying if you agree with the following statement:
>
> *People accuse the entertainment industry of being superficial, but it employs a great many people and is an essential part of our lives.*
>
> Write your **essay**. (You should write between **220** and **260** words.)

2 Model answer

> As the so-called celebrity culture has increased over the last few years and salaries for Hollywood actors run into millions, many people have questioned the point of the entertainment industry. For many, acting has always been playing at work, and is not considered to be a real job, but perhaps those critics have not looked beyond the surface of what the entertainment industry gives us.
>
> There is no doubt that aspects of the industry are very superficial. When we get wrapped up in film or pop stars' lives and when we see them running into problems despite all their money, it is easy to think that they are all rather spoilt and do not deserve the enormous sums of money that many of them get paid. In addition, we all know that entertainment is not critical to our survival in the way that food production or the transport industry are.
>
> However, if we look below these surface issues, we can see that the entertainment industry has grown enormously worldwide over the last few decades. TV is now in every home and pop records can be downloaded from the Internet. This makes entertainment a multi-billion dollar industry providing employment for millions of people at a time when more traditional jobs are decreasing through mechanisation. Furthermore, this giant industry is our modern approach to relaxing, vital for all of us who work hard.
>
> While the entertainment industry has a glossy and superficial surface, underneath it is a serious business and one that is vital to all our well-being.

Explain why you think the argument in the essay title is an issue.

Use complex sentences.

Remember to use topic sentences at the beginning of each paragraph.

Use formal or semi-formal language.

Give examples to justify your argument.

Use linking words to help the reader.

Remember to use topic sentences at the beginning of each paragraph.

Give examples to justify your argument.

Use formal or semi-formal language.

Use linking words to help the reader.

Give your personal opinion in the last paragraph.

Use complex sentences.

USEFUL LANGUAGE

Introduction
It is hotly debated …
Many people today say that …

Presenting an argument
Explaining why:
For this reason, …
As a result, …
Therefore, …
This is due to …
Expressing contrast:
On the other hand, …
In contrast, …
However, …
Nevertheless, …
Although …
While …

Explaining someone else's opinion:
According to …,
It is said that …
Some people say that …
Many people feel …
Others think that …

Conclusion
Giving your opinion:
I agree that …
In my opinion …
I am in favour of …
It seems to me that …
On the whole …
Overall …

Points to Remember

Always make a plan for your essay.

Example plans:

A

introduction
reasons supporting the statement
further reasons supporting the statement
conclusion with my view

B

introduction
reasons supporting the statement
reasons against the statement
conclusion with my view

C

> **Paragraph 1:** *Introduction: outline the problem. You could also explain more about the problem, give some background information or some reasons why we should be interested.*
>
> **Paragraph 2:** *Suggest a possible solution. You should then discuss the benefits of this solution, and also some of the difficulties involved.*
>
> **Paragraph 3:** *Suggest another possible solution. You should then discuss the benefits of this solution, and also some of the difficulties involved.*
>
> **Paragraph 4:** *Conclusion: state your opinion about which solution you consider the best, summarising the reasons.*

3 Sample task, answers and comments

Task

> In class, you have been discussing films. Your teacher has asked you to write an essay on the following topic:
>
> *To what extent do you think video-sharing sites, such as YouTube, are destroying the audience for commercial films?*
>
> Write your **essay**. (You should write between **220** and **260** words).

Answer

There is no doubt that the popularity of video-sharing sites has grown. This has been enormously in recent years. People now spend a lot of time watching videos on these sites. The question is how far this will affect cinema audiences. In the moment people seem to spend more time watching their TV or computers. The video-sharing sites have an enormous appeal. You can watch something funny or you can share videos with family and friends. It is also our opportunity to see famous stars doing something silly. Some of these videos are much more interesting than films we see at cinema. We feel involved. Resulting many people may prefer this way of choosing their own material. And they watch in comfort of their own home. On the other part, only cinema can provide the noise and scale of film. That makes them special. I'm not sure that video sites will ever rival this. Commercial films will have to think about offering something extra. Nevertheless, I'm sure they will survive as there will always be market for this. The special effects and drama only commercial cinema can give. Also we like to see certain actors.

I think the sites will not affect audience for cinemas. Films will have to make sure they always offer something extra. This is to get us to watch them.

Comments

The content is relevant with good development of topic.

The organisation is poor with inappropriate paragraphing and some inappropriate use of cohesive devices (one long paragraph and one very short one, *And they watch …*).

There is a good range of vocabulary and satisfactory range of structures but sentences are short and simple and there are some problems with articles (*at cinema, watch in comfort of, affect audience*).

The register is appropriate for the target audience.

The target reader would be informed.

Band 3

Writing Reference

Contribution

(For work on contributions, see pages 52 and 139.)

 1 Task

> A friend of yours is writing a book on attitudes to animals in different countries and has asked you to write a contribution. In your contribution you should say what kinds of domestic animals are popular, explain the attitude people in your country have to animals generally and suggest whether you think attitudes to animals should change or not and why.
>
> Write your **contribution to the book**. (You should write between **220** and **260** words.)

2 Model answer

Introduce the topic and say what you are going to describe.

In general, all kinds of animals are popular in Britain and it is very common to keep a pet in your home. Particular favourites are dogs and cats, but many people also keep fish, rabbits, hamsters and mice. Horses are also very popular as many people ride and keep their horses in nearby fields or stables.

Try to give a general rather than a personal view.

Make sure you give the information asked for in the question.

The British consider animals to be part of the family and some treat them as if they were human. People keep dogs, not so much to guard their home, but as company or as a pet for their children. Cats are also viewed this way and a lot of older people like to have cats. In general, children keep the smaller animals – often in the home or even in their bedroom – but adults also like to keep pigeons or greyhounds in order to race them. We also have a lot of animal charities in Britain, principally the RSPCA, which is evidence of how concerned we are for animal welfare.

Furthermore, we are keen to support charities which protect endangered species. In addition, there are several protest groups who organise demonstrations against animal experimentation.

People say that, in Britain, we care more about animals than people and maybe this is the case. I think we should care about animals, but one way in which the British should perhaps change is in their attitude to animal charities. People give these charities a lot of money when really the money should be spent on humans who are in trouble around the globe, especially children.

Make sure you give the information asked for in the question.

USEFUL LANGUAGE

Describing general facts
Overall it is true that …
It could be said that …
Generally, most people …

Predicting the future
It may be the case that …
It could be that …
It might mean that …

Talking about change
improve
different from
progress
alter

Pointing out benefits
There is no doubt that …
The advantage is that …
The upside is that …
It will give … the opportunity to …
You will be able to enjoy …
There is no better way to …

Points to Remember

Adjust your style according to what the contribution is for. For example, if it is for a piece of research, it may need to be very objective. If it is for a guidebook, it may need to be more persuasive.

3 Sample task, answers and comments

Task

> You see this announcement in a travel magazine.
>
> I'm writing a guidebook for students and would like contributions to my book. In your contribution please describe what a student visitor could do in your region without spending much money, give general advice on visiting our country and persuade students to visit your region.
>
> Write your **contribution**. (You should write between **220** and **260** words.)

Answer

My town is a great place for students to visit as it has so much packed into such a small area. Lots of students come here every year and they always enjoy themselves.

First, you can see the castle, which is really interesting. Tickets are expensive, but it is worth to see. For an extra charge, you can go on a special guided tour to learn all the stories. Then if you buy a tickets for one of the big sports games while you are here such as rugby or football, you will be able to see inside our fantastic stadium. It was only built a few years ago and is really incredible.

If you visit my country I suggest you bring clothes for wet weather as it rains a lot. An umbrella is a good idea. Also you should try about typical food. In my town the best restaurant is on Cowbridge Street, here you can eat very good typical food. You will find people are very friendly and helpful so do not worry about this. You can easily speak to local people if you get lost.

We welcome visitors so do come to my country and we can show you many exciting things. Students always have a good time as there are so many young people in my town. Every minute of your day will be full of interesting things to do. So please visit us!

Comments

This fails to mention where the country or region is and it does not address the point about suggestions which are cheap for students. It is more of a general guide. Note: good language will not compensate for missed content points.

There is good organisation and linking.

There are some good expressions (*packed into*) and range (*You will find …*).

Accuracy is generally good, though there are some awkward sentences (*Then … stadium*).

It is appropriately semi-formal and consistent in tone.

The target reader would not be informed as they would not know where this place/country is nor how to visit the region without spending too much money.

Band 2

Writing Reference

Competition entry

(For work on competition entries, see page 158.)

1 Task

You see this announcement on the web:

Culture shock

We are running a competition for people to participate in a new reality TV series. The winners of our competition will have to live in the jungle for six months, where you will have to learn to grow crops and survive.

If you are interested, please write and explain why you want to participate, what you expect to learn and why we should pick you.

Write your **competition entry**. (You should write between **220** and **260** words.)

2 Model answer

I would love to participate in this programme! I would be fascinated by the idea of going into the jungle to live and learn a completely different way of life and see how this contrasts with my life back home. I have been looking for a way to change my life as I think the way I live is quite normal and boring. Everything is done for me and everything is available. Also I would like to be able to see how I could live without all the material things I am used to.

> Start with an engaging sentence.

> Use a separate focus for each paragraph.

> Make sure you cover all the points you are asked for.

I would expect to learn a lot from the experience, not just about how to survive on what surrounds me, but about how to live in an alternative way and to feel more at one with my surroundings. I am sure I would find out many things about myself and perhaps develop a more informed point of view on the diversity between cultures. I know it would give me a completely altered perspective on my life back home.

You should pick me for this show because I am independent and outgoing and also I think I am very resourceful. I would be more than happy to live on limited resources and to discover how we can live more simply. I am at an age where I am flexible and adaptable and prepared to take on board new ideas. I would throw myself wholeheartedly into the project and I think I would probably change a great deal, which would be interesting for your viewers.

> Use a separate focus for each paragraph.

> Make sure you sound enthusiastic in order to convince the judges.

> Give lots of examples and reasons to support your entry.

> Make sure you cover all the points you are asked for.

USEFUL LANGUAGE

If you selected me/my choice, ...
I would definitely make the most of ...
I am sure I would be ideal because ...
This opportunity would allow me to ...
You would not regret selecting me for this ...

Points to Remember

- The most important thing is that you have to persuade the judges. Do this with concrete reasons rather than appealing to them emotionally.
- Try to explain why your entry is more deserving than anybody else's.

3 Sample task, answers and comments

Task

> You see this announcement on a website.
>
> ### COMPETITION!
> Our website is running a competition to select a building to include in a site we are creating about important buildings round the world. If you want a building in your town or city to be selected, then write to us outlining the function of the building, explaining why it is important to your town or city and saying why it should be selected to be in our programme.
>
> Write your **competition entry**. (You should write between **220** and **260** words.)

Answer

I want to propose the Cardiff Millennium Stadium as a building to be included in your website. The stadium was opened in 2000 and is used for sport, mainly rugby and football, and for concerts for big music bands or singers. It is an amazing building because it has a sliding roof so on sunny days it can be open to the sky and on rainy days the roof can be closed.

The building is a very important part of Cardiff. This is mainly because it symbolises how important rugby is for the Welsh people. However, it is also a fantastically beautiful building in the centre of town and since the stadium has been built so lots of other new buildings have been built around it. Another reason why the building is important to the town is that it has been increased business in the town centre, as more shops and restaurants are needed to cater to people coming to matches and concerts.

The stadium should be selected to appear on the website as it was the first building of its kind. It was a new design for a stadium with beautiful white arches. It is huge but when you are inside you are close to the events. It has also become an icon for the city and for the national game of Wales. Very few buildings can do what this stadium does, which is to dominate the skyline and the life of the city. For this reason alone, it should be included on your site.

Comments

All points are covered with good expansion.

It is well-organised into clear paragraphs and there is good use of cohesive devices.

There is a good range of natural language, both vocabulary and structure.

There are some errors (*built so lots …, has been increased business*).

It is written in an appropriate style and tone with good persuasive language.

The target reader would be clearly informed and would consider choosing the building.

Band 5

Writing Reference

Reference

(For work on references, see page 15.)

 1 Task

> A friend of yours is applying for a job with a travel company as a tourist guide for English-speaking tourists visiting your country. The company has asked you to provide a character reference for your friend.
>
> The reference should indicate how you know the person. It must also include a description of the person's character and the reasons why he or she would be suitable for the job.
>
> Write your **reference**. (You should write between **220** and **260** words.)

2 Model answer

Start with the appropriate formal language.

To whom it may concern

Katarzyna Kowalski — *State the full name of the person you are writing about.*

Katarzyna and I have been working together in the same English Language School for almost five years. — *Say how you know the person.*

Her job at the school is Social Programme Organiser and over the five years she has been at the school, she has proved herself to be an extremely hard-working and valuable member of the team. She undoubtedly has a strong sense of responsibility, is always punctual and very rarely takes time off sick.

I feel sure that Katarzyna would be an excellent tourist guide, particularly because of the way she deals with people. She is a natural leader but not at all bossy. Everyone who works with her respects her; as a colleague, she is considerate and easygoing and gets on well with everyone. She has — *Use a variety of interesting language to describe the person.*

a reputation as a good team player, not only being extremely organised, but also showing sensitivity and awareness of other people. — *Use a variety of interesting language to describe the person.*

On first meeting Katarzyna, you might think that she is a little shy, but as you get to know her, it becomes clear that in fact she is just a little quiet at times. She has grown in confidence during her time at the school and is more than capable of dealing with pressure and managing her own time, which she does professionally and without fuss. — *Divide your reference into appropriate paragraphs.*

For all the reasons that I have outlined, I believe that Katarzyna would be an asset as a tourist guide in your company. I therefore have no hesitation in recommending her for the position. — *Finish by summarising your overall opinion of the person's suitability for the job.*

USEFUL LANGUAGE

Beginning the reference
To whom it may concern

Main part of the reference
Maria and I have been working together for over five years.
In her present job, she has proved herself to be very responsible …
He is a valuable member of the team.
She has a reputation as an extremely organised person.
She undoubtedly has a strong sense of responsibility.

Ending the reference
For all the reasons I have outlined, I …
I have no hesitation in recommending her for the position.
I believe he would be a great asset to your company

3 Sample task, answers and comments

Task

> A friend of yours has applied for a job as a child-minder for a family of three children. The successful candidate will have sole responsibility for looking after the children (aged between seven and fourteen) for the duration of the summer holidays.
>
> In your reference, you should say how you know the person. You should also include information about their personal skills and qualities, any relevant experience they have and the reasons why you think they would be suitable for the job.
>
> Write your **reference**. (You should write between **220** and **260** words.)

Comments

All the required points are covered.

It is generally well-organised.

There is a good range of vocabulary.

The writer hasn't been consistent with formality: sometimes good (*For all the above reasons, I sincerely believe that ...*) but hasn't started appropriately and is sometimes rather informal (*she is having a great time*).

There are some small mistakes with grammar (*I know Giovanna ..., ... finds her being a cheerful, enjoy taking out the children*) and spelling (*responsable, undoutedly, sinceerly*)

It has an overall positive effect on the reader.

Band 4

Answer

A reference about Giovanna Lorenzo

I know Giovanna for a long time - probably over ten years. She is a very good friend of mine and we have also worked together in a café, being a waitress.

In her job as a waitress, she is always very organised and punctual. She is never late for work in all the time we have worked there. She has a very good attitude to her work and her colleagues, and has proved herself to be an extremely hard-working and valuable team-player. Everyone who works with her finds her being a cheerful and supportive person.

I think that Giovanna would be an excellent person to care for children, particularly because as well as being very responsable, she is also creative and fun. She has two younger brothers and she has often had to take care of them. She undoutedly loves them very much and when I have seen her with them, she is having a great time.

Giovanna has many interests which I think would be useful when looking after children. Her main hobby is sport and she is always playing tennis or something like that. She has a reputation as a very energetic person and she would certainly enjoy taking out the children and playing with them.

For all the above reasons, I sincerly believe that Giovanna would be a fantastic child-minder and I don't hesitate to recommend her to you.

Information sheet

(For work on information sheets, see page 97.)

 Task

> You have been asked by your college director to write an information sheet giving information and advice to students about how to get the most out of being and studying at the college.
>
> The title of the information sheet is *Making the most of your time here* and must include information and advice on the following:
> - different English courses
> - the range of social activities
> - the best type of accommodation.
>
> Write the **information sheet**. (You should write between **220** and **260** words.)

 Model answer

Making the most of your time here

Your time here at Rookfield College could be one of the best times of your life. So make sure that you make the most of it! — Include a short introduction.

English courses — Use sub-headings where appropriate.

You will have a General English course for three hours every morning. In the afternoons, there is a choice of three more specialised courses: 1 Business English 2 English for Tourism and 3 English for Academic Purposes. It is important that you choose the right course for you. If you're not sure what to choose, make an appointment to talk to the Director of Studies to discuss your options.

Give clear information and/or advice as appropriate.

Social activities

In order to make the most of your time here, it is essential that you get involved in the huge range of social activities on offer. Taking part in these activities is an excellent way of getting to know people and practising your English informally, as well as having fun. In a typical month, the activities range from cinema visits, coach tours to other cities, ice-skating, football in the park and lots more. Pick up a leaflet about this month's activities from the Reception Desk.

Be clearly organised.

Accommodation

Students at the college usually stay in 'Homestay' families, which the vast majority find very friendly and welcoming. Staying with an English family is a good way of finding out more about another culture, making friends and practising your English.

Include a short conclusion — *If you need any more information or advice, don't hesitate to ask any member of staff at the college for help. They want you to have the time of your life at Rookfield College!*

USEFUL LANGUAGE

It is important that you …
In order to …, it is essential that you …
It is advisable to take care when …
You should make sure that …
Pick up a leaflet about … from the Reception Desk.
You can contact a member of staff by ringing …
If you're not sure what …, make an appointment to …
If you need any more information or advice, don't hesitate to ask …

3 Sample task, answers and comments

Task

> You are a member of a sports club which has members from many different countries. The club has recently extended both its sports and recreational facilities. The manager has asked you to write an information sheet for English-speaking members, encouraging them to use the new facilities.
>
> In your information sheet:
>
> outline why the club was extended
>
> describe which new facilities are available
>
> explain how members will benefit from using the facilities.
>
> Write the **information sheet**. (You should write between **220** and **260** words.)

Answer

'Club Active' now has even more!

You are a member of 'Club Active' and therefore you will know that there has been a lot of building work happening over the last year. Now, the management is pleased announcing that the new, improved club is up and running.

A bigger, better club

Five years ago, 'Club Active' decided to do various member surveys to find out not only what did members like about the club, but also what were they disatisfied about and the club has used the results of the surveys and because of that it has now been extended and includes a fantastic range of new facilities.

New facilities

Two of the most impressive improvements at the club are the swimming pools and the gym. 'Club Active' now has two swimming pools: an Olympic-size swimming pool as well as a diving pool. Additionally, the gym is now double the size of the previous one and includes even more of the most up-to-date equipments and there are also more personal trainers available to help you plan your workouts.

Even more benefits

Swimming is known to be one of the best of all-round types of excercise you can get. Now you can benefit from this at 'Club Active' by including swimming in your weekly excercise programme. The additional space in the gym means it will never be overcrowded. You can also take advantage of a personal trainer to help you keep motivated and not give up.

That's why these are just some of the new improved facilities at 'Club Active'. Come along and book a guided tour of the new, extended club. You won't be disappointed!

Comments

There is an appropriate balance between the three points required in the task and good development of ideas.

It has good layout, headings and organisation of paragraphs.

There is a range of vocabulary and expression.

There are some inaccuracies in grammar, cohesive devices, spelling and punctuation, though generally these don't impede communication:

Grammar: *is pleased announcing, find out what did members like, the best of all-round*

Cohesive devices: *and because of that it has now…, Additionally, the gym is …, That's why these are …*

Spelling mistakes: *disatisfied, excercise*

Punctuation: some very long sentences, e.g. second paragraph

It is generally appropriate in tone and register.

It would have an overall positive effect on the target reader.

Band 4

Article

(For work on articles, see pages 35 and 42.)

 Task

> Your sports club magazine is including a special section on role models in sport. You have been asked to contribute a short article profiling somebody involved in sport or a sportsperson you know about.
>
> Write the **article** describing some of the achievements of this person and why you think he/she is a good role model for young people. (You should write between **220** and **260** words.)

2 Model answer

Include an attention-grabbing title.

Include quotes, questions, images, etc. to make it more interesting.

The most gifted player ever?

With movements described as 'ballet-like', Roger Federer is one of the beautiful players to watch. He makes everything look so easy. Not only that, but his achievements to date are phenomenal. I'm sure you agree with me that he is quickly becoming an important role model for young people and one of sport's all-time greats.

Use informal language to involve the reader.

Born in 1981, in Switzerland, Federer started playing tennis at the age of six. Since turning pro in 1998, he has won eleven Grand Slam titles, including the Wimbledon trophy five times. He holds the all-time record for the most consecutive weeks as the top-ranked male player. He is considered by many of his contemporaries to be the greatest tennis player of all time. The legendary John McEnroe admires Federer hugely, quoted as saying he is 'the most gifted player ever'.

Include quotes, questions, images, etc. to make it more interesting.

Not only has Federer achieved an incredible amount in a relatively short career, but I think he also displays many qualities to be admired. On the professional circuit, he has gained a reputation as a serene and focused player, not prone to emotional outbursts. Despite some setbacks, like the death of his coach in 2002, Federer has remained determined and modest.

Give your own opinion.

To sum up, I'd like to suggest that Roger Federer is a great role model for young people today. He has an impressive list of achievements, even at his relatively young age. His behaviour both on and off the court is impeccable and his matches are a joy to watch.

Summarise your opinion/ feelings at the end.

USEFUL LANGUAGE

Not only has he ..., but he also ...
He is considered to be ...
He has gained a reputation as ...
Despite some setbacks, ...
I'm sure you agree with me that ...
To sum up, I'd like to suggest that ...

Points to Remember

There are different ways of finishing an article:
- return to the beginning (paraphrasing the introduction or using similar words or imagery)
- a summary or conclusion
- a question
- a quotation
- an image or picture

Letter

(For work on letters, see pages 55 and 129.)

 1 Task

> The director of an international language school has written to your company asking if you would be interested in taking part in a work experience scheme and offering temporary summer work to students.
>
> Your manager has asked you to write a letter to the director outlining the kind of work your company does, explaining what kind of work experience the students could get and suggesting the type of person who might be interested.
>
> Write your **letter**. (You should write between **220** and **260** words.).

2 Model answer

Start the letter appropriately. — Dear Sir

Thank you for your letter asking about the possibility of temporary work with our company. I am pleased to say that we would be very interested in getting involved with this work experience scheme.

Firstly, let me explain a bit about the kind of work our company does. We are primarily a travel agent. Most of our time is spent with customers: helping them to book tickets; advising them on travel plans; suggesting holiday alternatives. We also have a small department which researches new destinations and reports back on them.

Make sure you include all the points required.

During the summer months, we are always very busy and would be delighted to offer temporary work to students who were interested in gaining some work experience. They could help in the office, doing various tasks like filing, inputting data into a computer and answering the phone. The other possibility is working with customers on the shop floor, helping them with their travel plans and bookings.

Divide your letter into clear paragraphs.

The type of person who would benefit from working with our company in this way would be someone who is interested in the tourist industry. Ideally, they would be committed to working in this field on a more permanent basis. Secondly, they would be someone who is able to work in a team, often under considerable pressure. Finally, the successful candidates would need to be able to communicate clearly and professionally with customers.

Make sure you include all the points required.

Thank you for approaching our company about this scheme and I look forward to hearing more from you.

Finish the letter appropriately. — Yours faithfully

Giacomo Pellini

Giacomo Pellini

Use appropriately formal/informal language.

USEFUL LANGUAGE

More formal

Thank you for your letter regarding …
I am writing in response to …
With reference to your letter of …
I am pleased to say that …
Firstly, let me explain …
Thank you for approaching our company about this scheme.
I look forward to hearing more from you.

More informal

Thanks for your letter.
It was great to hear from you.
Sorry it's taken me so long to reply!
How are you? I hope you're well.
Please write back soon.

Writing Reference

Review

(For work on reviews, see page 21.)

1 Task

You see this announcement on a website:

> Have you been to a restaurant that is special or different?
> If so, write a review for our website. Your review should
> describe the restaurant and its atmosphere, explain why
> the restaurant is different or special and say whether or
> not you would recommend it to other people.

Write your **review**. (You should write between **220**
and **260** words.)

2 Model answer

The Ninja restaurant ⎯⎯ *Use a title as a review is a type of article.*

Give personal information or use a question to catch your reader's attention.

Would you like a truly unforgettable experience to remind you of your visit to New York? A visit to the Ninja restaurant may stay with you for a long time! The Ninja restaurant is a themed restaurant which is supposed to represent a ninja mountain village in Japan.

Give some basic information about the restaurant/ CD/play, etc.

Use plenty of modifiers and adjectives to help the reader understand your experience.

Waiters dressed in ninja costumes take you through a series of dark, narrow tunnels to a small cave where you have your table. It looks a bit like a prison cell as there are latticed doors which the ninja waiters slide backwards and forwards as they deliver the dishes. The atmosphere is strangely gloomy but exciting. The menu has more than a hundred choices and each plate is placed on the table by the waiter's ninja sword. There is a lot of interesting fish, including a deliciously fresh seafood salad. Pudding includes a rather unusual green-tea ice cream.

Compare the restaurant/ CD/play, etc. with others.

What I was impressed with was the speedy service, which was better than at many similar novelty-type restaurants.

The special feature of this restaurant is that the waiters can perform magic tricks at your table, which is a great talking point. In fact, it is worth visiting the restaurant for this entertainment alone. The downside is that it is extremely expensive and you may prefer to eat Japanese food in more elegant surroundings.

Give reasons for your point of view.

The Ninja restaurant is not typical of New York, but it is the kind of startling experience that you might expect in this city. I'd recommend it just to experience a different way of enjoying food!

Remember to include a recommendation, even if it is negative.

USEFUL LANGUAGE

Giving identifying information
The restaurant has just opened …
This is the Kooks latest album …
The hotel is situated close to the beach …

Describing your experience
    Things you liked:
    relaxed atmosphere
    incredibly efficient service

    Things you didn't like:
    uninteresting menu
    surprisingly empty restaurant

Saying what was different or interesting
… much better than …
… not nearly as good as …
It was disappointing compared to …
One of the cheaper places to eat …

Giving a recommendation
I would certainly recommend …
I don't think I would recommend …
Go and visit/see/buy …!
Although it is interesting, it is not worth the money …

Set text

(For work on set texts, see page 149.)

In Question 5 of the Cambridge CAE exam, you may answer one of two questions based on your reading of one of the set books. You may be asked to write an article, an essay, a report or a review. You do not have to answer Question 5. If you do, make sure that you know the book well enough to be able to answer the question properly.

 1 Task

> You see this announcement in a book magazine.
>
> > We are inviting our readers to send in articles on books they have read recently. Choose a book you have read and write an article for our magazine saying how the title of the book connects to the story, explaining which was the most interesting aspect of the book for you and whether you would recommend it to our readers.
>
> Write your **article**. (You should write between **220** and **260** words.)

2 Model answer

Give some details about the book you have read.

Think carefully about organisation so that the separate points in the question are well-balanced in your answer.

'The Enigma of Arrival' is the story of a young Indian man who arrives in the UK as a student during the 1950s. In the story, the narrator describes the process of moving from one place to another both physically and mentally. Most of the book is about his life in rural England. In this sense, the book connects to its title as it describes in great detail the process of how, when a person leaves one country and arrives in another, they develop into a different person because the arrival is not just geographical but emotional and spiritual as well.

I think the most interesting aspect of the book is the record of the main character's development as he gets used to

Remember to cover all the points in the question.

Remember to cover all the points in the question.

a strange landscape and way of life. It causes him to reflect on his previous way of life, and the book moves through time, describing England's decline over the period when the main character lives there.

Mention examples from the book where relevant.

There are some excellent descriptions in this book of landscapes and of a way of life, and it is thought-provoking as it considers how living in different places changes us. I think anybody who has tried to live somewhere else or who is thinking of changing where they live would be interested in this book, but it also gives a very good glimpse into life in England several decades ago. It is extremely well-written and I would definitely recommend it.

Think carefully about organisation so that the separate points in the question are well-balanced in your answer.

Don't just tell the story of the book.

USEFUL LANGUAGE

The book describes/recounts …
The main character is appealing/unappealing because …
The book/character/landscape makes you think about …
The story gives you a different view of …
This book is worth reading because …
I would definitely recommend this book because …
Overall the book is disappointing because …

Pearson Education Limited
Edinburgh Gate
Harlow
Essex CM20 2JE
England
and Associated Companies throughout the world.

www.pearsonelt.com/exams

© Pearson Education Limited 2009

The right of Elaine Boyd and Araminta Crace to be identified as author of this Work has been asserted by them in accordance with the Copyright, Designs and Patents Act 1988.

First published 2009
Second edition Published 2012
ISBN: 978-1-4479-2933-8 (Book and CD pack)
ISBN: 978-1-4479-4007-4 (Book for pack)

Set in Cronos Pro Light 10.5/11.5

Printed in China   GCC/01

Authors' Acknowledgements

The authors would like to thank everyone at Pearson Education who was involved with this project for all their hard work and professionalism.

Elaine Boyd would also like to thank her sons Ben and Jamie Allen, for their patience while she was writing and being great boys.

Araminta Crace would also like to thank her daughters Lola and Petra, her sisters Charly and Emily and her mum Gay for all their love, energy and support.

Publisher's Acknowledgement

The publishers and authors would like to thank the following people and institutions for their feedback and comments during the development of the material:

Will Moreton, Spain; Dorota Adaszewska, Poland; Steven Miller, Mayfair School, London, UK; Kate Leigh, Spain; Roy Webster, UK (writing reference section); Iain Campbell, UK (writing reference section)

We are grateful to the following for permission to adapt or reproduce extracts from the following copyright material:

Aitken Alexander Associates for *The Enigma of Arrival* © V.S. Naipaul 2002; Amazon for 'The Diceman' (online review by Budge Burgess) © 2008 Amazon.com Inc. and its affiliates. All rights reserved; BBC Magazines for 'Blue sky thinking' and 'Total recall' by Ian Taylor, published in January, and March 2007, 'For and against' published in March 2007, 'Every step you take' by Mark Blackmore, published in Autumn 2006, 'The carbon coach' by Jheni Osman, published in May 2007, and 'Do you look like a Bob or a Brian?', published in August 2007; BBC News Online for 'My London: hit-and-run kindness' by Danny Wallace, published 11 August 2003, 'The rise of clip culture online' by Michael Geist, published 20 March 2006, 'Bonfire of the brands' by Neil Boorman, published 29 August 2006, 'What not to wear at work' by Tom Geogeghan, published 27 June 2007, 'Are you Dave Gorman?' by Dave Gorman and Danny Wallace, published 28 June 2006, 'Hot topics – the science of chocolate', published 17 November 2004, 'Publishers reject classic titles', published 19 July 2007 and 'Welcome, I'm your virtual receptionist, published 20 November 2000, at bbc.co.uk/news; BMJ Publishing Group for 'The luck factor' by Clare Hughes, published in *Student BMJ* 2003; Classical Comics Ltd for 'The classical comics story', by Clive Bryant, published in February 2007; Linda Curtis for 'The science of luck', published on http://onpurpose-coach.com/; David Higham Associates for extract from 'Nature: you clever little beasts', by Windsor Chorlton, first published in *BBC Focus* in September 1996; The Institution of Engineering and Technology for 'Hero hour' by Keri Allan, published in *Flipside* magazine in September 2007; Guardian News Service for: 'Welcome to the world of nano foods' by Alex Renton, published in the *Observer* on 17 December 2006 © Copyright Guardian News & Media Ltd 2006, 'The tribesman: former marine Bruce Parry' by Sam Wollaston, published on 17 September 2007, 'Who would live in Britain?' by Philip Suggars, published on 26 July 2006, 'Wacky workouts', by Peta Bee, published in the *Guardian* on 27 February 2007, and 'Making a move: Australia', by Roger Maynard and Jane Hooton, published on 27 January 2007, 'How to get your brain up to speed' by Denis Campbell, published in the *Observer* on 2 December 2007 © Copyright Guardian News & Media Ltd 2007; 'Reaping the harvest in Canada,' by Johnny Scott, published on 5 May 2008 © Copyright Guardian News & Media Ltd 2008; Penguin for extract from *Great Expectations* by Charles Dickens (Penguin Readers); Media Wales Ltd for 'Clash of the siblings' by Rin Simpson, published in the *Western Mail and Echo* on 18 April 2007; New Way Productions Ltd for 'The power of hypnosis in advertising' by Barrie St John, in www.hypnoshop.com; Terri Ann Laws and the Silva organisation of Loredo, Texas, for 'What is the IMI mind power plus training?' in www.internationalmindinstitute.com; New7Wonders for 'The New 7 Wonders of the World' www.new7wonders.com; NI Syndication Ltd. for 'Simon Cowell to make "Pop idol" movie, published in the *Times* on 2 August 2007, and 'How to give your brain a workout' published in the *Sunday Times* on 15 July 2006; Channel 4 and Objective Productions Ltd for 'Someone's lying', licence courtesy of Channel 4; OhGizmo.com for 'Dinner in the sky' by Andrew Liszewski; *Radio Times* for 'Unsung heroes' by Benji Wilson, published July 2006 and 'Tip-top Test' published in September 2007; Telegraph Media Group for 'Two men in a boat' by Cassandra Jardine and 'Red Riding Hood' by Sanjiv Bhattacharya, published in the *Telegraph Magazine* on 17 February 2007; University of Wisconsin-Madison, for 'The pet cure' by David Tenenbaum, published on http://whyfiles.org; J.M. Wanes & Associates for 'Dressing for interview success' by Joe Hodowanes.

Every effort has been made to trace copyright holders but this has not proved possible in every case. The publishers would be happy to hear from any copyright holder that has not been acknowledged and would be pleased to rectify the omission in any subsequent edition of this publication.

The publisher would like to thank the following for their kind permission to reproduce their photographs: (Key: b-bottom; c-centre; l-left; r-right; t-top) www.dreamstime.com: Asist 99c; Copestello 135tl; Forwardcom 79tr; **A&M Photography** 116l, 116r; **Alamy Images**: Frankie Angel 96r; blickwinkel 166 (dog and owner); Danita Delimont 99bl; Directphoto.org 17bl; Matthew Doggett 28cl; EuroStyle Graphics 59br; Greece 17c; Martin Harvey 166 (leopard); Images of Africa Photobank 47c; wales Alan King 111c; Ray Laskowitz 59c; Megapress 64b; Edward Moss 89c; David Noble 10b; Nick Onken 151c; Mark Scheuern 167tr; Alex Segre 141tr; Robert Slade 87; Jack Sullivan 168b; Colin Underhill 30tl; **Copyright © 2008. The American Society for the Prevention of Cruelty to Animals (ASPCA). All Rights Reserved.**: 103 (Russell Simmons); **Arenapal**: Marilyn Kingwill 69c; **BBC Photo Library**: 89br, 103 (Gorillas), 141bl, 143; **Sean Benham**: 22l; **Martha Camarillo**: 47tr, 48; **Classical Comics Limited**: 38; **Corbis**: Richard Baker 126t; Laszlo Balogh 166 (polar bear); L. Clarke 92r; Creasource 30tr; moodboard 92l; Tom Nebbia 51l; Eric Nguyen 79c; Reuters 99tl; Reuters/ Corbis 47bl; Staffan Widstrand 144l; **Dinner in the Sky (www.dinnerinthesky.com)**: 19; **DK Images**: 111bl; **Dr. Mitchell Joachim**: 108; James Dunlop, founder & designer of myhab: 122b; **Expedia.co.uk**: 79bl; www.eyevinearchive.com: Brendan Smialowski/The New York Times 122tr; **FIVB**: 27bl; **FremantleMedia Stills Library**: 66; **Garuda Indonesia Air Lines**: 17tr; **Gekkomat**: 135r; **Getty Images**: AFP 7c, 27tr, 37c, 64r, 90tl; 103 (Live Earth), 121bl, 121c, 121tr, 133tl, 141c; A.B 127; Evan Agostini 168c; Tony Anderson 39; AKA Images 144c; China Photos 8l; Renee Comet 24tl; Denis Felix 165cl; Hermann Erber 27br; Blasius Erlinger 167bl; Ken Fisher 10t; Judith Haeusler 24br; Chris Jackson 72; Jeffrey Mayer 99tr; Bobby Model 144r; Patrick Molnar 70 (Steven), 166 (Steven); Pascal Le Segretain 27tl; Marco Simoni 81bl; Jim Smeal 13tl; Carl de Souza 32t; Siri Stafford 119; Brent Stirton 121tl; Paul Vozdic 91t; **Glenn Dearing Photography**: 101; **Photo courtesy Google UK**: YouTube 59bl; **Ronald Grant Archive**: Thomas Hawk: 47tl; **Christopher Herwig**: 63; **Melissa Hom**: 21r; **Intel Corporation**: 131tr; **iStockphoto**: binagel 7tr; Cebolla4 131bl; creacart 167tl; David H. Lewis 28br; Lucato 131tl; perkmeup 99br; Photawa 133b; Prill 111br; **Jeff Moore (jeff@jmal.co.uk)**: 7bl, 111tl; **Jupiterimages**: Natalie Behring 167cr; David Troncoso 64tl; **Karushi Management Limited**: Bob Glanville 8r; **Kobal Collection Ltd**: Columbia/ Marvel/ The Kobal Collection 55; Dreamworks/The Kobal collection 55; Lucasfilm/20th Century Fox 68; Warner Bros. / The Kobal Collection/ Bailey, Alex 43cr; Warner Bros/ The Kobal Collection/ Mountain, Peter 17br; **Moviestore Collection Ltd**: 22r; **NASA**: NASA 43tl; **Nemock, LLC**: 74; **Ninja New York (www.ninjanewyork.com)**: 25 Hudson St, NY, NY 10013 (212 274 8500) 21c, 21l; **PA Photos**: 62; AP 27c, 34, 165br, 168t; **Penguin Group**: Penguin Books Ltd / © DACS / courtesy Fondazione Giorgio e Isa de Chirico, painting by Giorgio de Chirico, *The Enigma of Arrival*, 1912, oil on canvas, Private Collection: 145; Viking / Cover photo of Al Gore: Eric Lee / Renewable Films; cover photo of Earth courtesy of NASA 103 (Al Gore book); **PH Publishing, YO16 6BT**: Illustrated by John Patience 37tl; **Photolibrary. com**: Blend Images Llc 155cl; Brand X Pictures 156; Comstock 158; Corbis 28bc, 67, 133tr, 151br, 152, 165bl; Digital Vision 165cr; GlowImages 70 (Peter), 166 (Peter); Image100 141tl; ImageSource 28tl; PhotoDisc 17tl, 165tl; Rubberball 37bl, 79br, 167 (painting); STOCK4B-RF 70 (Maria), 166 (Maria); Stockbyte 70 (George), 166 (George); Upper Cut 124t; Westend61 126bl; **PunchStock**: Brand X Pictures 7br; ImageSource 37tl; Stockbyte 151bl; **Radio Times Magazine**: Mark Harrison 32bl, 32r, 33bl, 33br, 33tl, 33tr; **Reuters**: Yuriko Nakao 161; Lucy Nicholson 13bl; **Rex Features**: 121br; Nick Cunard 122tl; Jonathan Hordle 114; NBCUPHOTOBANK 131c; Sipa Press 13r; George Sweeney 96l; Terry Williams 89bl; **D Talapin & A Rogach, University of Hamburg, Germany**: 23; **Routledge**: "Persuasion in Advertising", John O'Shaughnessy & Nicholas Jackson O'Shaughnessy, 2004 (www.tandf.co.uk). Many Taylor & Francis and Routledge books are available as eBooks (www.eBookstore.tandf.co.uk) 75; **Science Photo Library Ltd**: Ted Kinsman 104; Laguna Design 69br; **shutterstock**: aaaah 28tr; Bruce Amos 79tl; Andresr 70 (Helen), 166 (Helen); Ryan Arnaudin 43b; Darren Baker 10c, 8bl; Arvind Balaraman 81cl; Germán Ariel Berra 90bl; Michael D Brown 8b; Bryan Busovicki 83t; criben 51c; Petronilo G Dangoy Jr 81bl; Sam DCruz 126br; Angelina Dimitrova 90r; Koksharov Dmitry 155tl; ErickN 81cr; Chistoprudov Dmitriy Gennadievich 136; GeoM 124b; Eray Haciosmanoglu 146; Amy Nichole Harris 80b; Margo Harrison 131br; hauhu 167 (Soduku); Lorraine Kourafas 47bc; Travis Manley 111tr; Marc Dietrich 151tr, 155bc; Michelle Marsan 30b; Glenn R McGloughlin 91b; Holger Mette 80t; Jeff Metzger 69bl; Mikhail Nekrasov 81tl; Petrafler 155br; Scott Rothstein 155tr; Ekaterina Shlikhunova 24tr; Maksim Shmeljov 89cr; Shutterlist 83b; Michaela Stejskalova 37br; Konstantin Sutyagin 7tl; Val Thoermer 165tr; USTIN 89tl; Vectorus 141tl; Ewa Walicka 155tc; Mark Winfrey 141br; Stavchansky Yakov 41; **Sima Products Corporation**: © 2008 / XL Theater 59tr; **Sony UK Ltd**: © 1999 Sony Music Entertainment Inc; Art Director: Giulio Turturro; Package Design: Laura Torres 69r; PlayStation 2 / Agency: TWBA, Paris; Creative Director: Erik Vervroegen; Copywriter & Art Directors: Sebastien Vacherot, Jessica Gerard-Huet, Loic Cardon, Ingrid Varetz; Photographer: Yann Robert 69tl; **Telegraph Media Group**: The Daily Telegraph 2005 / Martin Pope 29; **Nini Tjäder**: 51r; **UNHCR**: R. Ek 103 (Angelina); **University of Cambridge, Computer Laboratory**: Alex Labeur 18

All other images © Pearson Education

Every effort has been made to trace the copyright holders and we apologise in advance for any unintentional omissions. We would be pleased to insert the appropriate acknowledgement in any subsequent edition of this publication.

Page Layout & Illustration by HL Studios, Long Hanborough, Oxfordshire.